PATHWAY TO
Rebellion
GALWAY 1916

WILLIAM HENRY

MERCIER PRESS

IRISH PUBLISHER – IRISH STORY

MERCIER PRESS

Cork

www.mercierpress.ie

© William Henry, 2016

© Preface: Tomás Finn, 2016

ISBN: 978 1 78117 403 6

10 9 8 7 6 5 4 3 2 1

A CIP record for this title is available from the British Library

Printed and bound in the EU.

More titles by this author:

A Place in Our Hearts: St Bridget's Terrace 100

Blood for Blood: The Black and Tan War in Galway

Coffin Ship: Wreck of the Brig St John

Éamonn Ceannt: Supreme Sacrifice (originally published as *Supreme Sacrifice: The Story of Éamonn Ceannt 1881–1916*)

Famine: Galway's Darkest Years 1845–1850

Fields of Slaughter: The Battle of Knockdoe 1504

Forgotten Heroes: Galway Soldiers of the Great War

Galway and the Great War

Galway's Great War Memorial Book 1914–1918

Galway Through Time & Tide, Vols I–IV

Hidden Galway: Gallows, Garrisons and Guttersnipes

Mervue 1955–2003

Role of Honour: The Mayors of Galway City 1485–2001

St Clerans: The Tale of a Manor House

The Galway Arms Golfing Society

The History of Mervue United 1960–2010

The Shimmering Waste: The Life and Times of Robert O'Hara Burke

Tír na nÓg: A New Adventure

For Anne Maria

True Friendship is a Gift from God

Sought by Many

Experienced by Few

CONTENTS

POBLACHT NA H EIREANN.

THE PROVISIONAL GOVERNMENT

OF THE

IRISH REPUBLIC

TO THE PEOPLE OF IRELAND.

IRISHMEN AND IRISHWOMEN : In the name of God and of the dead generations from which she receives her old tradition of nationhood, Ireland, through us, summons her children to her flag and strikes for her freedom.

Having organised and trained her manhood through her secret revolutionary organisation, the Irish Republican Brotherhood, and through her open military organisations, the Irish Volunteers and the Irish Citizen Army, having patiently perfected her discipline, having resolutely waited for the right moment to reveal itself, she now seizes that moment, and, supported by her exiled children in America and by gallant allies in Europe, but relying in the first on her own strength, she strikes in full confidence of victory.

We declare the right of the people of Ireland to the ownership of Ireland, and to the unfettered control of Irish destinies, to be sovereign and indefeasible. The long usurpation of that right by a foreign people and government has not extinguished the right, nor can it ever be extinguished except by the destruction of the Irish people. In every generation the Irish people have asserted their right to national freedom and sovereignty : six times during the past three hundred years they have asserted it in arms. Standing on that fundamental right and again asserting it in arms in the face of the world, we hereby proclaim the Irish Republic as a Sovereign Independent State, and we pledge our lives and the lives of our comrades-in-arms to the cause of its freedom, of its welfare, and of its exaltation among the nations.

The Irish Republic is entitled to, and hereby claims, the allegiance of every Irishman and Irishwoman. The Republic guarantees religious and civil liberty, equal rights and equal opportunities to all its citizens, and declares its resolve to pursue the happiness and prosperity of the whole nation and of all its parts, cherishing all the children of the nation equally, and oblivious of the differences carefully fostered by an alien government, which have divided a minority from the majority in the past.

Until our arms have brought the opportune moment for the establishment of a permanent National Government, representative of the whole people of Ireland and elected by the suffrages of all her men and women, the Provisional Government, hereby constituted, will administer the civil and military affairs of the Republic in trust for the people.

We place the cause of the Irish Republic under the protection of the Most High God, Whose blessing we invoke upon our arms, and we pray that no one who serves that cause will dishonour it by cowardice, inhumanity, or rapine. In this supreme hour the Irish nation must, by its valour and discipline and by the readiness of its children to sacrifice themselves for the common good, prove itself worthy of the august destiny to which it is called.

Signed on Behalf of the Provisional Government,

THOMAS J. CLARKE,

SEAN Mac DIARMADA,   THOMAS MacDONAGH,
P. H. PEARSE,   EAMONN CEANNT,
JAMES CONNOLLY.   JOSEPH PLUNKETT.

Acknowledgements

Thanks to the following people for their support with this book: my wife Noreen, sons Patrick and David, and daughter Lisa. Sincere thanks to Dr Tomás Finn for writing the preface to this book. I would also like to express my grateful appreciation to the National Library of Ireland, Dublin; James Hardiman Library, NUIG; and County Galway Library, Island House. Thanks also to the staff members of the various libraries: Kieran Hoare, Michael Faherty, Marie Boran, Liam Frehan, Gerard Thornton, Maureen Moran and Mary Kavanagh; and to Hugh Beckett and Noelle Grothier in the Military Archives.

To all in the media organisations who have supported my work over the years: the staff members of the *Galway Independent*, Galway Bay FM, Raidió na Gaeltachta, the *Connacht Tribune*, *The Tuam Herald* and the *Galway Advertiser*. Thanks to all those who gave excellent publicity to this and various other projects: Declan Dooley, Hilary Martyn, Mike Glynn, Judy Murphy, Brendan Carroll, Dave Hickey, Joe O'Shaughnessy, Declan Furey, Stan Shields, Ronnie O'Gorman, Declan Varley, Tom Kenny, Keith Finnegan, Tom Gilmore, Jim Carney, Peadar O'Dowd, James Casserly, David Burke, Des Kelly and Máirtín Tom Sheáinin.

Thanks also to Loretta O'Kelly, Jonie Fallon, Fidelma Holland, Connie Gavin, Brid Ryan, Bridie Connell, Mary O'Malley, Mary Boyle, Mary Melia, Evelyn Flynn, Noel Skehill, Laura Walsh, Brendan Holland, Mona Holland,

Luke Silke, Michael Morrissey, David Morrissey, Paul Faller, Ronan Killeen, Finbarr O'Regan, Ambrose Joyce, Tony Claffey, Johnny Molloy, Seán Molloy, Mary McDonnell, Tom and Josephine Leonard, Marie Boran, Professor Padráig Ó Machain, Kathleen Davis, Elizabeth Byrnes, David Henry, Brian Quinn, Seán McDermott, Tom Lenihan, Sergeant Major Richard 'Dick' O'Hanlon, Private Padraig McDonnell, Sergeant P. J. Maloney, Mártin Concannon, Aoife Concannon, Sylvester Cassidy, Bernadette Forde, Maryann Vaughan, Dom and Mary Dunleavy and the Killererin Heritage Society.

Sincere thanks the following for all their support: Mary Waller, Mike McDonagh, Karolina Pakos, Tom Small, Dick O'Hanlon, Marita Silke and Anne Maria Furey for proofreading my book. Special thanks also to Jacqueline O'Brien for her long hours over many years of research and support with this and many other projects.

Sincere thanks also to Mary Feehan and all the staff at Mercier Press for their support and expertise, and for publishing this book.

PREFACE

On 18 November 2010, following the Irish government's decision to enter the 'bailout', *The Irish Times* asked whether it was for 'this' that the men of 1916 died. What exactly those individuals did, and how and why they acted, often in ways that were out of sync with those closest to them, are some of the issues considered in *Pathway to Rebellion*. Immersed as Ireland is in the decade of commemoration and the centenary of 1916, the consideration given to the Rising in Galway, why it occurred and its impact, is timely.

Anniversaries and commemorations are, of course, a key part of the context in which this and other works have appeared. Hitherto, areas outside of Dublin in 1916 have received little attention. One exception is the chapter on the provincial Rising in Charles Townshend's *Easter 1916*. Given that the most successful fight, as recounted by Townshend, was the one that took place in Ashbourne, County Meath, the lack of attention given by professional historians to this subject seems unfair. And yet, with the notable exceptions of Meath, Galway and perhaps Wexford, little seems to have happened beyond Dublin. One factor that was common to these places was that they had leaders with the ability to organise their men. However, whereas Richard Mulcahy in Meath recognised the need to take the conflict to the enemy, in Galway Liam Mellows lacked Mulcahy's authority and tactical awareness. Yet, by comparing these two are we doing a disservice to Mellows and the performance of the rebels in Galway? The failure to land arms in Kerry was critical to the way events unfolded in Galway, as well as in Limerick and Clare. Moreover, common to all parts of Ireland outside the Dublin area was confusion in the orders coming from the leadership in the capital, as well as communication problems within regions, indecision, a lack of weapons and the absence of a co-ordinated approach.

Given the importance of Easter 1916, it is not surprising that its effect on Ireland and its relationship with Britain is contested. With it emerged a new generation and political class which would come to dominate the nation and state, but questions remain as to why the Rising happened and what its destructive as well as its constructive consequences were. What were the forces that impelled some men and women towards rebellion, yet led many more to fight for Britain in the First World War? Could the result of the 1918 general election have happened without the Rising – in short, was it necessary for independence to become a reality? Did it mean that the division of the island was now a certainty? Was the choice between independence and unification, or is that to simplify a much more complex issue?

An important part of this decade is to seek answers to these questions and to remember key events, but also to consider others that have not been given the same attention. It thus provides the context in which historians can produce local studies, such as this work by William Henry. When read in conjunction with the work of Charles Townshend and, among others, Roy Foster's *Vivid Faces: The Revolutionary Generation in Ireland, 1890–1923* and *A Nation and not a Rabble* by Diarmaid Ferriter, this study can prove instructive as to how the rebellion came to happen in 1916 and how it then informed the nation and the states that came into existence.

The question asked at the start of this preface was also asked by a woman at the Easter commemoration in Galway in 2010 for those who had died in 1916. William Henry's recollection of this and his answer to her, that while this may not be the Ireland they fought for, it is more important than ever to remember these individuals and their ideals, and for everyone to strive towards these, illustrates an empathy with those of whom he writes and speaks. In identifying a range of issues, including the people who acted in the way they did, he is to be commended. His personal knowledge of Galway and passion for its history gives rise to a dramatic and illuminative account of the origins and impact of the 1916 Rising in the county. Those who are concerned with the past will find much of interest in the latest book by William Henry.

Tomás Finn,
Department of History,
NUI, Galway.

INTRODUCTION

This book, as its title *Pathway to Rebellion: Galway 1916* suggests, traces the origins of the rebellion in Galway in a way not previously explored. The story of unrest in rural Galway during the fifty years before 1916 shows that the county had a history of being one of the most troubled in Ireland. One must remember that the Ireland of this period was under the control of an unjust landlord system. It was inevitable that trouble would arise and it did, in the form of resistance to eviction and in land agitation. This manifested itself most notably during the Land War and the Plan of Campaign in the 1880s, and by the turn of the twentieth century most of the county's inhabitants were no longer willing to suffer injustice in silence. They had become organised and united under various nationalist movements, including the Land League and the United Irish League (UIL). Under these banners people felt more secure and became ambitious about their future and that of the country.

Even in Galway city during this period there was sometimes unrest and open hostility between the police, the military and the civilian population, although some believe that this was caused by troublemakers rather than being politically motivated. It has even been suggested that most of the trouble was fuelled by alcohol. Nevertheless, this hostility could not be ignored and there was clearly some anti-British feeling at work. However, over time this feeling seems to have subsided and by 1916 the vast majority of people living in Galway city were against the Rising and strongly supported government policy. Only a handful of rebels in the city took part in the action. Galway was not alone in this, as many of the big towns condemned the rebel action and supported the police and military.

In contrast, in many parts of rural Galway, where people had felt the weight of injustice for generations, support for the Rising was high. The insurrection in Galway was really a rural uprising and in many cases it was the children and grand-children of the people involved in the earlier resistance move-ment and land agitation who turned out in open rebellion in 1916.

The 1916 Rising had only been made possible by the for-mation of the Irish Volunteers in 1913. This allowed, in a sense, the establishment of an Irish army, which had not been seen for centuries. Although it was a part-time force, the movement was strong and well disciplined. The response to the Volunteers was very positive countrywide, although some would say that this was because of the involvement of John Redmond in the movement. Leader of the Irish Parliamentary Party, he had a lot of influence throughout the country.

In one way the formation of the Volunteers came at an ideal time for the authorities, with the outbreak of the Great War less than a year later. Through the Volunteer movement, Ireland had many young men partly trained militarily and this suited the British war effort. When war was declared in August 1914, John Redmond facilitated British recruitment for the front lines by pledging the support of the Volunteers to the conflict. However, his actions caused a split in the movement and while a huge majority followed Redmond and formed the National Volunteers, a smaller, much more focussed group, committed to Irish nationalism, remained. Their numbers were small when compared with the thousands of Irishmen fighting on the Western Front and in the other theatres of war in the European conflict, but this is not surprising when one considers the intense recruiting campaigns held across the country. The postponement of Home Rule, which had been the burning question in Irish politics for years, and the possibility of conscription led these men along the path to rebellion. Home Rule and its limited independence were no longer enough for the hard-line nationalists, who were led by the Irish Republican Brotherhood (IRB), and they decided to take the chance presented to them by the war to stage an uprising.

The mobilisation of the rebel forces and the attacks in various places detailed in this book show just how much (or little) of Galway was affected by the Rising. The immediate reaction of the police and British authorities in the city is also uncovered, as is the extraordinary support they received from the population. There were hundreds of arrests in the round-up of rebel suspects that followed the rebellion, but rather than decrying this, many of the men felt safer in the custody of the British military than being exposed to the public reaction against them. The men who rebelled were condemned, assaulted and subjected to verbal abuse in the days following the Rising. Those who managed to evade capture went on the run.

However, in the aftermath of the executions of the Rising's leaders in Dublin, attitudes and public opinion changed dramatically. The traitors of yesterday were suddenly the heroes of today. The homecoming they received on their release from internment was in total contrast to the reception they had had just after the rebellion, when they were viewed as traitors and troublemakers. The mood of the country had certainly changed, changed utterly. The actions of these men had paved the way for a new and independent Ireland, but it would take a bitter and bloody struggle to gain the independence sought in 1916.

When first setting out on this project I did not envisage that the final result would be a book of this size. However, the sources explored when compiling this work, including contemporary newspapers, books, interviews, letters and witness statements from the Bureau of Military History (BMH), which were recorded by the survivors between 1947 and 1957, contained a wealth of important information that deserved to be included.

It should be pointed out here that, while the BMH witness statements are invaluable for the study of this period of Irish history, there are some difficulties with them. Some of them differ when recording the same event and do not match exactly regarding information and timing. This is understandable as the statements were recorded many years after the rebellion. While they may have seemed accurate to the individual involved, others remembered an event differently. One example of a total mismatch between two statements recording the same event can be found in the accounts of Brian Molloy (company captain, Castlegar) and Thomas Courtney (intelligence officer, Castlegar). Molloy stated that when his company mobilised early on the morning of Tuesday 25 April 1916, Thomas Courtney arrived from the city and informed them that two of the rebel leaders, George Nichols and Micheál Ó Droighneáin, had been arrested in Galway. According to Courtney's statement he arrived in Castlegar at about 6 a.m. that same morning and was told by Michael Newell (second-in-command, Castlegar) that Brian Molloy and Patrick Callanan had gone to Moycullen. Therefore Courtney could not have met Molloy that morning. One could argue that Molloy was recording information given to him by Newell when he returned from Moycullen. However, there is also the fact that Courtney could not have informed anyone of the arrests of Nichols and Ó Droighneáin on that particular morning as this did not take place until later that day.

Other discrepancies arise between witness statements. One of these stated that it was in Limepark that Fr Thomas Fahy caught up with the rebels with news from Galway. Another account indicates that he joined the rebel column when they arrived in a place called Coxtown, which was about a mile from Limepark. Still another statement recorded that Fr Fahy caught up with the rebels at Monksfield. Fr Fahy himself stated that he reached the rebel column on the road to Limepark. There are also problems with differences in the spelling of names of people and places in a number of statements. These are just some examples of the issues that arose while compiling this book, which resulted in a lot of cross-checking of statements to try to build up a clear and accurate account of the events, which I hope I have achieved.

I would like to end this introduction on a personal note. *Pathway to Rebellion* was an amazing book for me to write, as in my childhood I knew some of the men who took part in this epic episode in Irish history. They were old at the time and like most children I never considered the freedom that I experienced as being earned by them, but I have come to appreciate it now. These were men of principle and integrity, and I am sure they would be disappointed with the lack of these qualities in the corridors of power today.

1

REBELLIOUS BEHAVIOUR

Looking back at the political climate in Galway towards the end of the nineteenth century and in the years leading up to the rebellion, one should not be surprised by the events of 1916. It has been said that Galway was one of the strongest areas of agrarian agitation in the country during those years. Not only were people rebelling against the crown forces, but they were also hostile towards the landlords and their agents.[1]

There was a long tradition of agrarian secret societies in County Galway, some dating from as far back as the early eighteenth century when a group calling themselves the 'Houghers' were active. By the late eighteenth century these had given way to the Whiteboys, sometimes referred to as Ribbonmen, an organisation that continued its lawless activities well into the following century. Perhaps their most famous member was Anthony Daly. He was hanged in 1820 on the hill of Seefin, located between Craughwell and Loughrea, after being accused of perpetrating attacks on the landed estates of Roxborough, Raford and St Clerans.[2] These attacks had their origins in the attitudes and practices of some landlords – it was not uncommon for landlords to seize crops from those struggling in poverty as payment of rent at that time. In many of these cases Ribbonmen sent threatening notes to landlords involved in such seizures, as well as in the mistreatment of tenants, warning them of the consequences if such practices continued. The Ribbonmen perpetrated violent assaults and robberies, and were also involved in nocturnal raids for firearms. Their area of activity stretched from north-east Galway to Loughrea and covered many other districts of the county, including Tuam, Mountbellew and Ahascragh.

By 1820 Galway was the most disturbed and violent county in Ireland and the most affected areas included Loughrea, Dunsandle and Roxborough. The attacks were causing the landlords and authorities such great concern that they held a meeting in Loughrea to set plans in place to crush the Ribbonmen. Many of those present were in favour of having the Insurrection Act of 1796 reintroduced. Among other things, this tough legislation had allowed the placing of any district under martial law by the lord lieutenant and the imposition of the death penalty for anyone administering an unlawful oath; it had been used with terrible effect during the 1798 Rebellion. Following the meeting, between 8,000 and 9,000 troops were drafted into the county to try to defuse the situation and repress those causing trouble. There was a series of battles between the Ribbonmen and the military, following which over 100 insurgents were captured and incarcerated in Galway Jail. The courts passed the death sentence on nine men, although six were later reprieved. Others received various terms of imprisonment, flogging and transportation.

Anthony Daly was one of those sentenced to death, for his role in the planning of rebellious operations in the area. One of the accusations against Daly had been the attempted assassination of James Hardiman Burke of St Clerans. Burke was not only a landlord, he was also the mayor of Galway at the time. Tradition tells us that Daly's only defence was simple – had he pulled the trigger, Burke would be dead. Despite being blind in one eye, Daly had a reputation of being an excellent shot. According to tradition, Daly was forced to sit on his own coffin during the journey to his place of execution. His hanging on 8 April 1820 had a long-term effect on the people and the locality.[3] It seems that Anthony Raftery, the renowned poet, was present at the execution and wrote about the hanging. A monument was later erected on the site of the execution. Over time, Daly became a folk hero, and his life and death are still remembered today, almost 200 years later. Some people believe that Daly was the first of the modern martyrs, a tradition which culminated in the 1916 executions.[4]

The agrarian struggle in Galway continued at a reduced pace following the death of Anthony Daly, and the famine years took their toll on those willing to stand up to oppression. However, in the years following the catastrophe of hunger, during which many landlords had continued to evict their starving tenants, a renewed struggle evolved. The main concern for people in Galway at this time was land rent and reform, and tensions were running high. Unfortunately those in authority did not deem the demand for fair rents important and this was apparent from the failure of the Landlord and Tenant Act, passed in 1870 to amend the law relating to the occupation and ownership of land in Ireland, to address this issue. The people could not tolerate this and the situation resulted in some of them taking the attitude that the only fair rent was no rent. After all, why should people pay rent for land that had been confiscated by landlords from their forebears?

The situation came to a head in the late 1870s when local and global problems caused a recession which meant that increasing numbers of tenants could not pay their rent. This led to the formation of the Land League in 1879 following a meeting in Irishtown, County Mayo. The League aimed to protect from eviction people living on smallholdings and to abolish landlordism in Ireland. Their tactics culminated in the so-called 'Land War' of 1879–82, where the League used tactics such as protest meetings, riots, assassinations and boycotts to prevent evictions and advance the cause of tenants.

By this time people were starting to show more courage in their struggle against the landlord system. This was apparent in the events surrounding the eviction of a man named Mike Fallon and his family in September 1880. Fallon was a tenant of the Persse family on the Roxborough estate. Over previous years he had suffered financially because of poor harvests. To make matters worse, Persse refused to pay him for work he had carried out on his house. When Fallon was unable to pay the rent, his horse and foal were seized as payment. As a result he became so ill that he was unable to farm the land. Persse then offered Fallon a position as caretaker, to remove him from the land, but he refused. He told Persse that he wished to hold onto the patch of land regardless of the situation, warning him that he had the Land League's support and that the days when landlords controlled these estates were numbered. Fallon was forced off the land, but, being a determined man, he refused to go without a fight. Between March 1881 and June 1883 he appeared before the courts some thirty-four times, charged with trespassing on the land which he considered his own. The fines exceeded the rent he owed on the property and Fallon found himself in prison on many occasions. However, while Fallon faced many problems, he found that he was not alone in his struggles. Forty prisoners in Galway Jail raised money for the Fallon family, while Michael Davitt, one of the key figures in the Land League, provided finance to have the Fallon children looked after on an ongoing basis.

Between 1881 and 1882 there were eight murders in an area stretching from Athenry to Loughrea. Those killed included a landlord, a soldier, a policeman, a land agent and a number of so-called 'land grabbers'. It was believed that the IRB shot these men. Following the killings, there was a large influx of police and military into the county, which only added tension to a worsening situation. The landlord who lost his life was Walter Bourke of Rahasane House. On the day he was killed Bourke had travelled to Gort to attend the Petty Sessions and obtain court orders to evict some of his tenants. Both he and his personal guard, Corporal Robert Wallace, were killed in an ambush at Castletaylor on the way home.[5]

During this period Constable James Linton was fatally shot and another policeman, Constable Kavanagh, was killed while investigating the death of a landlord's son in Letterfrack. It was inevitable that the police would be targeted, because while some had shown themselves to be humanitarians, others had displayed utter brutality towards the people. It was reported that in some areas of unrest, police had viciously punched young girls in the stomach and breasts, and used the butt-end of their rifles freely on anyone they came in contact with during confrontations. One woman in Carraroe, who was not involved in the League or the unrest, received a bayonet thrust to her neck, and it was claimed that she was not the only innocent victim of police brutality. People in Moylough were baton charged by police, with many receiving head wounds. Many of these attacks were unprovoked.[6]

In 1881 the British government introduced measures that would lead to the end of the Land War in the summer of the following year. One was a policy of brutal repression of the Land League, which was proscribed. The other was the 1881 Land Act: this allowed tenants to apply for rent reductions to the courts, which could be fixed for fifteen years, and also introduced the possibility of land purchase. As the situation on the ground improved, the League lost its support.

However, evictions were still the cause of much resentment and it is evident that the authorities were certainly not heeding or listening to the voice of the people. Dispossession was still a huge threat hanging over families and, with the end of the Land War, in many cases people felt that they were once again alone in their struggle against this injustice. Nevertheless, things were about to change. On 20 August 1886 resistance to evictions reached boiling point in Woodford, County Galway. That day an attempt was made to remove Thomas Sanders from his home, but the sheriff and his men met with strong resistance after a number of Sanders' supporters barricaded themselves into the house. As the police and bailiffs attempted to force an entry, they came under attack from the men inside, who used stones, sticks, gaffs, boat-hooks and boiling gruel to repel them; even a beehive was thrown at the attackers. The police were forced to retreat after two hours with nothing to show for their action except wounds and embarrassment. The defenders then erected a green flag on the roof of the house and began preparing for another attack.[7]

The incident became known as the 'Siege of Sanders' Fort' and it received huge publicity over the following days. The man behind the eviction was the most notorious of all the absentee landlords, Hubert George de Burgh-Canning (Lord Clanricarde), who, despite his immense wealth, lived a miser's existence. Across the county, Sanders' supporters numbered in the thousands and to impede police and troops from reaching Woodford, roads were dug up and trees knocked across them, and a bridge was also destroyed. The ringing of church bells warned that the police and military were close and brought people out to support Sanders. Over the following week the authorities called in reinforcements and by 27 August some 700 police, two companies of troops and forty emergency men had reached Woodford and were engaged in the siege.[8] Although Sanders and his men were eventually overcome, their resistance was widely publicised and captured the imagination of many nationalists both at home and abroad.

The events at Woodford sent thousands of people onto the streets of Galway city in support of the man who had made a stand against the police. Local priest Fr Fahy had actively supported the men involved in the Woodford standoff and for this he was brought to court. On the day of his trial some eighteen men supporting Fr Fahy were arrested for 'riotous conduct'. All received prison sentences and Fr Fahy was taken to Galway Jail. He was greeted by hundreds of well-wishers when he arrived from Woodford and initially, for the most part, it was a peaceful demonstration.

However, when his supporters arrived in Galway by train some time later, it was a very different matter and trouble was clearly expected as they were placed under a heavy police escort. The police and military faced a dangerous situation from the increasingly rebellious conduct of the crowd. Head Constable Wynne, who was in charge, forced the people back and succeeded in making a division between them and the prisoners with their escort. However, when he tried to rejoin his party, he came under attack. The police escort quickly marched the prisoners towards Galway Jail, but the crowd became angrier and started to launch missiles indiscriminately at the police escort; some of the prisoners were also hit. Upon reaching the jail, the police formed a line in front of the gate and the prisoners were marched through. The attacking crowd reacted even more violently and volley after volley of stones was fired at the police, injuring a number of them. Prison wardens also felt the fury of the crowd as stones were thrown at the prison gates, making a loud continuous crashing sound as they struck home.

The attack on Wynne continued and more police were injured. Orders were given to fix bayonets and prepare to charge the crowd. As the police surged forward in military formation, men, women and children ran in panic, and many of them fell and were trodden on by others. Wynne became worried about people being seriously injured and so he rushed forward and halted the police attack. About a dozen men were arrested and taken to the police barracks in the Newtownsmith area of the city. However, some of the mob regrouped and attacked, showering the police with stones before they could reach the relative safety of the barracks. Once inside the barracks Wynne decided to have his men switch their rifles and bayonets for batons. Perhaps he was nervous of people being killed if his men had firearms. They then rushed out of the barracks and attempted to baton-charge the crowd, only to be met by a further hail of stones. The police regrouped and charged again, this time forcing the mob to retreat towards the city centre.

The violence continued in the streets as stones and batons on each side found victims. Shop windows were also smashed as the crowd ran through the streets. People disappeared down side streets, lanes and alleyways. The police halted and re-grouped, before marching through the main streets. As they marched down Shop Street they were again attacked, with stones and bottles being thrown from every conceivable place. The police sustained more injuries before they were able to force the rebels to retreat yet again. Meanwhile, the police at Galway Jail were still under attack.

Police reinforcements were called into service from out-lying areas, but it took hours to bring the situation under control. Strong police patrols had to be maintained throughout the night and over the following days, to make sure calm prevailed, but this was not the last riot Galway would see over the issue of land.[9]

The following is an extract from a poem 'In the Year of '86' about the event. It was published in *Forgotten Campaign* in 1986 and is believed to have been written by a reporter from the *Pall Mall Gazette* following the Woodford eviction:

> The next was Fr Fahy
> Who couldn't see his people die
> From hunger and starvation
> To save them he did try
> For doing this for six long months
> He pined in Galway jail
> He said 'I did commit no crime
> I'll not go out on bail'.

> When he arrived in Galway town
> He was met by thousands there
> The people all had turned out
> Their voices rang through the air
> Twice they thought to rescue him
> And then with stones and sticks
> They attacked the jail in Galway town
> In September '86.[10]

2

A GARRISON TOWN

While the violence in the city during this period was influenced by events in the countryside, such as Woodford, this was not the only cause of unrest in the city. Trouble between the people and the military, and between the military and the police, was also a problem.

Galway has always been a garrison town, with a military presence there from at least as far back as the sixteenth century. During the late eighteenth and nineteenth centuries troops were housed in the Shambles and the Castle Barracks, both located in the city. However, over time these buildings became unsuitable for the accommodation of soldiers and there were many complaints from the local military, so the War Department decided to have a new barracks erected. An area was chosen at Renmore, just outside the city, and work began in the 1870s. By February 1880 the construction of Renmore Barracks was complete and troops began to move into the new military complex. Renmore became the Connaught Rangers' depot, and it also provided accommodation for other regiments such as the Suffolk Battalion and the 14th Battalion of the Prince of Wales' Own Regiment. However, the older military establishments in the city stayed in use despite the adverse conditions.[1] Many of the troops socialised with the civilian population and attended various events during this period.[2]

In December 1881 a row broke out between the police and soldiers in William Street after a soldier who had over-indulged in alcohol started abusing a policeman. The argument developed into a fistfight and a number of other soldiers joined in the attack. The policeman drew a sword and began slashing to keep them at a distance. A number of other policemen arrived and, following a sharp scuffle, the soldiers were arrested.[3]

In 1885 disturbances broke out after soldiers from the 14th West Yorkshire Regiment based in Renmore Barracks arrived in the city. Trouble erupted with some young men who were attending a bonfire in Frenchville Lane close to Galway Railway Station. After the clash the soldiers made their way through the city, smashing several windows and causing more trouble. They were set upon by a crowd of civilians, but the police arrived on the scene and calmed the situation. Over the following nights crowds of civilians thronged the streets awaiting the soldiers' return, as they were determined to attack any who ventured out from the safety of their barracks. However, all remained quiet, helped by the fact that the soldiers had all been confined to barracks. Just over a week later 120 of the troops who had been involved boarded the train for Cork on the first leg of a journey to their new posting in India.

Despite this, the trouble in the city escalated and girls who were seen in the company of soldiers also became targets. Many had their bonnets and shawls pulled off and trampled on in the mud. Even the wives of soldiers were not safe and received the same rough treatment. It was reported that one woman was attacked in the centre of Galway when she was out walking with her soldier husband. The unruly mob, led by a priest, almost stripped the woman of her clothing. Her husband tried to reason with them, but he was simply pushed aside. Another attack took place in College Road when a gang of about twelve men set upon two soldiers of the Border Regiment in the company of two girls. They tried to escape, but another gang of men came from the opposite direction and joined in the attack. The soldiers were thrown to the ground and kicked and had their uniforms torn. As in other attacks, the girls had their bonnets and shawls ripped off and kicked about the street. One of the attackers later admitted that they had only done as the clergy instructed.

It was a difficult situation to address because some clerics, assisted by some 'very zealous' young men, were involved in the attacks. In trying to justify their actions, the clergy said that they were worried about the virtue of their flock. One stated that he would not 'give the females of our faith to the unbridled licence of any regiment'. While saving the young women's virtue was the excuse used, some of those involved were simply anti-British and were prepared to inflict injuries on the military and anyone they felt was supporting them.

The police were called in to try to sort out the situation. Some of the men involved were taken before the magistrates, but this didn't solve the problem as they were only punished with small fines. There were calls for the Church authorities to help restore public order, but they were slow to react. Some priests were guilty of grossly illegal acts when they encouraged others to commit disorder and the problems continued for some time.[4] This tradition of clerical involvement in rebellious acts was kept up later when a number of priests became involved in the Irish Volunteers and the Rising in Galway.

The attacks on the military did not help an already volatile situation as they meant that some soldiers felt justified in becoming involved in public disorder. In June 1888 soldiers of the Welch Fusiliers attacked a shop owned by Thomas McDonagh in Flood Street. The trouble started earlier in a public house, where they had an argument with a local man. After the man left the pub the soldiers followed him, determined to give him a beating. He made his way to Flood Street hoping to escape, but the soldiers were closing in on him, so as he passed McDonagh's shop he decided to take refuge there. The owner and some of the customers in the shop helped him by closing and locking the doors, but when the soldiers arrived outside, they began attacking the shop. Although they smashed the windows and pulled the shutters off the building, the people inside the shop managed to hold the door securely closed.

What happened next was truly horrific. When they failed to gain access, the soldiers turned their attention and rage on a donkey and cart tied to a pole just outside the shop, and beat and kicked the unfortunate animal until it collapsed. They then proceeded to jump on its body before leaving the area. This same group of soldiers, stationed at the Shambles Barracks, was known to break shop and house windows on a regular basis. Although the military authorities in Galway claimed to be appalled by such cruelty, the soldiers were not held accountable for their actions, which angered the people of the city.[5]

Although Queen Victoria's birthday was in May, it wasn't celebrated in Renmore Barracks until early June. The event was held in the parade ground in Renmore Barracks as they did not want it to be tarnished, which was a distinct possibility if they organised it in the city. The celebrations went off as planned and the cheering troops could be heard at a great distance as they chanted, 'Long may she reign', a wish they hoped would be echoed across the world where the 'sceptre of England holds sway – the great dominion on which the sun never sets'.[6]

Resentment against the Welch Fusiliers took a shocking turn on 18 September 1889, when Private Mark Owens was fatally stabbed during a fight between soldiers and civilians. He was taken to a medical unit in Renmore Barracks where he died a short time later. The soldiers had been drinking in a pub in Middle Street and while returning to barracks they spotted a boy playing his mandolin in the street and some girls dancing to the tune. The soldiers, eight of them, joined in and began dancing with the girls, who were frightened and wanted nothing to do with them. One of the soldiers fell, the music stopped immediately and his comrades helped him to his feet. The girls ran away down the darkened street. Two of the soldiers began shouting offensive names at them while the others continued on their way, walking towards Buttermilk Lane. A man who was standing at the corner of the street observing the situation began shouting abuse at the soldiers in defence of the girls. One of the soldiers ran at him, knocked him to the ground and began kicking him. There was a lot of shouting and soon other civilians who were passing came to the aid of the man and began throwing stones at the soldiers. The fight escalated and Owens was stabbed. He fell to the ground and as he tried to regain his feet, his comrades dragged him away while still under attack. Enraged because of the stabbing, they began smashing windows in Buttermilk Lane, but this only brought more people onto the street. The soldiers were now in serious danger as the crowd grew in numbers and hostility. The police arrived to try to calm the situation, but were too late to save Private Owens, who was bleeding profusely and later died of his wound. The inquest held at Renmore Barracks stated that Owens died from a 'Punctured wound in the right side inflicted by some person unknown'. His attacker remained 'unknown', except, possibly, to his friends. It was recommended that members of the regiment should be confined to barracks until their departure from Galway could be arranged.[7]

In July 1890 trouble almost broke out between the police and the Connaught Rangers, after the police ordered a drunken man to go home. He became angry and attacked one of the policemen and was promptly arrested. The incident occurred in Lombard Street, just outside the Shambles Barracks where a member of the Connaught Rangers was on guard duty. While the man was being taken away, he shouted to the soldier that he had served with the Rangers abroad and needed his help. It seems that there was an unwritten rule between the Rangers that they would always defend each other. The man's call for help had the desired effect, as the soldier left his post and challenged the police. A number of other soldiers who were making their way to the barracks at the time also became involved. It was obvious to the police that these men were in the mood for a fight.

A crowd gathered and began inciting the soldiers to violence. However, the sound of the police whistle brought more constabulary to the scene, among them the head constable. Once order had been restored, he went to the Castle Barracks and made an official complaint to the military commander, who was responsible for the troops stationed in the city at that time. The commanding officer immediately dispatched armed troops to the Shambles, where the soldiers who had caused the trouble were arrested and placed in the guardroom. Another detachment of Connaught Rangers was then dispatched from Renmore Barracks to take over duties at the Shambles.

There was more trouble in November that year when soldiers carried out a number of attacks on police in several places around the city. In one of these they used belt buckles to inflict injuries on the policemen. Some soldiers began calling out in support of nationalists who had been imprisoned in Galway Jail, men such as William Smith O'Brien and those being held for political reasons and agitation. Eventually, the Rangers had to retreat, as more constabulary arrived and organised themselves in baton-charge formation. Nevertheless, the trouble continued over several nights.

That same month, a detachment of troops who were bound for India decided to have a little action in the city before leaving. On the night in question they attacked the constabulary with stones at Eyre Square. The disturbances continued the following night and a policeman, Sergeant Boylan, had his skull fractured during the trouble. Eventually, the soldiers were forced to return to Renmore after police reinforcements arrived.[8]

There were conflicting reports regarding the Rangers and their relationship with other British regiments. It was reported that in one incident in the city some members of the Connaught Rangers tried to provoke a fight with members of the Suffolk Regiment. This was denied by the military authorities, who claimed that both regiments were on good terms.

There seems to have been a trend in most of the attacks involving the military. The Connaught Rangers were in conflict with the police, while civilian aggression was directed towards the English and Welsh regiments. It was also reported that Galway was the only town in the country where civilians were openly attacking military personnel at this time. The fact that the soldiers of the Connaught Rangers were mainly from the west of Ireland might explain their attitude during these particular troubles. Many of them would have seen or experienced the injustices of the landlord system. They were the only Irish regiment in the British Army to mutiny against authority during the later War of Independence.

Over the following years efforts were made by the military and the local authorities to ease tensions and by 1916 the tide seems to have turned in favour of the military. However, this was not the case in the county, where resentment against the ruling classes and their supporters continued to grow, even after the turn of the twentieth century.[9]

3

THE SPREAD OF RESISTANCE

There had been great hostility in County Galway towards the landed-gentry classes during the second half of the nineteenth century because of injustice and evictions, and the fact that the police, and sometimes the military, assisted the landlords in their actions caused serious resentment towards these organisations. The loss of a home and the means of sustaining an income were major blows to already poverty-stricken families and evictions caused a lot of animosity in communities across the country. In some cases this loss of property triggered a strong response, leading to an increase in acts of violence throughout the county. For instance, in 1878 a man was shot and a policeman and court clerk were wounded in Clonbern. It is highly likely that armed and well-organised members of the IRB, a secret nationalist organisation committed to achieving an Irish Republic by any means, infiltrated the agrarian movement to ensure attacks against landlords and their agents were carried out.

The availability of the arms that were used in this type of attack in Galway may seem remarkable for that time, but there had been gun-running in Galway since the Fenian rising of 1867. The main people involved in the illegal arms trade were Mark Ryan, Matthew Harris and John O'Connor Power. It has been estimated that membership of the Fenian movement in

Galway city alone in the 1870s was possibly as high as 1,000. In 1873 Ryan travelled to England where he was actively involved in sending arms to Ireland, and many of these weapons ended up in Galway. One reason that these men were able to obtain weapons so easily was that during the early 1870s the war office decided to dispose of surplus arms and many of these guns found their way into the hands of Fenians in Ireland. One of the shipments included six revolvers sent to a man named John Scanlon in Loughrea. During the Land War, Loughrea was one of the leading areas of political agitation in Connacht.

In 1879 John Devoy, a leader of the Clan na Gael movement in the United States, arrived in Ireland for a tour of the country. During his time in Connacht, he attended a number of meetings organised by the IRB and estimated the strength of the organisation to be about 24,000 members, made up mainly of men from the farming community. He too promised to arrange for the importation of guns before returning to America and it was later claimed that weapons were being sold openly in east Galway.[1] Devoy would later play an important role in the lead-up to the 1916 rebellion.[2]

Despite the fact that the IRB was a supposedly secret society, the police were monitoring local members in County Galway to try to uncover any hostilities it might be planning. The police relied heavily on informers for this intelligence-gathering. Following the appointment of Clifford Lloyd, who was very suspicious of the IRB, as Special Resident Magistrate in 1882, additional police were drafted in to allow the regular force to carry out all their duties. In some areas police masqueraded as civilians among the crowds attending fairs and other such gatherings, so they could watch suspects, and some new members of the IRB noted that they came under observation very shortly after joining the organisation. Police reports to Dublin Castle from 1882 regarding IRB suspects included the names of Michael Shaughnessy, Peter and John Broderick, John Lynskey and John Kelly, who were all from the Athenry area. In the Loughrea district that year five men were taken into custody – John Sweeny, John McCarthy, Thomas Cunningham, John Farrell and John O'Loughlin. Matthew Harris was also identified in these reports and was described as an agent of a secret society and a man with revolution as his objective.[3]

While rebellion in Ireland is characterised by dates such as 1798, 1803 and 1916, there were many rebellious acts by people during the late nineteenth and early twentieth centuries in Galway. One of the most important events during this time was the Plan of Campaign, a renewal of the Land War that had petered out in 1872. This campaign was promulgated in Woodford by Matt Harris and John Dillon, both members of parliament, and a number of others, on 17 October 1886 before a crowd of some 4,000 people.[4] It has often been described as a forgotten campaign because it was overshadowed by later events such as the 1916 Rising and the War of Independence. However, the Plan of Campaign was hugely important as it gave people hope that they would eventually gain control of the land of their birth. It paved the way for the transfer of ancestral land from the landlords back to the tenants through social agitation, a sense of justice and parliamentary reform. The campaign was not without its obstacles, even between the people involved, as there were differences of opinion and rivalry among them. However, it was nonetheless a crucial phase in the struggle for the ownership of land. The silent people who had continued to suffer in the years following the great famine would be silent no more. Those involved in the campaign reminded the authorities that, as in the Woodford eviction, people were no longer prepared to suffer the injustices of the past. In fact, within thirty years of the Plan of Campaign over two-thirds of the population owned their own land, which had formerly been in the possession of landlords.[5]

Despite the efforts of the campaigners, there were still problems with some landlords, who enjoyed the continued support of the authorities. Some of those involved in the campaign issued warnings to people who were doing business with the offending landlords, threatening to boycott them. Violence was never far away during those years. In 1887 a man named Halloran was set upon by a number of people close to Lough Cutra Castle near Gort. He was beaten with sticks and had his skull smashed with a stone. Halloran was left to die on the side of the road, but was later found and taken for medical treatment. It was believed that despite several warnings he had continued to befriend a man who was being boycotted by members of the campaign.[6] Such violent attacks did not diminish support for those involved in the Plan of Campaign and resistance to unfair rulings or injustice by the authorities continued to grow throughout the latter years of the nineteenth century.

As well as the activities of the IRB and the physical unrest in the countryside, there was also an increase in cultural and political activity in the late nineteenth century. Ireland was moving forward with a renewed pride in its national identity, which was evident in the foundation of organisations such as the Gaelic League and the Gaelic Athletic Association. These organisations united people and communities, and re-awakened Irish identity. Many people, both young and old, found a powerful self-realisation through their involvement with these organisations, and they had a loyal following in Galway county.

Since the Land League had effectively disappeared, it was inevitable that other radical organisations determined on challenging the status quo and land issues would form and flourish among the native Irish. These were no longer limited to the poorest tenants, but instead started to include people of higher social status within their ranks. The most important of these organisations was the United Irish League (UIL), founded by William O'Brien in 1898. Formed in Connacht, its aims were to have large estates divided and redistributed among those who needed more land to improve their modest incomes. One must remember that Ireland in the late nineteenth century was still a country of small farmsteads, with many people in rural areas still living in mud-walled cabins. For the most part the population continued to depend on the potato as a means of survival and one bad crop could cause great distress for the majority of people. The UIL attracted tenant farmers on smallholdings and provided them with their only hope of acquiring additional land, as the Plan of Campaign had run its course by this period.[7]

William O'Brien was originally from Mallow, County Cork, and had been a member of the Land League and editor of the *United Irishman* newspaper. It was his disillusionment with the Irish Parliamentary Party, sometimes referred to as simply the 'Irish Party', that triggered his establishment of the new movement. Ireland's leading nationalist political party, which was supposed to be fighting for the rights of Irish people in Westminster, had been rendered ineffective after the split caused by Charles Stewart Parnell's affair with Kitty O'Shea and his subsequent death. O'Brien felt that a new political movement to fight for the rights of tenants was now needed.

By the end of 1898 the UIL had spread from its foundation in Westport across Galway to Roscommon and Sligo. Its inaugural meeting in County Galway was held on 18 October 1898 in Headford, where Rev. Canon Barrett was elected president and W. Kyne was appointed vice-president. Following a second meeting at Headford, a number of resolutions were passed calling on the government to introduce a new bill for the compulsory purchase of land. This was to allow people living on what was described as 'wild mountain uncultivated' land the opportunity to live and work on good holdings and 'thereby do away once and for ever with the terrible cry of famine'. The UIL also condemned the government for suppressing public meetings. Another announcement from the new movement was a pledge stating that in future elections they would only vote for a candidate who was a member of the League and a practical supporter of the organisation.

Abbeyknockmoy was the next area to unite under the banner of the League; this took place on 31 October 1898. The UIL spread swiftly across the county to places such as Athenry, Dunmore, Monivea, Caherlistrane, Milltown, Donaghpatrick and Castlegar, among others. At the Monivea meeting the speakers called on all nationalist members of parliament to play a more active role in the new organisation and stop 'squabbling amongst themselves' and unite. All the meetings of the new movement seemed to have had well-prepared agendas, which would indicate that there was good communication between the various branches. This is not surprising given that representatives from the different branches attended each other's meetings. Such was the support for the movement that North and South Galway Executive Committees had to be set up to organise the various areas into a united front. Some of these places became hotbeds of nationalism over the following years.[8]

From its inception, the UIL proved to be a powerful force amongst the people, as membership gave them a sense of security in a period when evictions were still commonplace for those unable to pay their rent. The Irish Party quickly realised the strength of the movement and, in 1900, under the leadership of John Redmond, decided to join forces with the UIL. Redmond declared himself president of the UIL and the organisation quickly became a vital wing of the Irish Party, proving to be a valuable financial asset. The union between these two organisations also proved positive for the UIL, as they now had a voice in Westminster, which resulted in them gaining concessions from the government. A number of land acts were introduced which were of benefit to the League's members and a worry to some landlords.

One of these landlords was Lord Ashtown of Woodlawn, County Galway, who believed that if the UIL was allowed to continue it would bring about the destruction of the entire landlord system in Ireland. In 1901 he organised a meeting between landowners and secured an agreement that if anyone working for them joined the League they would be dismissed from employment. These were harsh measures, but deemed necessary in order for the landlords to remain in control and destroy the movement. Because of this decision, it was inevitable that trouble would arise, and it did, at Gloves near Athenry.

It began with a young man named Pat Fitzpatrick, who lived with his father, mother and a nephew on rented land at Gloves. He worked for a large landowner named J. Monaghan, who owned Gloves House and estate. Monaghan dismissed Fitzpatrick upon hearing that he had joined the UIL and also ordered him out of the house, but Fitzpatrick refused to go. The landlord then set about implementing the eviction process, which included the use of police and military to force Fitzpatrick and his family to vacate the house. In the process the bailiff and his men tried to remove a donkey from Fitzpatrick's yard, but the animal proved difficult to handle. In fact, they couldn't catch the donkey, much to the amusement of the crowd that had gathered in support of their neighbour. The crowd began cheering for the animal and this infuriated the police. A baton charge followed, resulting in a number of people being badly injured. There was a lot of anger as several of those injured were elderly men and women. The Fitzpatrick family were then forced from their home.

While the landlord and the authorities had achieved their aims in the short term, this action only served as a reminder to many people of the insecurity they still faced daily. A short time later a man named Holland provided a home for Fitzpatrick and his family in the townland of Tallyhoe. The descendants of this benevolent landowner are the present owners of Holland's Shop in Williamsgate Street, Galway.[9]

Trouble of this kind continued into the early twentieth century and other members of the UIL found themselves being targeted by landlords because of their political affiliations. One of these was Martin Ward, and his resistance would soon become infamous.

4

INDEPENDENT FUTURE

A remarkable and powerful display of resistance against the authorities began on 29 May 1906 in Loughrea, when an attempt was made to evict the well-known businessman Martin Ward from the premises and house he occupied. The incident became known as the 'Siege of Loughrea' and this eviction was also triggered by Hubert George de Burgh-Canning.

In 1890 Ward had rented property from de Burgh-Canning, which included a house and business premises in Church Street in the town. Over the following years, he built up a successful business through hard work over long hours. Ward had been assured that he would never be evicted as long he continued to pay his rent. He spent a substantial amount of his own money on renovating the general store and house as they were in a dilapidated condition when he first moved into the premises. By 1905 the business was proving very successful, but suddenly, the following year, he received an eviction notice.[1]

While some people were surprised by this move, others were not. After all Ward was secretary and former president of the UIL in Loughrea and this was believed to be the reason for his being evicted. He stated this in a letter to the chief secretary of Ireland on 25 May 1906, when he also warned him that he would defend his home and livelihood with all his strength. The people of Loughrea were outraged at the idea of

Ward being evicted and began organising public demonstrations to show their support. They also put in place a plan of action should the authorities move against Ward.[2]

The night before the eviction Ward and some of his closest supporters gathered in the shop and prepared to defend the premises. News had already spread of the eviction notice and by morning the roads leading to Loughrea were crowded with people making their way to the town. There they were greeted by a green flag with a harp emblazed upon it floating proudly over the store which, along with the house, had all its doors and windows barricaded. A substantial force of police also arrived, under the command of County Inspector Tyacke, and they cordoned off the streets leading to the premises. However, a large group of men and boys had already taken up positions inside the cordon, behind the railings of a church close to the besieged building, and they began shouting abuse at the police, which continued for several hours. The siege began shortly afterwards, when Ward refused orders to surrender.

Hundreds of additional police were drafted into the town, along with bailiffs armed with battering rams and axes. The store was soon under attack, but the defiant band of local men defended their position well. Armed with pots of boiling gruel – hung over blazing fires and maintained at scalding temperatures – pikes, swords, sticks and stones, they put up a heroic stand. When the police and bailiffs came within striking distance, they were showered with the boiling gruel. The cheering people soon drowned out their screams of agony as they excitedly shouted their support for the men behind the barricades.

Volley after volley of stones was then thrown at the attackers, who were forced to retreat while the men of the shop garrison waved national flags and shouted 'No surrender'.

While Inspector Tyacke sent for even more reinforcements, a police scouting party made their way to the rear of the premises. They returned and reported that a room at the back of the store had been left unguarded. Tyacke immediately ordered District Inspector Duffy to take thirty men and attempt a surprise attack at the rear of the building. However, they had to smash a window to gain access, which attracted the attention of the defenders. They rushed to stop the constabulary and one of them grabbed a bottle and hit a policeman on the head forcing the man to retreat with blood streaming down his face. The remaining policemen were then joined by some of the bailiffs and they began to force their way into the building.

Meanwhile, fighting raged through the streets, lanes and alleyways of the town as people clashed with police. The police regrouped and baton charged the crowds of demonstrators. There were severe injuries on both sides, but eventually the sheer mass of well-armed police managed to restore order. While Ward lost his battle for the store, he managed to hold position in the house.

On 31 May more police poured into Loughrea. It was estimated that the entire force numbered almost 1,000. However, they held off attacking 'Ward's Fortress', as it had become known, until additional reinforcements arrived. There was an atmosphere of violent tension as the rebel garrison in the building grew stronger, with new men arriving to relieve the others in guarding the windows and doorways. Later that day a bow of black crêpe was hung on the door of the besieged building with the inscription 'In Memory of Michael Davitt – No Surrender', as the great Land League campaigner had died the previous night.

The Bishop of Clonfert, Dr O'Dea, was extremely concerned and even offered Martin Ward a site for a new house, but by then the situation had developed into a political and nationalist conflict. Ward and the people of Loughrea were not going to surrender one inch of ground and were determined to stand firm and united in their cause. More and more volunteers poured in from places as far away as counties Mayo and Clare to support the besieged garrison. Many were also making their way to Loughrea from around Galway county. Public demonstrations of support for the besieged men continued in Loughrea every night and parades led by brass bands marched through the streets where bonfires raged. The men in the barricaded building were in jubilant spirits, singing nationalist songs including the great rebel song of Connacht, *The West's Awake*.

In the House of Commons John Redmond warned of the mounting unrest in Loughrea and spoke of the blatant disregard for tenants in Ireland. British Prime Minister Sir Henry Campbell Bannerman sent Sir Anthony McDonnell, the under-secretary for Ireland, to Loughrea with an offer of 'an olive branch' and a promise of a £10 subscription to the fund that had been set up for Martin Ward. The 'olive branch' was a promise to change the law regarding the protection of tenants, and a local committee, which included members of the UIL, was formed to meet with McDonnell and the British government representatives. In his statement McDonnell told Ward that he had won and there was no point in going on. He also said that his resistance had impressed on the government the necessity for the introduction of legislation to prevent such recurrences in future. During negotiations Ward refused to hand over the keys of his home and premises to the landlord's agent, but instead gave them to Sir Anthony McDonnell. In an interview many years later, Martin Ward stated that while the legislation was passed, 'the ten pound note stayed in Sir Anthony's pocket'.[3]

What happened at Loughrea was a powerful show of strength and resistance by the people and was in a sense a rebel defiance of authority. A victory parade was held and some people marched through the town, while others gathered around the bonfires that blazed in the streets. This was a victory for the people and one that cannot be underestimated, as it led to the Town Tenants Act being passed a year later, in 1907. It was also the first time in many years that the newspapers in London carried stories regarding the situation in the west of Ireland.[4] Some people believe that this absence of news about resistance had been instigated by certain members of parliament because of the people's reaction following the eviction of Thomas Sanders and the Plan of Campaign.

A year after the 'Siege of Loughrea', Sinn Féin, another important organisation, began to emerge in County Galway. Arthur Griffith had formed this new nationalist political party in 1905. Its first president was Edward Martyn of Tullyra

Castle, Ardrahan, but he did very little political work in County Galway, so it fell to others to promote the new party. The movement found fertile ground in the old secret-society areas where the Ribbonmen had once flourished.[5] Shortly after its foundation a branch of the party was set up in County Galway by a blacksmith named Tom Kenny from Craughwell, who was an extreme nationalist and a prominent member of the IRB. He went on to play an important role in the Irish Volunteers and the Easter Rising.[6] Some believe that the Rising in Galway would not have taken place without Kenny. He influenced hundreds of small farmers, tradesmen and labourers through his open political beliefs, and this resulted in many of them joining the Volunteer movement. However, his violent agitation caused concern among the local middle class, some of whom were members of the UIL.[7]

In 1910 trouble erupted between Kenny's Sinn Féin supporters and members of the League at Craughwell, which resulted in a number of public fights. It seems that the police always sided with the League members against the Sinn Féiners. The situation became so serious that Seán MacDiarmada travelled from Dublin to try to reconcile the two sides. Despite his best efforts the attempt failed and he returned to Dublin. However, these problems seem to have faded over time; at least the physical attacks stopped.[8]

Agrarian agitation against landlords was ongoing at this time and many men suspected of being involved were arrested and imprisoned. But there was strong support for these men – for example in October 1910 some 200 men from the Kinvara area turned out to harvest the corn for families whose adult males were in prison because of their involvement in land agitation. The depth of feeling was such that, despite members of the Catholic clergy calling on people to turn away from these activities, the support continued. So strong was the resistance that Gilbert Morrissey, one of the men who was active during the Rising, said that arms were never put away in Galway before 1916 and if the people were not fighting against British forces, they were making a fair stand against their henchmen, the landlord class, and their agents and bailiffs. The chief secretary for Ireland, Augustine Birrell, noted in the House of Commons that those involved in these acts of defiance were being protected by the people.[9]

Despite this, by 1910 the UIL had begun to lose credibility, as some people believed that it was not living up to the purpose for which it was founded. In that year Martin Finnerty from Gurteen, near Ballinasloe, formed the United Estates Committee. Finnerty had also been a founder member of the UIL, but over time he had become disillusioned with the organisation. He was of the opinion that large farmers were taking over the League and because of this, people living on smallholdings were being overlooked when it came to the redistribution of land. He was not alone in his views and found many people who were prepared to join him. At the second meeting of the United Estates Committee, held in Athenry during February 1911, delegates arrived from many areas indicating strong support for Finnerty. He was elected president for the second year running and was given great credit for being a 'sterling nationalist and always found working on behalf of the tenant farmer'.[10]

Another possible reason for the move away from the UIL was the fact that during 1910 its leadership had terminated its support for aggressive agitation and the members felt that the League was no longer acting in a strong enough manner to achieve its goals. The new organisation took a more militant view on the land issue than the UIL and openly advocated violence against landlords to force them to redistribute their land.[11] While the League managed to maintain a healthy membership, there is no doubt it could have been stronger.

It is tempting to think that all of this agitation may have been unnecessary if Home Rule had been introduced when it was first suggested. Home Rule had been the dominant issue in Irish politics for decades, but the government had failed to pass it into law twice in the past. However, following the 1910 general election, this changed when Liberal Prime Minister Herbert Henry Asquith found himself in need of the support of the Irish Party in order to stay in power. An agreement was reached, with the price of Irish support being Home Rule for Ireland. An act was passed by parliament the following year, which deprived the House of Lords of their traditional power to obstruct legislation.[12] It seemed that there was now nothing to stop Home Rule being introduced, and with the prospect of Irish rule in Ireland, it seemed that the changes for which the Land League, the UIL and the Irish Party, as well as the people, had been fighting for so long would finally be made possible.

5

THE IRISH VOLUNTEER FORCE

The first obstacle to Home Rule came from Unionists in the north of Ireland, who set up the Ulster Volunteer Force (UVF) early in 1913 to oppose, by force if necessary, the imposition of a Dublin-based government on Ulster. The UVF quickly armed itself as the British authorities turned a blind eye. Once this happened it became clear to nationalists that a similar force would have to be established by them to counter the threat posed by the Ulster organisation. A meeting to discuss the formation of the Irish Volunteers was held on 11 November 1913 in Wynne's Hotel, Dublin, where it was decided that there would be a public meeting on 25 November at the Rotunda Rink in the city. It was a large venue that could cater for 4,000 people. The fact that some 7,000 turned up indicates the overwhelming support for the new movement. Patrick Pearse and Eoin MacNeill addressed the large crowd and emphasised the importance of forming the Volunteers. The meeting proved more successful than even the organisers had hoped, with some 3,000 men signing up for service immediately. It was decided through an election process that Eoin MacNeill would become chief of staff of the new organisation.

The success of the Irish Volunteers continued and it spread across the country like a prairie fire. Within ten months the

Volunteer ranks had swollen to over 170,000 men. While other organisations had shown various degrees of strength, the newly formed Irish Volunteers was a powerful military force, an army in real terms, and it took every opportunity to display its numbers in public. Gone were the days of secret societies, with the exception of the IRB, which took full advantage of the new organisation. IRB men infiltrated its ranks, as the Volunteers provided them with a military force which they hoped to use to achieve their republican aims should the opportunity present itself. The objective was to have their members placed in strategic positions within the Irish Volunteers and some of them, including Patrick Pearse, Éamonn Ceannt and Seán MacDiarmada, took on vital posts within that organisation. As director of communications, Ceannt was crucial to the rebellion, not just in Dublin, but countrywide. Being a Galwayman, he developed close ties with the Volunteers in the west of Ireland.

John Redmond had initially been against the formation of the Irish Volunteers and even tried to discourage people from joining. However, once he saw how powerful support for the new movement was, he requested that some of his nominees be placed on the Executive Committee. This request was refused at first, but was accepted at a meeting of the Provisional Committee of the Volunteers on 16 June 1914, and twenty-five of his men were given positions. While the majority of the IRB members were against Redmond's proposal, they allowed his men to become involved rather than cause disunity within the organisation. Redmond was now in a strong position and over time gained a great deal of control over the Volunteers, which later caused problems for the organisation.[1]

Many men in the west of Ireland welcomed the formation of the Irish Volunteers. On 12 December 1913 the first meeting of the Volunteers in Galway took place in the town hall. Among the speakers were Eoin MacNeill, Roger Casement and Patrick Pearse. Casement told a packed hall that their main objective was to win Home Rule, but that the movement had also been formed to protect them from the Ulster Volunteers. When MacNeill addressed the crowd he said the Irish Volunteers had been formed to carry out the wish of the Irish people, which was to gain an independent and undivided country. In reality it was, he said, a defence force for the people of Ireland.[2] The meeting was a huge success and some 600 men joined the Volunteers after it. By October 1914 there would be over 8,300 members across the county.

As in Dublin, the IRB had a lot of influence in the organisation in Galway, through two of its prominent members: Tom Kenny, the blacksmith, and George Nichols, a coroner and solicitor from University Road in Galway city.[3] Following the formation of the Galway branch of Volunteers, George Nichols became its president, Seamus Carter was elected secretary and Frank Hardiman, another member of the IRB who joined the Volunteers on the organisation's formation in Galway, was the treasurer. Hardiman had declined to join the IRB on at least two occasions, but when Seán MacDiarmada asked him in 1913 he accepted. They acquired a drill hall in Williamsgate Street from John O'Donnell, a former MP who had obvious sympathies with the nationalists. Nichols was also the Centre in the local branch of the IRB and was already friendly with Frank Hardiman. Two other IRB men who became involved were Dr Thomas Walsh and Louis O'Dea.[4]

The IRB Circle in Galway city consisted of about fifteen members. Their meetings were irregular and were held in various locations, including the old Shambles Barracks.[5] How they managed to secure a room in the barracks is not known considering it was a British military establishment. However, the Gaelic League also held meetings there and perhaps it was through this organisation they gained entry to the barracks. They could not have identified themselves as being members of the IRB, as the military would certainly never have entertained them. Incidentally, the term Centre was a special title and was given only to men of great integrity and honour in the IRB. These men were privileged to act as the leader of a group known as a 'Circle' within the organisation.[6]

Roger Casement, who spoke at the initial meeting in Galway, was a well-known humanitarian and had also been involved in highlighting the plight of the poverty-stricken people of Connemara over previous years. In the months following that meeting, many young men in Connemara also joined the Volunteers. Even in such a remote part of the country drilling and exercises became part of their weekly routine. Connemara had seen much hardship and suffering, which possibly encouraged enlistment into the Volunteers. One might also wonder whether Casement had a personal influence on the men in this area.

One of the men who became involved in the movement in Connemara was Pádraic Ó Máille. He was born in 1878 in the Maam Valley, the son of a sheep farmer. The family were educated above national school level after their father employed a private tutor, who taught them at home. While his brothers attended university in Galway, Pádraic remained on the family farm. His brother Thomas later became professor of Irish Studies at the university. Ó Máille became involved in the Gaelic League at an early stage of his life and joined Sinn Féin shortly after its formation. He was also a member of the IRB and was fully supportive of its objectives.[7] His uncle, Tobias Joyce, presided over a meeting in Leenane to establish a branch of the Volunteers there. Some months later Peter McDonnell was elected as captain of the company, but there was opposition from Ó Máille, who wanted the position. When he failed to overturn McDonnell's leadership, he formed his own company in opposition. General Headquarters became involved and eventually Ó Máille's company was dissolved. Nevertheless, Ó Máille continued his involvement in the movement.[8]

Another man involved in the Connemara branches of the Volunteers was Micheál Ó Droighneáin, who was present at the initial Galway town hall meeting. Ó Droighneáin later recalled that Patrick Pearse helped him with the formation of a local unit in the Irish College near Spiddal. William Pearse also attended. Their first route march took them through Spiddal village and a lone piper, Colm O'Lochlainn, led them. A photograph was taken of the Volunteers that day, but it later disappeared.[9]

Patrick Pearse was very familiar with Connemara as he had been visiting the area regularly for many years. According to Fr Michael Corcoran, the curate of Rosmuc between 1908 and 1910, Pearse visited there annually on his holidays. Fr Corcoran was friendly with Pearse and later gave the following description of the rebel leader:

> … he was quite gentlemanly-looking in appearance. Good-looking too … his photograph is nearly always in profile: I have heard that this was because his features looked best in profile. He was very gentle and peaceful and, to my mind, the very last man that anybody could think of making commander-in-chief of an army … a man whose idea it was that the Irish people and nation should be distinct. And I often picture him as having – even in conversation – a far-away look in his eyes, as if he were thinking continually of some other thing … I was amazed in 1916 to hear that he was one of the leaders of the insurrection.[10]

Fr Corcoran said that Pearse was mostly alone at the cottage where he stayed, but he remembered that one year he had a visitor, Mary Hayden, who later became a celebrated historian. She shared a lot of interests and spent time with Pearse in Connemara. His clerical friend said that while Pearse was in favour of Ireland being an independent nation at that time, he did not display any signs of a man who would later lead an armed rebellion. His main concern seemed to be the restoration of the Irish language. Pearse obviously loved Rosmuc as he built a cottage there in *circa* 1903.[11]

Éamonn Ceannt was also a regular visitor to Connemara and indeed the Aran Islands. His wife Áine and their son Rónán often accompanied him. Most of his time was spent in Spiddal, where he played the pipes at ceilidhs being held in local houses. Outside politics, Ceannt was also deeply interested in the Irish language and had a great love for the west of Ireland. He spent as much time as possible in Connemara and developed a close friendship with Micheál Ó Droighneáin.[12] Ceannt and his family often stayed in his home during their visits to the west of Ireland. Ó Droighneáin organised meetings with the local IRB men.[13]

Like the UIL many years earlier, the Irish Volunteers quickly attracted young men in various areas across the county. One of the men who had joined the Volunteers from the start was Patrick Callanan from Craughwell. He was known as the 'Hare'; some people said he earned this name because he proved a difficult man to trap, although others assigned different reasons. According to one source it was Callanan who instigated the formation of a company of Volunteers in Clarenbridge. Callanan was by this period a staunch nationalist, having joined the IRB in April 1905. He later said he found it strange that shortly after joining the IRB, new members were questioned by police regarding agrarian outrages. These men had never been questioned by the police before – informers were obviously at work within the secret organisation. However, Callanan became a bit disillusioned by the IRB and later said that he felt the majority of older members were only interested in acquiring land rather than furthering the nationalist ideal.[14]

While cycling home from Galway one evening Callanan stopped at Clarenbridge, where he saw some twenty young men gathered at the gable-end of Jordan's public house in the village. Having spoken to them he realised that they were potential candidates for the Volunteers. The following day he cycled to Galway and met with George Nichols, asking him to come to Clarenbridge the following Sunday because a hurling match had been arranged for that day and there would be a good crowd in attendance. That Sunday turned out to be a fine day and George led Volunteers Tom Flanagan, Charlie Costello, Michael Allen, Seamus Carter, Peter Reynolds and the newly formed Volunteer band (formerly the Sinn Féin band) out of Galway. The group, including a number of other Volunteers, marched to Clarenbridge and upon arrival the band paraded into the field where the hurling match was being played. A platform had already been set up and the organisers and speakers mounted the stage and took their place as a crowd gathered before them. The meeting proved successful, with most of the young men present enlisting.[15]

Later that evening Patrick Jordan, a veteran of the IRB and the Land League, presided over the company's first meeting and more men joined up at this point. Shortly afterwards Éamonn Corbett from Kileeneenbeg was appointed as captain of the unit. From the beginning most of these Volunteer groups were trained by British army reservists, which was not surprising. After all, military training could not be achieved without experienced soldiers and the only ones available were in the British Army.[16]

Other Volunteer units were also set up in areas such as Maree, where Mike Athy was appointed company captain. Willie Burke and Francis Carney from the same area were appointed as junior officers.[17] Some of the men involved in the Ardrahan Volunteers were Patsy Shaughnessy, Joe Burns, Peter Noonan, Michael Silver and Pádraig Ó Fathaigh. The training for these men included marching in military formation from Labane to Ardrahan and parading openly in front of the RIC barracks. There they sang various nationalist songs and one they wrote themselves, now largely lost to time, although some of the surviving lyrics include 'Charging with fixed bayonets we terrify every foe, For the glory of old Ireland we're as brave as buccaneers, We're a terror to creation, the Ardrahan Volunteers'. Other songs they sang were *A Nation Once Again* and, of course, *The West's Awake*, which contains references to Ardrahan.[18]

Another man involved with this branch was Peter Howley from Limepark near Peterswell. His fight against the constabulary began at Peterswell in 1909, when, along with his brothers Patrick, William and Michael, he clashed with the police. The brothers believed that a policeman had been listening at the door of a public house where they were having refreshments. One of the brothers struck the policeman, who ran back to the barracks for help. When the constabulary returned they were armed with guns, but the Howley brothers, using just shovels and spades, forced them to retreat to the safety of the barracks. The police discharged their weapons, but none of the brothers were hit. Two of the policemen were badly injured and a warrant was issued for the arrest of the Howleys. Two of them eventually served a number of months in prison.[19]

There were close ties between some of the Galway units, not simply because of politics, but also because of sports. In Castlegar, just outside Galway city, there were many young men involved in hurling who were well-known to the men in Clarenbridge, Athenry and many other areas throughout the county. This sporting connection helped the spread of nationalist ideals.

One of the Castlegar Volunteers was Brian Molloy. Molloy had been a member of the Castlegar branch of the IRB since it was formed about 1907 and he would go on to play a leading role in Galway during 1916. Dick Murphy, a strong activist, had sworn him into the Castlegar IRB, which numbered about thirty men who were actively involved in agitation against the landlord system. Over time Molloy became suspicious because following incidents in the area he was questioned by the police: this had not happened to him before he joined this secret society. This reflected Patrick Callanan's experiences and supports the suggestion that there were informers at work within the IRB.[20]

One of Molloy's friends from the area was Thomas 'Sweeney' Newell. He was present in the town hall the night the Irish Volunteers were formed in Galway. Both he and another friend, John Conroy, joined the Galway City Volunteers immediately. Newell already knew the officers who were elected that night, including George Nichols, Seamus Carter, Tom Flanagan and M. J. Allen. When the Castlegar Company was formed a short time later, Newell was appointed 1st lieutenant and Michael

Burke 2nd lieutenant. Again their training was completed under the guidance of British army reservists.[21]

The Volunteers in Tuam were formed on 22 February 1914 at a meeting held in the Gaelic Rooms in Bishop Street. About 300 people attended and they were addressed by a number of speakers, among them George Nichols and Bryan Cusack from University College Galway. Many of those attending signed up and were enrolled in the organisation. They were informed that training would begin the following Sunday and they were to assemble in a yard provided by a local man named Tom Sloyan. The Volunteers enlisted the help of a soldier, Captain Charles Phillips from Dunmore, and he put the men through their paces in drilling, but after the first day of training it was clear that more instructors were needed. Three other men, Stephen Shaughnessy, Michael Kennedy and Dan Flanagan, were appointed as instructors. A short time later the Volunteers made their first appearance on the streets of Tuam as they marched to the town hall. Upon arrival a meeting was held during which the officers and committee were elected. Dr T. B. Costello was elected president and during his inaugural address he said that none of the men were to seek personal gain from their involvement in the Volunteers and they were not to accept any inducements of land or otherwise from anyone. He continued by saying that the Volunteer movement was based on patriotism and that members should be prepared to suffer for their country.

As membership in Tuam increased, a larger parade ground had to be found and the Tuam race committee solved this problem by providing an ideal site at Parkmore. Some of the training involved manoeuvres through the streets of the town during the hours of darkness, with the Volunteers taking Tuam street by street from an unseen enemy. The problem with some of these nocturnal activities in the town was that they disturbed mothers trying to get their children to sleep. There were also day exercises and marching through the streets, where both the public and police watched with interest the growing numbers. It seems that they were all impressed by the discipline of the men. Plans were also put in place to purchase uniforms and equipment as funds became available. Many of the men were partially equipped and it was hoped to complete this requirement by the end of the year. Under the guidance of Dr Costello, classes in first aid were organised, an important part of any army.

On 7 June 1914 the company completed one of its first route marches, to Brownesgrove, over three miles from Tuam. The plan was to connect with Volunteer units from Dunmore, Kilconly and Kilbannon. Once they joined forces, a large display of drill and exercises took place under the command of Captain Phillips. The total headcount of the Tuam Volunteers had reached about 1,000 by August of that year and among them were most of the members of St Jarlath's hurling team.

On 29 June 1914 a large force of over 2,000 Volunteers assembled in Athenry. The inspector-general of the movement, Colonel Maurice Moore, attended and Sir Henry Grattan Bellew accompanied him. Some 5,000 people turned out to see what many considered the army of Ireland. A number of marching bands were in attendance, which added to the military atmosphere.[22] Moore was a brother of writer George Moore, and their family home was Moore Hall in County Mayo, which was later used as a safe house by the IRA. Maurice Moore supported the Free State during the Civil War and allowed the hall to be used by their troops. In February 1923 the IRA burned it to the ground. In 1964 members of the old IRA had a plaque erected on the ruined house, which some say was an apology, in memory of Maurice Moore, for its destruction.[23]

The town of Athenry was decorated with flags, banners and buntings for the great event. One of the banners was hoisted across the main street and declared 'Home Rule or Else'. The O'Rahilly, one of the most respected officers to be killed in 1916, also attended. A review was held in the 'Park', which later became Kenny Park, named after Tom Kenny.[24] During his address, Moore told the Volunteers that he was very pleased with the turnout and glad to see that they were at least partially supplied with equipment. However, he also said that a soldier's equipment was not complete without firearms and ammunition and he hoped to remedy this situation by the end of the year. He reminded them that the exercises in which they were now engaged were extremely important. These were lessons in discipline and it was this obedient manner that made the difference between an armed crowd and soldiers who follow orders.[25] One of the Volunteer officers who attended the rally that day was Stephen Jordan from Athenry. He had joined the IRB in 1906 and was sworn into the organisation by Richard Murphy who was Centre of that branch. Jordan later stated that the assembly of Volunteers addressed by Moore at Athenry seriously alarmed the British authorities in the west.[26]

6

A DIVIDED FORCE

According to one report the Irish Volunteers' membership in Galway city and county was 1,938 in June 1914 and consisted of twenty-four branches. By the end of July there were forty-two branches consisting of 3,704 members. This figure had jumped to 5,191 in August, making up fifty-four branches, and it continued to grow as it did in other counties.[1] However, when Britain declared war on Germany on 4 August 1914, this had serious consequences for the Irish Volunteers. During his speech before the House of Commons the previous day, John Redmond advised the government that they could withdraw their troops from Ireland as the Irish Volunteers would defend the country. Parliament took his words as a pledge of total support for Britain's war effort. War was declared the following day and unsurprisingly this changed the government's priorities. The burning issue in Ireland over previous years had been the implementation of Home Rule, but the government decided to suspend this for the duration of the war. Redmond agreed with this decision and began encouraging the Irish Volunteers to enlist in the British Army.

With the suspension of Home Rule, unity among the Irish nationalists was at stake. There had already been growing concern among the Volunteers over the Home Rule issue, as many feared that it might never be implemented because of the strong opposition from Ulster unionists. The suspension of Home Rule and Redmond's words of support for Britain were not acceptable to many hard-line nationalists.[2] There was also growing concern among nationalists who did not support the war over the number of Volunteers who had already gone or were on their way to the Front.

On 25 October 1914 an Irish Volunteer convention was held in the Abbey Theatre, Dublin. By then the battles of Mons, Aisne and Marne had already taken place and the first battle of Ypres was raging, leaving mounting casualties, among them Irishmen who had supported Redmond. There were 160 delegates attending the conference, who had to carry back the mood of the meeting to their respective Volunteer units. During his address to the convention, Eoin MacNeill stated that the training and equipping of the Volunteers was for the service of Ireland, in Ireland, and he felt that maintaining this was the only way of forcing the government to follow through on the issue of Home Rule. He also made reference to Redmond, saying that since the formation of the Irish Volunteers he had tried to gain control over the organisation and now he wanted them to support Britain in the war in Europe. Indeed, some people labelled Redmond as a recruiting officer for the British Army.[3]

In his bid to win Volunteer support for the war, Redmond promoted the Home Rule card, using it as an inducement or prize to be claimed when the war was over. He also reminded the leadership of past achievements on land issues. Speaking of the wrongs perpetrated on the Irish people in previous years, he said that this was in the past and that they should forgive the injustices of those times. He believed they should concentrate on the present situation, pointing out that they had already emancipated the farmer, housed agricultural labourers and won religious liberty and free education. He also said that they had laid the foundations for national prosperity, but warned that all of these achievements were now in danger because of the war. A short time after the convention, the Irish Volunteers split, with the vast majority of the men following Redmond and becoming the National Volunteers. This left about 12,000 who retained the name and the aims of the Irish Volunteers.[4]

In Galway, Frank Hardiman received a request to organise a meeting to discuss the matter in the town hall. This was signed by Martin McDonagh, a prominent businessman, Luke Duffy, who later became a senator, P. J. McDonnell, James Pringle and Martin Reddington. The idea was to place the entire Galway Volunteer Force under the control of John Redmond, but the meeting was a disaster because, echoing the situation elsewhere, the Galway Volunteers were divided, again with most of the men supporting Redmond, but others refusing to do so.[5]

The National Volunteers in Galway made their headquarters in the Temperance Building, Prospect Hill. The chairman was Máirtín Mór McDonogh, with P. J. McDonnell serving as vice-chairman and T. J. Lydon as secretary. Their motto, 'Defence Not Defiance', speaks volumes when one considers the political climate at the time. It seems like a clear message not only to their followers, but also to those who remained with the Irish Volunteers.[6] The UIL, the membership of which had by then become indistinguishable from the Irish Party, also expressed its total confidence in and support for Redmond.[7] It could no longer be considered an independent organisation and eventually suffered the consequences of this unity with Redmond.[8]

A meeting of the Tuam Volunteers took place on 14 November 1914 to decide which side to follow, MacNeill or Redmond. The secretary, Liam Langley, gave a brief account of the movement since its formation and stated that one of the objectives of the Volunteers was to secure the rights of the Irish people. This was the pledge of the men who had joined the organisation and nothing had happened to change this aim. He reminded the meeting that some £200 had been collected for equipment and had not been spent as intended. Langley also said that the time had come for them to make a decision, to stay with the original ideals or place themselves in the defence of the British Empire. The president, Dr Costello, said that he regretted any split in the movement and added that there should be no ill feeling afterwards. A number of other speakers addressed the meeting and expressed their opinions, after which a vote was taken. MacNeill won with a majority of sixty-four votes to eleven. Costello then resigned because he did not agree with the result.[9]

In north Galway the majority of the Volunteers remained true to the Irish cause, and this was also the case in east Galway. However, there was a backlash against some of the people who opposed Redmond. One man living in Loughrea who attracted the attention of the civil and military authorities was Allen

Ashe, who worked for the Ordnance Survey Department. He was an opponent of the British Army recruitment campaign and a strong supporter of the Irish Volunteers. During the height of the tension leading to the split, he attended a meeting where a resolution was proposed congratulating John Redmond on his success regarding the Home Rule issue. Ashe opposed the resolution and is believed to have said that Redmond had sold out the Volunteers 'for a scrap of paper, as Home Rule was not introduced'. Redmond's supporters attempted to eject Ashe from the meeting, but others prevented this. Ashe later said that he made no remarks about a 'scrap of paper', but did say he mentioned that Home Rule was not an adequate measure. He also stated he was not disrespectful to Redmond or those involved in the recruiting campaign, but had reminded people that the Irish Volunteers were formed for the defence of Ireland.

Following this, two local informers gave evidence to the police about Ashe being a leading anti-recruitment campaigner. In December 1914 Ashe was dismissed from his employment and lost his pension. Worse still, the circumstances surrounding his termination prevented him from securing employment elsewhere. He appealed his dismissal to the lord lieutenant of Ireland on the grounds that he had worked for the Ordinance Survey department for some twenty-three years without a blemish on his record. Ashe also said that his brother was away at war fighting in the service of His Majesty. Despite his appeal and support from a number of prominent Dublin MPs, his dismissal was upheld because the government believed that he had been disloyal.[10]

According to one source, there were almost 10,000 Volunteers in Galway consisting of 110 companies at the time of the split. Although the numbers of men remaining loyal to MacNeill were high in the north and east of the county, the majority in other areas followed Redmond. Most of those who remained with MacNeill in east Galway were IRB members and this was the same in Galway city.[11] That MacNeill had lost a lot of support in the city was evident from attacks perpetrated against members of the Irish Volunteers by Redmond supporters. Thomas Courtney from St Bridget's Terrace recalled that one evening a mob attacked a small group of Irish Volunteers and tried to take their rifles. Following the attack, Seamus Carter, a member of the Irish Volunteers, received a jail sentence because he defended himself. A few nights later some of the men from Castlegar arrived in the city to attack the National Volunteers, but Courtney advised them against this action as the only outcome for them would be a jail sentence, which was futile to the cause.

Shortly afterwards Courtney transferred from the city to the Castlegar unit and soon after he was appointed as an intelligence officer for the Irish Volunteers. In the weeks that followed he attended a meeting to plan disruptions at a military recruitment gathering to be held in the town hall in Galway. These plans were a complete success, despite some twenty-five policemen on duty both inside and outside the town hall, as the Volunteers enlisted the help of students from University College Galway, who were only too happy to let off dozens of stink bombs in the premises.[12] Volunteer Thomas Hynes and

Seamus Carter cut the lighting and had also helped make the stink bombs. The smell was so bad that people almost crushed each other trying to get out of the building. Some of the Volunteers outside were in fits of laughter as they watched people smashing windows and shoving their heads out for fresh air. The premises could not be used for over two weeks such was the brutal odour.[13]

A month after the split the Volunteers in Tuam gave a strong indication of where their loyalties lay when they commemorated the anniversary of the 'Manchester Martyrs'. One of the speakers giving a lecture was Major John MacBride, the celebrated Boer War hero. He had led the Irish Brigade against the British in that war and commanded great respect amongst nationalists countrywide. The commemoration began with the Volunteers assembling at the square in Tuam under the command of Anthony Griffin and M. Kennedy. The Kilbannon Company soon joined them and a detachment of Na Fianna Éireann also attended, led by Seán Forde. Once assembled, they all marched to Oakmount on the road to Dunmore and were joined there by the Dunmore Volunteers under Captain Tom Kilgarriff.[14] Kilgarriff later acted as a brigade intelligence officer in north Galway and was a highly respected man throughout nationalist circles.[15] They again lined up in marching formation and returned to Tuam. Upon arrival in the town they were met by a torch-lit procession of their supporters, who were led by a lone piper. They marched through the streets until they reached the town hall, where the lectures got under way, and MacBride spoke about the Fenians and their contribution to Ireland. The celebrations were closed with the singing of 'A Nation Once Again', which they described as the national anthem. The units then disbanded and the Dunmore Volunteers marched back home, a total journey of some sixteen miles both ways.[16]

The Athenry Volunteers also commemorated the 'Manchester Martyrs'. It seems that some of the men there were issued with three rounds of ammunition to be discharged into the air when the order was given. They marched through the streets of the town, passing the police barracks. Once the men reached the appointed position, they fired off the three volleys, shattering the silence of the town. The Volunteers then waited to see if the police would arrive, but nothing happened. They then marched back to their assembly point and were dismissed until the next meeting. As regards the split in the Athenry Volunteer unit, one of the members of the company, Frank Hynes, said that only 'two old members of the council' and 'most of the milk and water Volunteers who joined when Redmond took over' followed Redmond.[17]

In Castlegar the entire company of Volunteers remained loyal to MacNeill. Their local officers were capable of training their own companies and no longer required the assistance of soldiers serving in the British Army.[18] They would later be joined by Sweeney Newell's brother, Michael. He had been a member of the IRB since 1908 and had made his presence felt within that organisation. He was involved in a number of incidents and attacks against landlord estates and so-called 'land-grabbers'. Newell was arrested on at least one occasion, but released without charge. However, because of continued harassment by the police, he was forced to leave Galway and went to Dunboyne in County Meath, where he joined the local company of Volunteers when it was formed in 1914. Like the Volunteers in Castlegar, Newell was bitterly disappointed when the organisation split its allegiance.

It was Christmas 1915 when Newell returned to join his colleagues in Castlegar.[19] He became vital to the Volunteers there, as he was totally committed to the movement and many of the young men looked to him for guidance. He was also a blacksmith by trade and began producing pikes for the local company. What he and the other Galway Volunteers couldn't have known was that the split had enabled IRB dominance of the Volunteers and the organisation had been set on the path to rebellion.

7

PATH TO REBELLION

Although Liam Mellows gained a strong reputation as a nationalist leader, his family background did not make him an obvious candidate for the republican movement, yet his name would become synonymous with the Volunteers in Galway. He was born on 25 May 1892 in Ashton-under-Lyne, Lancashire, England, as his father, William Joseph, was a British soldier and was stationed there at the time. William had married Sarah Jordan from Wexford on 8 December 1885 in Fermoy, County Cork: she was working as a dressmaker there when William was stationed in Fermoy. In 1889 he was transferred to Glasgow and then a few months later to Lancashire. Their first baby, Jane, was born in 1886 and their second child, John, was born in Lancashire, but did not survive. Liam was the third child born to the couple. In 1895 William was transferred again, this time to Fairview in Dublin. The couple had two more children, Frederick and Herbert, both of whom were born in Dublin. Herbert was more commonly known by his nickname, Barney.

There are doubts about Liam having lived in Fairview for any length of time, as his health was a cause for concern and he was sent to live with his grandfather, Patrick Jordan, in Wexford. His grandfather was a land steward on the Beaumont estate at Hyde Park near Castletown; he had known many of the men involved in the 1798 Rebellion and often spoke of them. Another man, Murtagh Kavanagh, who was a gardener on the estate, was also a great storyteller. He would tell Mellows of the United Irishmen and of the injustice perpetrated on Ireland and its people. Mellows spent five years living in County Wexford. It is believed that he was taken to the 1798 Centenary Commemoration in Gorey, where hundreds of the descendants of the rebels were present. Liam later attended military school at Wellington Barracks in Cork, but by 1900 the family were back living in Dublin, although they began spending the summers in Wexford and Liam always found it difficult when returning to Dublin.

After moving back to the capital, Mellows' father sent him to Portobello garrison school in the hope that he would become an army officer. Mellows began reading more and more books on Irish history and was often found daydreaming – when asked what he was thinking about his reply would be 'Ireland' as he was becoming very republican-minded. He finished school in 1907 and began working as clerk in the Junior Army and Navy Stores in Dublin. The fact that he refused a military career greatly disappointed his father.

In the summer of 1911 Mellows bought a copy of *Irish Freedom* and began visiting Tom Clarke, the old Fenian who had a newsagent's shop in Great Britain Street. Through Clarke, he became involved in Na Fianna Éireann and met Con Colbert and Éamon Martin, with whom he became friends. A short time later, Mellows was given the rank of lieutenant and also joined the IRB. Mellows, along with many other young members of the nationalist movement, believed that, regardless of the introduction of the Home Rule Bill, they would still have to fight against Britain. In 1913 he was promoted to captain in Na Fianna Éireann and later that same evening he announced to his mother, 'I'm going to be another Robert Emmet.' As a senior member of the Fianna, Mellows spent months travelling to various parts of Ireland promoting the movement and in 1914 was given the responsibility of supervising the distribution of the arms that were landed at Kilcoole.

Following the split in the Volunteers, a meeting was held to try to rebuild the movement under MacNeill. Provisional instructors were appointed, of which Mellows was the first, and he was asked to take responsibility for the Galway area. On 31 October 1914 Mellows left Dublin and travelled to Athenry, where he set up his office. The officer in charge of the Athenry Volunteers at the time was Larry Lardner, who also ran a bar in the centre of the town. Lardner helped Mellows secure accommodation in a boarding house owned by a woman named Broderick.[1] While based in Athenry, Mellows met with some of the other local leaders, including Tom Kenny. The authorities were well aware of Kenny's powerful influence in the nationalist movement and the chief secretary for Ireland is reputed to have said, 'Is Ireland to be governed by a water bailiff [Major John MacBride] in Dublin and a blacksmith in Galway?'

The appointment of Mellows to reorganise the Volunteers in County Galway caused tension in the local leadership, as they felt that they were being undermined. Both Lardner and Kenny were initially suspicious of him, but he fitted in very well with the Volunteers and was soon highly respected by them. Fr Thomas Fahy, who later became chaplain to the local Volunteers, was very impressed by Mellows and his determination and commitment to the idea of rebellion.

The following is an interesting description and first impression of Mellows recorded by Martin Newell (no relation of the Newell brothers of Castlegar), one of the Volunteers in Clarenbridge: 'Soon after my transfer to Clarenbridge, the company was visited by Liam Mellows. He was very boyish-looking and full of enthusiasm for his work. He impressed us tremendously by his determination and, looking at his slight figure and boyish appearance, we wondered where all his determination came from'.[2] Perhaps it was because of his appearance that some of the local leaders were initially unsure of Mellows' ability.

Under the guidance of Mellows there were a lot of changes and reorganisation, and the county's Volunteers were split into four brigades: Galway, Athenry, Gort and Loughrea. He also encouraged more men to join, particularly men who were considered extremists. When one looks at the geographical distribution of the organisation it is clear that the movement was much stronger in the east of the county.[3]

During the winter months, intensive training was given at Athenry and Mellows wanted the Volunteers to have a number of their own military instructors in place by the spring of 1915. These men included John Cleary, Frank Hynes, Stephen Jordan, Jim Barrett, Seán Broderick and, of course, Larry Lardner. The company met nightly in Murphy's Hall in the town, where drilling took place most nights; on other occasions there were political and military lectures on how to drive the British out of Ireland. When the weather was fine, Mellows cycled throughout the surrounding townlands to make contact with other nationalists and ensure that preparations were being made for the establishment of additional companies. He was also encouraging young men to join the IRB. His plan of having instructors in place by the spring materialised and with improved weather conditions the men could now drill in the fields.[4]

However, it was not all politics and nationalist activities for Mellows in Athenry, as he became involved with a girl from the town. During an interview in the late 1990s, the late Kitty Lardner (daughter of Larry Lardner) said that Mellows was a regular visitor to their home. It seems that they were secretly engaged to be married, but following his execution by the Free State in 1923, she left Ireland and never married.[5]

Mellows used his knowledge from his days in military school to reorganise the Volunteers into a better fighting force. Joe Howley from Oranmore joined the Volunteers during the early summer of 1915; he attended a lecture on military tactics delivered by Mellows in the town hall in Athenry and was very impressed. Following the lecture, field exercises were arranged between various units to put their tactical training into action. Tom Kenny, who was also chairman of the GAA County Galway Board, organised sporting fixtures for the same day as the Volunteer exercises. When Kenny was requested by Patrick Callanan, who was now the brigade chief of scouts, to change the fixtures, he refused, saying, 'You are killing the best movement we ever had – the GAA'.[6] There is no doubt that Kenny was a true nationalist, who believed in an independent Ireland, but his decision suggests that the GAA was equally or indeed more important to him than the Volunteer movement. Gilbert Morrissey, who had set up a branch of the Volunteers at Rockfield, once asked Kenny if he was in favour of a rebellion. He replied that he was against the idea as personally he felt the time was not right for such action.[7] Kenny's decision could also have had something to do with his opinion or suspicion of Mellows.

One of the most worrying issues for the Volunteers was the intense recruiting campaign being run by the British Army in the various towns around the county. Seán MacDiarmada, a frequent visitor to Athenry and the surrounding area, addressed a number of meetings with Mellows in the early months of 1915. The police were watching both men and making notes of their seditious speeches. No move was made against them initially, but that was about to change.[8] On 16 May Mellows was involved in an anti-recruiting meeting in Tuam with MacDiarmada. During his speech, MacDiarmada left the authorities in no doubt about his attitude towards the war in Europe, and spoke out passionately against the British government. He spoke about their condemnation of German atrocities in Belgium, reminding those attending the meeting that this same government had conveniently forgotten their own atrocities committed at Bachelor's Walk (the people who were shot dead by British troops following the Howth gun-running episode). MacDiarmada told the audience that he had just returned from England, where he saw ample work created for young men, yet in Ireland the only employment available to them was to join the army and die fighting for Britain. He was also concerned about conscription and warned that the Volunteers would fight this at any cost. He maintained that he represented neither pro-German nor pro-British views, but would fight against either side to protect Ireland. In a note of sarcasm he asked, 'If Britain rules the waves, where was she when the *Lusitania* was sunk?' Before concluding he said that Britain's 'difficulty' was Ireland's 'opportunity' and that they should take advantage of this situation. As MacDiarmada finished his address, the police forced their way through the crowd and arrested him under the Defence of the Realm Act 1914; he was the first person in Ireland to be arrested under this act. He was imprisoned in Mountjoy, but this did nothing to quench his quest for freedom – as soon as he was released, he was back on the campaign trail for Irish independence.[9]

The meeting in Tuam continued after MacDiarmada was taken away, with Mellows addressing the crowd.[10] Before being arrested MacDiarmada had managed to pass his revolver to Mellows. However, he also had a notebook containing a list of the names of the IRB Centres, which worried Mellows as it would be disastrous for them if the police found it. Mellows asked Volunteer Liam Langley to accompany him to the police station, where they were allowed to see MacDiarmada. The plan was for Langley to cause a distraction while Mellows took the list from MacDiarmada – it worked and Mellows managed to throw the paper into an open fire in the station without the police becoming suspicious.

Following the Tuam meeting, the police kept Mellows under even closer observation. He was aware that they were watching him and began to antagonise them by cycling openly through the streets in full Volunteer uniform. Although being followed regularly, he always managed to elude his pursuers, which annoyed the police even more. Finally they decided they could not tolerate his behaviour any longer, and on 11 July 1915 the British authorities issued orders for Mellows to leave Ireland immediately.[11] The directive was served under the Aliens Restriction Act.[12] They served him with the order at his lodgings in Athenry and he left for Dublin as if to comply with the demand. He stayed at the home of his parents where his mother fed him for two days unbeknownst to his father, who opposed the path his son had chosen. Instead of leaving the country, Mellows made his way to Wexford, but was arrested a week later and sentenced to three months' imprisonment in Mountjoy.[13]

Back in Galway the local units continued as best they could without Mellows and during August 1915 Alf Monahan arrived from Dublin to help with the training and organisation of some of the Galway Volunteers. Monahan, originally from Belfast and a member of the IRB, had joined the Volunteers when they were formed in that city. His military training was completed under an NCO of the Royal Artillery, a former member of the Orange Order. Monahan was first sent to Cavan, but was arrested and imprisoned in Belfast a short time later and when he was released after three months he was sent to Galway.[14]

The appointment of Fr Harry Feeney as curate in the parish of Clarenbridge that same year also had an effect on the Volunteers. He was fully behind the movement and did all in his power to support and encourage the men. He provided his house for meetings and for the manufacture of bombs.[15] Fr Feeney, originally from Two Mile Ditch near Castlegar, was known to attend night gatherings of Volunteers in the Athenry area.

Training intensified and field exercises were held between various units from around the county. By then the Volunteers were being instructed in signalling, scouting and engineering classes in addition to the drilling and weapons instruction that was now a regular part of the training.[16] Some of the men were rising through the ranks; by Christmas 1915 Brian Molloy had been appointed captain of the Castlegar Volunteers.[17] Éamonn Corbett had also shown his natural military ability over the previous twelve months and had been helping Liam Mellows with the training of Volunteers, so he had risen to the rank of brigade adjutant under Larry Lardner.[18] The Galway Volunteers were being readied for action, but none of them knew just how soon this would come.

8

A REBEL CALL

A very important call to arms for nationalists took place in Dublin on 1 August 1915 – the funeral of the Fenian Jeremiah O'Donovan Rossa in Glasnevin Cemetery. Patrick Pearse delivered the oration in front of thousands of nationalists who had gathered to pay their last respects to O'Donovan Rossa. His speech at the graveside was a masterpiece and left all those present with a deep respect for him as he concluded the oration by saying, 'Life springs from death; and from the graves of patriot men and women spring living nations ... They think that they have foreseen everything, think that they have provided against everything; but the fools, the fools, the fools! – they have left us our Fenian dead, and while Ireland holds these graves, Ireland unfree shall never be at peace'. It was a defining moment for Pearse and his words brought a powerful sense of pride to the nationalist movement.[1] His speech was also heard as a rebel call by many of the young men present.

According to at least one source, most of the oration was written by Pearse while staying at his cottage in Rosmuc in Connemara and completed on the train while travelling back to Dublin.[2] The journey was not very pleasant because it seems that Pearse became involved in a row with a drunken man on the train. The man was smoking in a non-smoking carriage and refused to extinguish the cigarette when requested to do so.

William Pearse had to restrain his brother to prevent him from forcing the man out of the carriage.[3]

About 400 Volunteers from Galway took part in the funeral cortège and were accompanied by a band from Galway city. Larry Lardner was in charge of the men from Galway and Daniel Kearns said that it was difficult to hear Pearse properly as they were behind the Dublin, Limerick and Cork companies.[4]

Pearse returned to Connemara later that month and visited Micheál Ó Droighneáin. A meeting was arranged with the Connemara companies and Pearse informed them that a rebellion would definitely take place; it was only a matter of time. Ó Droighneáin established an IRB Circle in Barna and Moycullen as well as a Volunteer company in each district. All of the Volunteer officers appointed were IRB men.[5]

Éamonn Ceannt also visited Connemara in August of that year, along with his wife and son, on his last visit to Galway. They stayed with Micheál Ó Droighneáin and the two men spent much time wandering along the beach at Spiddal and walking in the mountains. In the evenings and sometimes at night Ceannt trained and advised the Volunteers in the use of weapons and completed night exercises with them. He was almost arrested one night while on his way to meet the Volunteers, when the constabulary stopped him because he didn't have a lamp on his bicycle. Ceannt had at first ignored the call to stop, but the policemen enforced their order. He would only answer their questions in Irish which caused confusion and while the police were annoyed with him, they decided to let him go and send a summons a month later. Ceannt also spent some evenings entertaining the locals by playing the pipes in various houses around the district.

One evening, while walking along the beach with Ó Droighneáin, Ceannt found a bullet. He picked it up and asked Ó Droighneáin if he had any knowledge of it. Before he could answer, Ceannt advised him that a rebellion was being planned and he wanted Ó Droighneáin's total assurance that Connemara would rise to the cause. Ó Droighneáin was fully committed, but said they needed guns. Ceannt promised to try to supply weapons before the Rising would take place. He also told Ó Droighneáin to be prepared and watch for signs, saying one of the issues that would trigger an immediate rebellion was conscription.[6]

The military recruiting campaign had intensified throughout Galway city and county during 1915 and the threat of conscription grew. In September 1915 the male population in the city continued to diminish because of the amount of young men enlisting in the army. The smaller towns and villages around the county were also being targeted for recruits. The methods and tactics used to encourage young men to join the army were extensive and the recruiting offices literally combed every part of the country to ensure that the military secured their numbers for the Western Front. People were warned that if the Germans should invade they would lose their land; no woman was safe from being raped or murdered by these brutal invaders. Girls were told not to be seen with a man unless he was wearing khaki or navy blue. There was also the promise of Home Rule, once victory had been achieved. Another major incentive was, of course, a regular army income. Many people today either forget, or choose to ignore, that there was enormous support for the war effort at that time and Galway Urban Council acted more or less as a recruiting committee for the military. This was much the same across the county, with local councils supporting the recruiting campaigns also. All of this caused much concern among the various nationalist movements, including Sinn Féin.

There had been Sinn Féin protest marches between 1914 and 1915, but they gained little or no support from the public and there were serious scuffles and name-calling between them and the supporters of the war. During one anti-recruiting meeting organised by Sinn Féin in Galway, a large crowd of pro-war supporters gathered in the street outside the hall in Williamsgate Street and stones were hurled through the windows of the building. A short time later, members of the Irish Volunteers and Sinn Féin marched out of the building in military formation and as they paraded through the town, the crowd followed, shouting abuse at them. As the nationalists reached O'Brien's Bridge they were forced to break formation and run because the crowd were becoming violent. The homes of Sinn Féin members were also targeted, with windows being smashed and doors damaged by people throwing stones.[7]

There seems to have been very little support for Sinn Féin in the smaller population centres also. In October 1915 Sinn Féin called a public meeting in Tuam to be held after the last mass on Sunday, when it was felt that there would be a large gathering of people. A platform was erected and three speakers prepared to address a disappointingly small crowd of between thirty and forty people. It was an anti-British/pro-German meeting. The crowd showed no signs of support for the speakers, and in fact some simply walked away and went about their business. Three policemen were watching, and one of them, District Inspector Comerford, mounted the platform and arrested one of the speakers as the few people remaining simply dispersed due to a lack of interest in the proceedings.[8]

On 31 October 1915 Liam Mellows was released from prison, just before the Volunteers' convention was due to take place. He was again elected to the Central Council and prepared to return to Galway. On 23 November the Volunteers held a huge rally in Athenry to welcome him back. There were a number of speakers, including Joseph O'Flaherty, who chaired the meeting, The O'Rahilly, Lawrence Ginnell MP and three strongly nationalist priests, Fr Connolly, Fr O'Meehan and Fr Feeney. Mellows was now even more popular, not just among the leadership of the Volunteers, but among the men themselves. The jail term had ensured widespread respect, which was clear from the hero's welcome he received west of the Shannon. During the meeting, Mellows was presented with a motorbike, which he would use for long journeys to surrounding counties and in the Connemara area. However, he stopped using it locally as the police were alerted to his presence by the sound – motorbikes were a rare means of transport in those days.

Mellows went to live in the home of Volunteer Frank Hynes and from there he planned his journeys to the various Volunteer companies. The police were clearly aware of some of his travels as one day he recognised two RIC men in civilian clothing on the road between New Inn and Kilconnell. He was on his way to Tullamore and continued on his journey; on the return he spotted two masked men at the same location. He turned down a boreen towards Woodlawn Station, but the men had obviously anticipated this move and were waiting for Mellows about a half-mile on the other side of the station road. They pulled him off the motorbike, but Mellows managed to kick one of them in the jaw and the other man ran. He then lifted the damaged motorbike and made his way back to Athenry. Mellows was seen by the authorities as the instigator of all the disturbances in east and south Galway and because of this he was under constant close police surveillance.[9]

In January 1916 the IRB Military Council began holding their meetings at Éamonn Ceannt's house at Dolphin's Barn, Dublin. Definite plans were being made for the rebellion and over the following weeks it was decided that the uprising would take place on 23 April 1916. Ceannt was appointed director of communications, which was one of the most important positions within the Volunteers. It was his responsibility to ensure a countrywide rebellion and it was vital that he had men who could be relied upon to ensure a successful revolt. From a Galway perspective, he certainly knew a number of the senior Volunteer officers, and kept their names and addresses in a diary along with details of their second-in-command. He was also a close friend of Liam Mellows and had every confidence in him.[10] The Irish Volunteers had rebuilt their organisation following the split, and this was evident from their massive show of strength in the St Patrick's Day parade in Galway city, when over a thousand men turned out to represent many areas of the county.[11] The following are some of the companies who were represented that day: Clarenbridge, Oranmore, Maree, Athenry, Ardrahan, Craughwell, Claregalway, Castlegar, Gort, Spiddal, Kinvara, Ballinderreen and Killimor. They all carried weapons of some type; most of them had shotguns, but there were also pikes and rifles on display. There were at least two police constables from each of the areas represented, positioned at various strategic points along the parade route, watching and making notes about the men bearing arms. While many of the Volunteers believed that the parade was a demonstration against recruitment for the British Army, some later felt it had been a rehearsal for the rebellion.[12]

A fourteen-year-old girl named Brid from Waterlane, Bohermore, watched the parade with interest. The following is an extract from a journal compiled following an interview with her in 1979: 'I woke early as I always do on some great occasion like this, mostly because I was too excited to sleep. When I went downstairs there was the usual bustle. All my younger sisters were nearly hysterical with excitement. The beginning of the parade was just as usual, but then we heard a huge cheer. Soon we knew the reason. Up the street came a body of men; some of them had rifles, others had guns and about twenty of them carried pikes. The pikes fascinated me but yet terrified me.'[13]

The parade route took the Volunteers through the main streets of the city and around by Newcastle, down by University Road and back to the assembly point near Eyre Square. They were subjected to a lot of abuse from people lining the streets, particularly from the 'separation women': the wives, daughters and girlfriends of the Irishmen serving with the British Army abroad. The lists of names noted by the police came in very useful in the aftermath of the rebellion and some of the rebels were later reminded of the type of weapon they carried that day in the parade. The determination of the Volunteers was evident by the fact some companies had to march long distances to take part in the parade. For instance the Clarenbridge Company marched to Oranmore and took the train to Galway from there.[14] Many of the pikes had been produced in Briarhill in the forge of Michael Newell, who worked late into the evenings and nights making the weapons, helped by his brother Sweeney. As there was always the danger of the police arriving, sentries were placed to warn of anyone approaching Briarhill.[15]

One of the Volunteers not present on St Patrick's Day was Thomas Courtney, who had been advised by the leadership of the Castlegar unit not to march in the parade. Courtney, who worked for the post office, was of more benefit to them gathering intelligence, which was after all his position in the Volunteers, so he was ordered not to attract attention to himself.[16]

In March 1916 Mellows was again arrested, this time in the house of Julia Morrissey, and was sent to Arbour Hill Barracks in Dublin, where he awaited deportation to England. It seems that Mellows was not charged with anything and there were public protests because of his arrest.[17] Alf Monahan was also to be arrested, but he escaped detection with the help of Fr Feeney and Sweeney Newell. Monahan, dressed as a priest, travelled to Oranmore with Fr Feeney, while Newell and another Volunteer acted as decoys, leading the police in the wrong direction.[18]

In the absence of Mellows, Patrick Pearse travelled to Athenry to inform the Volunteer officers of their objectives when the rebellion broke out – to secure territory as far as the River Suck and hold the eastern border of the county. They were also to try to occupy Galway city and take control of it. Once these objectives had been achieved, they were to travel to Dublin to join the fight there. While Larry Lardner told Pearse that he felt these plans were possible, others attending the meeting disagreed strongly. Pearse then agreed to modify the plan, opting for them to hold a line along the River Shannon instead. They were to be supported by their comrades from Ulster, whom he said would join them. Again there were disagreements, as this plan was not practical given the distance between these two Volunteer units and the fact that the men from Ulster would have to pass through militant unionist territory. The decision finally agreed on was that they were to take military action when they received communication that Dublin was out in rebellion. Pearse told them to take as much territory as possible and then await further orders.

In reality Pearse's proposals were not realistic as they were indecisive and lacked any clear objectives. Such a lack of planning was sure to cause problems when the Rising began.[19] This was certainly a serious error on the part of the leadership in Dublin, particularly Pearse, as it was in a sense leaving the outcome of the rebellion in the west to chance. This meeting also left the situation open to differences of opinion, and without clear, well-defined plans, the rebels could not hope for much success.

9

ORDERS AND COUNTERMANDING ORDERS

The arrest of Mellows was a serious blow to the Volunteer movement in Galway and, now that a date for the rebellion was set, it was crucial to the IRB that they stay in close communication with him as he was expected to lead the rebellion in the west. Mellows was allowed to choose his own place of exile and decided on Leek in Staffordshire, where he had relatives. Some sources indicate that Mellows relayed details of his destination through his brother Barney to Seán MacDiarmada.[1] However, another source clearly states that it was through his mother and Áine Ceannt that this information was passed on to the rebel leadership. The plan was for his mother to visit him every few days, as it seems to have taken him some time to decide on the location. She would then relay the details to Áine Ceannt, who would pass the information to her husband. The IRB would then put an escape plan in place.

Even though Mellows was staying with relatives in England, his movements were restricted and the police kept him under constant surveillance. While he could trust his hosts, he still needed an effective plan to escape without the police becoming suspicious. His brother Barney bore a striking resemblance to Liam and agreed to exchange places with him in Leek. He travelled there with Nora, the daughter of James

Connolly. Shortly after reaching the house where Mellows was staying, both men retired to one of the bedrooms where they exchanged clothing and Liam was given the return sailing ticket for Ireland. He then set out on the journey back with Nora and on arrival in Dublin was placed in the home of Frank Fahy, whom he had met in Athenry.

The IRB were aware that if the police in England realised that Mellows had escaped, there would be a major search for him in Ireland, so as a precaution he was supplied with clerical clothing to use as a disguise should the police become aware that he was in Dublin.[2] He stayed with Fahy for three days and was visited by some of his old friends from the Fianna, including Con Colbert. He then made his way to Pearse at St Enda's, where, along with Éamonn Corbett, they discussed plans for the rebellion in Galway. Corbett and Mellows were informed at the meeting that a consignment of arms from Germany was to be landed in County Kerry on Good Friday morning. Roger Casement was travelling with the arms and would ensure that the Volunteers in Kerry received them. These arms were then to be sent to the Volunteers in the west. The plan included the hijacking of a train to get the weapons to Limerick from where they would be taken by road to Gort. There the Volunteer companies from south Galway were to assemble when the arms arrived and this would signal the start of the Rising in the west. Orders were also issued to destroy public communications in all areas of eastern Galway. Portumna was to be one of the main objectives and, if successful, the rebels in this area were to cross the Shannon and proceed towards Dublin.[3]

On the Monday morning of Holy Week, Éamonn and Áine Ceannt decided to visit the Pearse family at St Enda's. They took their son along with them. Shortly after arriving they went to the garden at the rear of the building where the fruit trees were in full bloom. Áine Ceannt remembered that everything was very peaceful as they walked through the sunny garden. Moments later they noticed a young cleric emerging from the trees and approaching them. He smiled as he came closer and soon Mellows was shaking hands with Áine and making a special effort to speak to Rónán in Irish. Patrick Pearse and his mother joined them shortly afterwards and soon lunch was announced. They all went into the dining room where they were greeted by William Pearse and his sister Margaret. They had a pleasant meal together with the topic of conversation moving across many subjects, from music to books. There was no mention of an impending rebellion.

Following the lunch Mellows, Ceannt and the Pearse brothers retired to one of the rooms to discuss the events of the coming week. Mellows was informed that dispatches would be sent out by Ceannt with the code words for the rebellion which were already decided: 'Collect the premiums'. Pearse would sign all orders. Before the meeting came to an end, words of encouragement were shared, but it was the last time that Mellows ever saw any of these men alive. The women waited in the garden; however, they avoided speaking of the weeks ahead. When Ceannt emerged from the house, he asked Áine if she would contact Mrs Mellows immediately and take her to see Liam that night, as Mellows was being sent to Galway the following day and this was the last opportunity for his mother to see him before the rebellion.[4]

The return of Mellows to County Galway was welcomed by the local leadership. Once he reached there, he changed from his clerical outfit to civilian clothing and made his way to the home of Joseph O'Flaherty in Loughrea. O'Flaherty was an old Fenian and had been a pallbearer at the funeral of O'Donovan Rossa in Dublin. Mellows had to remain under cover as the Volunteers could not afford to lose him again, particularly being so close to the insurrection.[5]

There was a lot of confusion among the Galway Volunteers that week, with no written orders arriving from Dublin as expected. The Volunteer officers, including Éamonn Corbett, Joseph Howley, Pádraic Fahy, Matt Neilan and their commanding officer, Larry Lardner, called a meeting in Fr Feeney's house to discuss the situation. Corbett told the men of the meeting with Pearse at St Enda's earlier that week, but it was decided that no rebellion could take place until they received written orders. When the orders did not arrive, Lardner decided to travel to Dublin on Holy Thursday to obtain official instructions for the rebellion. Unfortunately when Lardner arrived in Dublin he could not locate Pearse or MacNeill. However, he did meet with Bulmer Hobson, a former IRB council member, who instructed him not to obey any orders unless Eoin MacNeill had signed them. This was disappointing for Lardner and he returned to Galway more confused than when he had left that morning.

Meanwhile the dispatch ordering the rebellion to go

ahead as scheduled had been sent by Éamonn Ceannt. One source claimed he entrusted the orders to Frank Fahy's wife, who brought them to Athenry where she was to give them directly to Lardner. She was unable to locate him as he was in Dublin at the time, but eventually met with Éamonn Corbett that evening and he took the dispatch from her and gave it to Lardner when he returned.[6] However, Margaret Browne claims in her witness statement that it was she who brought the dispatch to Athenry on Thursday evening after she was asked by a priest, Fr Hannon, in Dublin to take two letters to Galway. One of these was to be delivered to the bishop of Galway and the other was for the archbishop of Tuam. The letters contained information about the arrest of leading Irish Volunteers and the seizure of certain buildings by the British. As she was making her way along the platform of Broadstone Station to board the afternoon train to Galway she was approached by Seán MacDiarmada, who asked her to stop off at Athenry and deliver a dispatch to Larry Lardner and then go to Galway and issue another to George Nichols. Upon arriving at Athenry, she made her way to Lardner's premises, but he wasn't there. His mother and brother received her and she entrusted them with the dispatch. A few minutes later the police arrived enquiring about her identity and the Lardner family said she was a visiting relative. After the police left, she slipped out through the back of the house and returned to the railway station to catch the next train. Having arrived in Galway, Browne stayed in the Railway Hotel and the following morning was met by a woman named Tina Power who would help her with the delivery of the letters from the priest. She completed all of her tasks and before leaving Galway, she met Nichols, who told her that the plans had changed.[7] Margaret Browne later married Seán MacEntee, a founder member of the Fianna Fáil party.[8]

There was obviously a lack of clarity as to the events of that day among the Galway leadership. According to Michael Newell, on Holy Thursday night he was with Brian Molloy and Tom Ruane of the Claregalway Company. They met the midnight train from Dublin in Oranmore Station where a meeting had been arranged with George Nichols. He was returning from Dublin with orders stating that the rebellion would start at 7 o'clock on Easter Sunday. He was also to inform Captain Alf Monahan, who was on the run at this time.[9] It seems strange that both Lardner and Nichols were in Dublin on the same day on the same mission without any knowledge of each other.

The plans apparently agreed between the officers that night included Molloy and Ruane uniting their forces and attacking the police barracks at Lydecan in County Galway. Having captured that barracks they were to remove all weapons, ammunition and equipment and then burn the building. They would then proceed to Loughgeorge and Killeen and carry out the same action against the police there. The plan included handcuffing all police prisoners and marching them ahead of the Volunteer column into Galway city, where they were to link up with the other companies from Connemara.[10]

In Dublin Bulmer Hobson had continued working at his office in Dawson Street after Lardner left for Galway that

Thursday evening. Sometime later two members of the Dublin Volunteers arrived and informed Hobson that the Volunteer companies around the country had received orders to start a rebellion on Easter Sunday. Hobson became alarmed and immediately went to see MacNeill to tell him. MacNeill was shocked and very much annoyed, and immediately travelled to St Enda's to confront Pearse and confirm if the rumours were true. After Pearse admitted that plans for the Rising were already in place, MacNeill became outraged and abusive. Being commander-in-chief of the Volunteers, he felt deceived by the IRB men. They argued for a time and before leaving, MacNeill warned Pearse that he would do all in his power to prevent the rebellion as he did not want the blood of the men on his hands.

Knowing that MacNeill was now a liability to their plans, the rebel leaders held an emergency meeting and decided that Pearse, MacDiarmada and Thomas MacDonagh would go and speak with him the following morning. Tensions were running high on both sides and when they arrived at the home of MacNeill, he would only meet with MacDiarmada. During the discussion, MacDiarmada informed MacNeill of the arms landing in Kerry and convinced him that the only way forward was rebellion. He also said that the authorities would arrest the leadership of the Volunteers once they became aware of the situation and there was now only one option open to them – to go ahead as planned. Having thought about their position for a short time, MacNeill decided to support the rebellion. The others then joined him for breakfast to discuss the coming events.[11]

That same morning, Good Friday, Mellows left Loughrea in the company of Éamonn Corbett and two other Volunteers, Patrick Walsh and Ned Newell, who were taking Mellows to a new location. There weren't enough bikes for them all so they each took turns carrying Mellows on their crossbars. They crossed the Dunkellin River into Killeeneen and Mellows was placed in a cottage close to the schoolhouse, owned by a Mrs Walsh. There he was given his uniform, which had been sent from Dublin by train.[12] All they could do now was to wait for news of the arms landing as the orders from Dublin had arrived. Although many people were aware that Mellows was back in Galway, he was anxious not to attract any attention, so he was for the most part out of contact with the companies.[13] Armed sentries were placed along the roads leading to the cottage where Mellows was staying and sentry duty continued throughout the weekend.[14]

Orders for the Rising reached the Spiddal Company on Friday. Volunteer Peadar Duignan told Micheál Ó Droighneáin that a woman named Peg Conlon was trying to locate him. She was a stranger in the area and had made a few discreet inquiries in the village before meeting Duignan. Ó Droighneáin was teaching in Furbo at the time and he recalled in his witness statement that he arranged to meet her in a house near Spiddal. She had travelled from Dublin by train and then cycled to Spiddal to deliver the orders.[15] Peg, originally from Glenamaddy in County Galway, moved to Dublin and married Martin Conlon in 1910, and both were involved in the nationalist movement, he as an Irish Volunteer and she as a member of Cumann na mBan. Her memory of meeting Ó Droighneáin differs slightly from his account, as she said that while she was making inquiries about him, he was pointed out to her as he made his way along the road with another man. They had hurleys and were on their way to play in some match. Once Peg was sure that the man to whom she was speaking was Ó Droighneáin, she removed the dispatch from one of her stockings and gave it to him.[16] It was from Ceannt and contained the orders for the rebellion.

Ó Droighneáin was a bit shocked as, while he was expecting to hear news of the rebellion, he did not believe it would happen so quickly. During that week he and his men had already collected as many arms as possible, including pikes from Newell's forge in Briarhill which, according to Ó Droighneáin, were secured just coming up to Easter Week. It was a long distance for them to travel without being detected by the police, but they managed to do so. The manpower at Ó Droighneáin's disposal consisted of twenty-four Volunteers from Spiddal, fourteen from Barna and about sixteen from Moycullen.[17]

According to Michael Newell, it was Holy Saturday when Ó Droighneáin collected the pikes and he said that he was very lucky as the police had been there shortly before he arrived. Newell had just finished making the last of the weapons that day when he had a visit from Fr Feeney. The police arrived while they were talking, but did not enter the forge when they saw the priest there. Although they called Newell out, he refused to go, saying that anything they had to say could be said from where they stood. The sergeant said he had information that Newell was making pikes and warned that if they caught him, they would charge him under the Defence of the Realm Act. The police then left and returned to the city. After they departed, Fr Feeney confirmed the plans for the rebellion on Easter Sunday and Newell told him that they were already aware of them and that the orders included confession for the Volunteers. Fr Feeney also said that there was a possibility of arms being landed on the Connemara coast.[18] This is interesting as it was mentioned in a number of later witness statements, but not, as far as I am aware, anywhere else.

Whatever plans had been laid, events in Kerry on Good Friday morning changed everything. All hopes of a successful rebellion disappeared beneath the waves with the loss of the *Aud*, some 20,000 rifles and a consignment of ammunition. When MacNeill heard the news from Kerry he changed his mind about supporting the rebellion and sent out Volunteers loyal to him with orders to cancel it, stating in the notice, 'Volunteers completely deceived. All orders for special action are hereby cancelled, and on no account will action be taken'. It was signed 'Eoin MacNeill, chief of staff'.

This left the rebellion leaders with little or no time to react and caused confusion across the country. Among the men who supported MacNeill and tried to prevent the rebellion was Arthur Griffith. MacNeill's orders reached Lardner on Saturday. Orders and countermanding orders were causing havoc for the local leadership, so an emergency meeting was called in the home of George Nichols in Galway.[19] Those who attended the meeting included Larry Lardner, Pat Callanan,

Tom Ruane, Matt Neilan, Micheál Ó Droighneáin, Éamonn Corbett, Pádraic Fahy, Fr Feeney and John Hosty. After a long discussion, it was decided that one of them would have to go to Dublin and meet with Pearse or MacDiarmada personally and clarify the situation. Hosty was chosen to travel, but time was running out, so in the meantime it was decided to go ahead with the original plans and strike on Easter Sunday.[20]

Not all of those attending the meeting were in agreement with following the orders from Pearse. One of these was Nichols, who, while not in favour of the decision, went along with this plan, but warned the others that they would all be slaughtered.[21] Although the officers agreed that Hosty should clarify the issue with MacNeill, Nichols pulled him aside before leaving and told him to go to see Pearse. Hosty travelled to Athenry with Lardner and took the 12.30 a.m. train to Dublin. He arrived in the capital shortly after 5 a.m. and took a sidecar to the home of Pearse. However, none of the men were there and the only person he spoke with was Margaret Pearse. She was unsure of the whereabouts of her two brothers, but sent Hosty to Rutland Street, where she thought he might find Patrick. When Hosty failed to make contact with Pearse he then decided to try to locate MacNeill. When he arrived at MacNeill's home, MacNeill's wife Agnes and the children were leaving for mass, but she brought him in to see her husband, who was still in the house. Another Volunteer officer, Seán Fitzgibbons, was also there. MacNeill informed Hosty that he had published the countermanding orders in the Sunday papers and that the Rising was cancelled. Hosty later stated that he also met Stephen Jordan and Tom Kenny while in Dublin, as they were attending a GAA Congress.[22]

There was as much confusion in Dublin as in Galway, and MacNeill contacted the newspapers because he was not satisfied with the hand-delivered countermanding orders. On Saturday evening he issued a notice to appear in the Sunday newspapers. His orders read, 'Owing to the very critical position, all orders given to the Irish Volunteers for Easter Sunday are hereby rescinded, and no parades, marches or other movements of Irish Volunteers will take place.' On Easter Sunday morning Pearse, James Connolly and the other leaders called an emergency meeting in Liberty Hall to discuss the situation. After much discussion it was decided to strike on Easter Monday at 12 noon and new orders were sent out to countermand those issued by MacNeill. However, the statement to the press cancelling manoeuvres had already killed off any hope of a simultaneous countrywide rebellion.[23]

10

EASTER MONDAY 1916

On Easter Sunday 1916 the morning newspapers were read with interest and disappointment by some people in Galway. The countermanding order from MacNeill was published, causing much concern amongst the rebel leadership.[1] That morning Micheál Ó Droighneáin reported that he saw a fleet of British warships in Galway Bay. However, this seems strange given that the rebellion had not started and there do not seem to be any other reports about British ships until mid-week. Nevertheless, he says he began to have grave misgivings about the plans for rebellion.[2]

During Holy Week the various companies of Volunteers in Galway had been told by their officers to make sure they went to confession on Saturday evening and received Holy Communion on Easter Sunday. They were advised to bring their arms, equipment and rations of food with them on Sunday. In some areas the girls of the Cumann na mBan prepared breakfast for the Volunteers in the church grounds after mass. As word spread that the Rising was cancelled, the Volunteer units were dismissed, but told to stay close to home and remain on the alert for a quick mobilisation.[3]

While some sources indicate that Mellows was at mass with Éamonn Corbett in Roveagh Church that day and was aware of the situation, another placed him in the cottage in

Killeeneen.[4] He could, of course, have been in both places depending on the time. According to Desmond Greaves in his
book *Liam Mellows and the Irish Revolution,* it was at the cottage that he received word that the rebellion was cancelled. It
seems it was Éamonn Corbett and Fr Feeney who brought
him the news on Sunday afternoon, saying that a priest had
arrived in Athenry by motorbike that morning with an official
dispatch from MacNeill calling off the rebellion. Although
Mellows was in total disagreement with MacNeill, he reluc-
tantly ordered the suspension of all military operations in
Galway. His mood was solemn, but this changed a little later
when another dispatch arrived. This one was from Pearse and
it informed the men that the rebellion was postponed rather
than cancelled. His reply to Pearse was simply that Galway
was always ready.[5]

The Castlegar Company under Brian Molloy had already
mobilised and was on its way to join the Claregalway unit
when a dispatch rider, Michael Walsh, arrived with word from
Lardner that operations were suspended until further notice.
They marched back to Castlegar, placed all arms in a barn belonging to the Newell family and were dismissed for the night.

Earlier that day Molloy had ordered Thomas Courtney to
find as many boats as possible and secure them in safe places on
the west side of the River Corrib to aid the Connemara companies in crossing the river without having to enter Galway
city, in case it was heavily occupied by British troops. Courtney
was chosen for this task because he was a powerful oarsman
and knew the river very well. As he was making his way back

to Castlegar to inform Molloy that he had successfully carried out his task, two Volunteers who did not recognise him captured him. This was not really surprising as it was dark and, being the intelligence officer for the unit at the time, he had always managed to keep a low profile. He was taken under armed guard to Molloy, who laughed at the idea of Courtney being their first prisoner of the rebellion.[6]

On Easter Monday morning a party of Irish Volunteers, supported by members of the Irish Citizen Army (ICA), assembled at Liberty Hall in Dublin. Those who gathered were prepared for war and rebellion was inevitable for all those present. The Army of the Republic was about to strike at the very heart of the capital in the hope that the country would rise with them. They were under the command of Patrick Pearse, Thomas Clarke, James Connolly, Seán MacDiarmada and Joseph Plunkett. Shortly before the appointed time for action, 12 noon, the combined Irish forces marched from Liberty Hall to the General Post Office (GPO) in Sackville Street.[7]

One of the first witnesses to the rebellion in Dublin was a sixteen-year-old girl named Katie Hoare from Galway. She had arranged to meet her sister, Sarah, who had secured employment for her in the capital. The date chosen for the beginning of her great adventure was Easter Monday 24 April 1916, and she took the morning train to Dublin. Before travelling they had exchanged letters and had arranged to meet at Nelson's Pillar at noon, so, having left Kingsbridge Station, Katie made her way along the quays to Sackville Street. Although she had never been away from home before, she found the then-famous landmark easily and, while waiting for her sister, saw a large group of armed and uniformed men marching up Sackville Street as they made their way towards the GPO. As the war was raging in Europe, and being from a garrison town, Katie took little notice at first. It wasn't unusual for her to see groups of armed soldiers in the streets. However, moments later she became aware that something was different by the manner in which they approached the GPO. After they entered the building she heard the sound of shots being fired, which frightened and confused her, and moments later she became concerned as the windows were smashed and she heard the screams of people making a hasty exit from the building. She said that after some time the leader and some of the soldiers emerged. He began to read aloud from a document he had in his hands. She later realised that it was Patrick Pearse proclaiming the Irish Republic. Although Katie didn't know it at the time, she was witnessing the birth of a nation. It seems that three days passed before she was finally located by her sister because of the barricades set up by troops and rebels. She had managed to find a place of refuge in a city engulfed in rebellion and she remembered those days for the rest of her life.[8]

The rebellion was now a reality and over the following days Dublin witnessed many deaths and much destruction. Having occupied the GPO, the rebels removed two British flags that flew over the building and replaced them with two Irish flags. One was green and bore the legend 'Irish Republic' in gold-and-white lettering. The other was the tricolour and the rebels raised it with great pride.

The GPO became the headquarters of the Provisional Government of Ireland and to ensure that the general public were aware of the reasons behind the rebellion, copies of the Proclamation were handed out to civilians in the streets and were also posted on various buildings. The first exchange of fire occurred at Dublin Castle, after a section of the ICA shot dead Constable James O'Brien, who had been on duty at the castle gate. Although the rebels forced the military to retreat from the castle's guardhouse, they failed to press forward with the attack. The castle was almost entirely at their mercy as there were only about twenty-five soldiers on duty at the time, but the rebels were unaware of this. Had they succeeded in capturing Dublin Castle it would have been an epic moment in Irish history.

By this time hostilities were breaking out all across Dublin city. The first British attack on the Volunteers in the GPO took place that afternoon when a group of British Lancers moved against the rebel position, but were repulsed. At the Four Courts the 1st Battalion of the Irish Volunteers under Commandant Edward Daly seized the building, set up a number of outposts, including one at the Mendicity Institution with Seán Heuston in command, and erected barricades in the surrounding area. A short time later a number of Lancers of the 6th Cavalry Reserve Regiment arrived on the scene. Their encounter with some of Daly's men cost them six or seven men, while the others fled.

As the GPO was being taken by the rebels, Commandant Michael Mallin was leading a section of the ICA into

St Stephen's Green, accompanied by his second-in-command, Countess Markievicz. The action began there as the rebels were taking control of the park. The countess shot a police constable dead as he attempted to enter the park area. Mallin also had barricades erected in the surrounding streets. It seems strange that he made no attempt to occupy the Shelbourne Hotel, as it would have given him a commanding view of the street and this was an error he later regretted. The British occupied the hotel, and by Tuesday, after some sharp exchanges of fire, Mallin and his remaining men were forced to retreat to the College of Surgeons.

By noon of Easter Monday Commandant Éamonn Ceannt had occupied the South Dublin Union complex, where some of the bloodiest fighting took place that week. The union was a large complex that resembled a fortified town surrounded by stone walls, so attacks there were costly for the British, with many lives lost. In contrast, Jacob's factory and the various rebel outposts in the surrounding area, which were under Commandant Thomas MacDonagh, remained relatively quiet during the rebellion.[9]

It was vital to get news of the rebellion in the capital out to the Volunteer companies around the country. Pearse and Ceannt did send out dispatches, but there was still a lot of uncertainty in Galway. Even today there are conflicting reports of how the dispatch arrived in Athenry. One source says that sometime after 1 p.m. on Easter Monday, Larry Lardner was speaking with some Volunteer officers, among them Liam Langley, who had arrived from Tuam requesting instructions, when a woman arrived from Dublin with a dispatch. This read, 'We are out from twelve o'clock today. Issue your orders without delay. – P.H.P.' According to this source the woman who delivered the order was Elizabeth O'Farrell, who was with the GPO garrison. Nevertheless, Lardner was suspicious of the dispatch because it only had Pearse's initials rather than his signature. He was fearful of more misinformation and did not issue orders immediately. It is not known for certain if he informed Mellows in Killeeneen.[10]

However, according to Stephen Jordan in his witness statement, it was a man on a motorcycle who arrived at the home of Commandant Lardner with news that Dublin was in rebellion. He was at Lardner's house at the time and said that he was ordered by Lardner to go to Galway city and inform George Nichols that the Rising was at last taking place. The orders were for Nichols to mobilise Galway city and Connemara. Having delivered the dispatch, Jordan returned to Athenry that night by train. He was met by Volunteer escorts and taken to the town hall where the company had mobilised.[11]

The afternoon train from Dublin brought definite news that the rebellion was under way. Lardner then sent word to Mellows and the other companies, and the schoolhouse in Killeeneen was the main assembly point for the Volunteers in this area.[12] This soon filled and others arriving at the school had to be accommodated in local houses until the order to move out was issued.

Mellows sent Volunteer Pádraic Fahy and three others to Kinvara to inform Fr O'Meehan, in charge of the company there, about the Rising. There was a lot of police activity in Kinvara when they got there, so Fahy went into the home of the priest alone as the police were watching the house. As Fahy was leaving they overpowered and captured him, but the other Volunteers escaped and made their way back to inform Mellows of the situation. Mellows decided that an attempt to rescue Fahy would be made the following morning, as he believed that the police would take him to Galway Jail. However, Fahy was taken to Limerick Jail instead, so no rescue could take place.[13]

That same evening Mellows told Patrick Callanan and Joe Fleming to instruct various companies to mobilise immediately. Callanan mobilised the Oranmore, Maree, Claregalway and Castlegar companies, but was unable to contact anyone in Galway city.[14]

Another Volunteer, Martin Newell, was sent by Éamonn Corbett to Clarenbridge with orders for all the men assembling there to proceed towards Killeeneen where Mellows awaited them. The officers, including Éamonn Corbett, Matt Niland and Fr Feeney, met with Mellows in Mrs Walsh's house that night to discuss plans for the morning. Newell later remembered that Mrs Walsh had an intense love of Ireland and was delighted that her house was being used as a headquarters by Mellows:

> She and her family were heart and soul with the Volunteers. From before the Rising and right through the War of Independence her home was 'open house' for the Volunteers

and IRA, and there was always a warm welcome for them. She was most self-sacrificing and it is well known that very often, having fed the Volunteers at night, she had nothing left for the family breakfast in the morning; but she was only too happy to help the cause of freedom. She adored Mellows and held him in the highest esteem.'[15]

While Volunteers were arriving at Killeeneen all evening, there were still some units unaware of the orders from Dublin. Volunteer Michael Kelly had a great knowledge of the countryside and Mellows asked him to deliver dispatches to companies that had not yet been informed of the situation. Another Volunteer, Patrick Kelly, was ordered to accompany him on his mission and both men were armed, with orders to fight policemen or military personnel who made any attempt to stop them. Having delivered the orders, they returned to headquarters, by which time it was Tuesday morning. However, they found Killeeneen quiet, as the Volunteers gathered there had already left – the Rising in Galway had started in earnest.[16]

11

MOBILISATION IN COUNTY GALWAY

Tuesday was really the day of mobilisation in County Galway. Several Volunteer companies had already converged on Killeeneen to join Mellows, and before they moved off that morning the officers addressed them to ensure that all were aware of the importance of the Rising and of the dangers that lay ahead. In his own way Éamonn Corbett lifted the spirits of the men when he sang the following song before leaving Killeeneen:

> For thee we stand, O native land,
> To thee we pledge devotion,
> Our love for thee will never be
> As boundless as the ocean,
> For ages passed, with voices massed
> Have poets hymned thy story;
> But soldiers now upon thy brow,
> Shall poise a crown of glory.
>
> Then forward for the hour has come
> To free our fettered sireland;
> 'Mid cannon boom and roar of gun
> We'll fight for God and Ireland.
>
> What matter if the road is long,
> We'll tread it to the end, boys;
> What matter if the foe is strong,

Our country we'll defend, boys.
The star of hope illumes the way
Our fathers trod before us,
God send the light of freedom's day
To dawn in splendour o'er us.

Then forward for the hour has come
To free our fettered sireland;
'Mid cannon boom and roar of gun
We'll fight for God and Ireland.

Out yonder leaps the beacon fire
To guide us through the valley;
Around us throng our martyred sires
To harken and to rally.
Strike home for God and Ireland now,
Strike home for all we treasure;
And if the foeman drink – we vow
To give him brimming measure.

Then forward for the hour has come
To free our fettered sireland;
'Mid cannon boom and roar of gun
We'll fight for God and Ireland.[1]

The rebels marched towards Clarenbridge about four miles away. On the way they seized some weapons and bicycles from an ex-policeman who lived along the route. The column halted as they came close to Clarenbridge and Mellows asked for twelve Volunteers to go ahead of the main force. Once it was established that there were no surprises awaiting them, the column entered the village. Their first objective was to take the police barracks, and they called on the constabulary to surrender.[2] There were seven policemen in the barracks at the time and it seems that one did open the door initially, but slammed it shut again after a Volunteer discharged his weapon. The police then retreated to the upper floor of the building.[3]

By the time Michael Kelly and his companion Patrick Kelly, who had followed on from Killeeneen, arrived in Clarenbridge, the attack on the barracks was under way. They had initially met a number of their comrades who had taken up positions at the rear of the Reddington estate in Kilcornan, located just outside the village. Having heard shooting they then made their way into the village and found the approach roads barricaded and manned by Volunteers.[4] Just before the attack started, a policeman cycling towards the village had come upon one of these barricades and was ordered to surrender. He attempted to pull his revolver, but was immediately shot and wounded, and was taken to the nearby convent where he received medical attention.[5]

When the two Kellys arrived in town, the Volunteers were firing on the barracks and Éamonn Corbett had a number of mills bombs which he used in the attack, but the Volunteers failed to dislodge the police.[6] The attack continued for a time with little effect and then the local parish priest, Fr Tully, appeared on the scene and asked Mellows to call it off. Fr Tully wished to avoid bloodshed at any cost and pleaded with Mellows, telling him that the police were unarmed. Mellows was then informed that his men had captured four policemen who were on their way from Kilcolgan. This seemed to satisfy him and so he suspended the action against the barracks, deciding to march towards Athenry and join forces with Larry Lardner. However, he felt that Oranmore had to be secured first, as it was closer to Galway city.[7]

By the time Mellows and his men reached Oranmore, the barracks was already under attack by the Oranmore and Maree companies; with the Clarenbridge Company the Volunteers now numbered about 130 men.[8] Joseph Howley began placing explosives under the bridge leading into the town and a large hole was dug in the centre of the bridge to impede the enemy should they advance on the village.[9] The barracks was occupied by Constables Smith, Foley, Barrett and Heffernan at the time of the attack. Two others, Sergeant Healy and Constable McDermott, were on patrol when the rebels made their move and both men tried to reach refuge in a house opposite the barracks, but the rebels captured McDermott.[10] Mellows then received word that a large force of police and military were on the way from Galway city by train, so he sent Volunteer Michael Cummins to the railway station, just outside the village, to see if the police had arrived and how many were in the group. By the time Cummins got there the train had pulled in and police were already assembling on the platform. When they spotted Cummins they opened fire on him.[11] He jumped onto his bike and cycled away 'in a stooped position', trying to gain cover from the stone walls along the road. He made it back to Mellows and told him that the police had arrived in force.[12]

Mellows ordered the men to fall in and told them that they

were going to join Commandant Larry Lardner and his men at the Agricultural College and Model Farm near Athenry. The college was about six miles from Oranmore. Mellows remained behind to cover the retreat and found cover behind the gable-end of Reilly's public house.[13] Some of his men were still placing explosives at the bridge when the police reinforcements arrived and in the exchange of fire that followed several policemen were wounded. One of the Volunteers was also wounded and was helped away by his comrades as Mellows covered their with-drawal, blazing away with his 'Peter the Painter' weapon. The police returned fire, but Mellows got away and was not pursued; he rejoined his men a few hundred metres along the road to march towards Athenry.[14]

When the police had secured Oranmore, the constables un-der siege were relieved. Later, stories of various incidents invol-ving the Volunteers began to emerge. The house where Sergeant Healy had taken refuge was actually the home of Constable Smith, who was trapped in the barracks. Healy said that the rebels had approached the house and asked him to surrender and the family in the house were terrified as the rebels began banging on the door. Healy fired a number of shots through the door, which forced the attackers to retire to a safe distance; no other attempt was made against his position. Pat Whiston, a jarvey from Galway city, had been in Oranmore when the re-bels arrived. He said some of them forced him to drive them to Athenry on his horse and cart where, according to his story, they held him captive until he managed to escape in the early hours of the following morning. Upon reaching Galway he informed a

119

newspaper reporter of his ordeal, saying that the rebels had fired on him as he made his bid for freedom. Similar stories were circulated about other encounters with the rebels at Oranmore.[15]

Another story that emerged about that Tuesday came from the Galway correspondent for the *Daily Mail*, who claimed that the rebel army had come within three miles of the city on that day, but were forced to retreat as a result of shell-fire from naval gunships in Galway Bay.[16] However, it was actually Wednesday before the ships began shelling what they believed to be rebel targets: this was later confirmed by Micheál Ó Droighneáin, who had been captured and was on board one of the ships, in his witness statement.[17] There is a possibility that Mellows' move against Oranmore may have been mistaken as an advance on Galway city itself, although the rebels' march took them away from the city along the Athenry road.

There was a huge amount of police activity in the town of Athenry as, upon hearing of the Rising in Dublin, the police called in their men from the outlying and isolated posts in the surrounding districts and then billeted them in houses in the vicinity of the barracks. There were normally about sixty policemen in Athenry, but numbers now swelled and made a rebel attack on the barracks impossible. This might have been the reason why the Agricultural College was taken over by the Athenry Volunteers; the town hall had been the insurgent's headquarters on Tuesday morning, but they vacated the building before the constabulary arrived. Mellows and his men arrived at the college later in the afternoon and joined Lardner. This meant there were over 500 men billeted at the college and rations were as essential as weapons, which resulted in several bread carts and a van loaded with tea and groceries being commandeered, while many farmers sent their daughters with freshly baked bread and canisters of milk to give to the rebels. The stock of weapons was now twenty-five rifles, 350 shotguns and a number of small firearms, and of course some pikes. Some of the men who gathered at Athenry to fight were not members of the Irish Volunteers and had no military training at all, but they expressed a wish to fight for Irish freedom now that the opportunity had presented itself.[18] Despite the police presence, the men stayed in the college for the night.

Elsewhere in the county other companies were in action. At about 3 a.m. on Tuesday, Patrick Callanan and Joe Fleming had arrived in Castlegar with mobilisation orders for Brian Molloy. He immediately asked Michael and Thomas Newell to assemble the men, and requested that Callanan accompany him to Moycullen to deliver the orders to the company there. They met with Captain Pádraig Thornton, told him of the fighting in Dublin and issued him with the mobilisation orders. Molloy also told him that he had arranged transport for them to cross the River Corrib without having to enter the city. However, there was obviously a lack of enthusiasm for the orders, and Molloy later stated that during the conversation he felt these would not be carried out. Unable to make contact with anyone from the Spiddal Company, Molloy and Callanan then went to University Road to call on George Nichols, but he wasn't home. There was a lot of police activity in the city so they decided to rejoin the Castlegar Company.

Upon reaching Castlegar they found the company already assembled and Molloy resumed command as they marched off towards Carnmore. On route they met up with the Claregalway Company.[19] The officer in command of Claregalway was Tom Ruane, born in 1884 and a native of Carnmore. Ruane was also a prominent GAA figure and was well known around the county through his involvement in sports. He was captain of the Claregalway hurling team from 1910 to 1916, when he led his men out in rebellion. He had joined the IRB in 1908 and continued to follow the nationalist cause from that time. Some of the other leading officers from the area included Nicholas Kyne, George Glynn and Patrick Feeney.[20] While most sources indicate that Tom Ruane was the senior officer in Claregalway, another record states that it was Nicholas Kyne.[21] Whatever the case, the two companies united and the march to Carnmore continued.

Having reached Carnmore most of the Claregalway Company camped there, while the men from Castlegar found shelter in Kiltulla. They were supposed to meet the Oranmore and Maree companies at Carnmore, but as there was no sign of them arriving, Molloy ordered a number of his men to fall in and they proceeded to Oranmore. When they reached Oranmore Station, Molloy received a dispatch ordering them to march towards Athenry and was obviously confused, as there was still no clear objective except to mobilise and join up with other companies. He sent Sweeney Newell, John Walsh and Pat Feeney to locate Mellows to clarify the orders. Molloy then marched back to Carnmore with the rest of his men. They were billeted in farmhouses in the area and settled down for the night.[22]

12

GALWAY CITY –
SWIFT ACTION

On Easter Monday evening Peg Broderick, a teenage girl from Prospect Hill in Galway, went for a walk through the city streets and noticed that a number of shops were closed, which was unusual for the Easter weekend. Peg later remembered seeing George Nichols and Tom Flanagan and thinking that they were very worried-looking; arriving home she mentioned it to her mother, asking her if there was something wrong. Her mother replied, 'The boys are out in Dublin; there is a Rising'.[1]

While there had been serious confusion in the Volunteer orders coming from Dublin, there was none in the police and military dispatches arriving in Galway. On Tuesday morning a wireless bulletin was received from the British Admiralty which stated, 'An attempt was made to land arms and ammunition in Ireland by a vessel disguised as a neutral merchant ship, but it was really a German auxiliary cruiser, acting in conjunction with a German submarine. The auxiliary was sunk and a number of prisoners were taken. Amongst them was Sir Roger Casement. Sir Roger was brought to London on Monday morning, and is now detained in custody.'[2] The British authorities reacted quickly in Galway city and arrested several key rebel leaders rapidly. It is obvious that the police knew exactly who they were looking for and where these people could be located.

In order to understand why the Connemara companies didn't mobilise in Spiddal and Barna, one must look at the events of both Monday and Tuesday. On Monday morning Micheál Ó Droighneáin was awakened at his home near Spiddal by a loud knocking on his door. Peter Fagen, a Volunteer from Barna, was delivering a message from John Hosty, who had gone to Dublin the previous Saturday to clarify the Volunteers' orders, saying that the Rising had been called off. Then, about 4 p.m., he had two other visitors, George Nichols and Liam Langley, who showed him orders from Pearse saying that the Rising had begun. Unsure about the orders, they decided to wait until there was more information available before taking action.

Ó Droighneáin was very disheartened and the following morning, Tuesday, he cycled into Galway city to see if there was any activity that would indicate that a rebellion was in progress, and noticed there was a large police presence on the streets. He went to McDonnell's Café in the hope of meeting someone he could trust and as he was leaving he met one of the Castlegar Volunteers, who told him he was making his way back to the village to join his company. He informed Ó Droighneáin that the rebellion had already started in Dublin so Ó Droighneáin immediately mounted his bicycle and began his return journey to update his men. As he cycled through Bridge Street, a Ford car being driven by County Inspector George Heard appeared heading towards him, so Ó Droighneáin kept his head down and continued pedalling as the car passed him. As he was cycling along Dominick Street, however, the car swept past him again, stopped a few yards ahead and a number of policemen armed with rifles jumped out and pulled Ó Droighneáin off the bicycle. He was taken to Dominick Street RIC Barracks where Heard questioned him. Not getting the answers he had hoped for, Heard began shouting at Ó Droighneáin, calling him a common scoundrel. He was stripped and searched and they found that he was carrying a loaded revolver and £20 in cash. A short while later he was taken to the main RIC barracks in Eglinton Street.[3] Ó Droighneáin's arrest was a major blow to the Spiddal Company and was probably one of the main reasons that they failed to rise.

Another Connemara unit, Leenane, reported that although word of the rebellion was sent to them, possibly from Spiddal, when they were out on training exercises on Easter Sunday, they never actually received the orders to mobilise. Volunteer Martin Conneely maintained that it was only on the following Sunday that they became aware of what had happened, when the RIC began placing public notices that the rebellion was over.[4]

It has often being asked why the rebels in the city didn't rise up like their comrades in the county. According to Frank Hardiman, the Volunteer branch in Galway city was in such a weak position it rendered a revolt almost impossible, but had they received definite plans, the men would have reacted as best they could. On Tuesday morning Hardiman left his home near the town hall and made his way to Shop Street hoping to gain some information. He saw George Nichols further down the street and as he approached him, Nichols said, 'Keep moving, don't be seen talking to me.' Hardiman decided to return home, but the police were waiting for him and he was arrested and taken to Eglinton Street Barracks.[5]

Shortly after arresting Ó Droighneáin, County Inspector Heard and his men went to the home of George Nichols, and he too was taken to the barracks in Eglinton Street. A short time later, Seamus Carter was arrested and joined his colleagues.[6] These arrests signalled the end of any hope for rebellion in the city.

The four Volunteer officers were handcuffed and taken to Galway docks where a Royal Navy ship awaited them. The journey was somewhat hazardous for the Volunteers, as word of the arrests had spread through the streets and crowds of angry people had gathered. The prisoners were pelted with mud, stones and generous rations of verbal abuse. Once on board the ship, Nichols spoke with the naval officer, asking him to produce written warrants for their arrest and imprisonment, but the officer paid little attention to him and simply replied, 'My word is enough, we are at war.' A short time later they were joined on the minesweeper *Guillemot* by another Volunteer prisoner, Pádraic Ó Máille from Connemara, who had been arrested while making his way home.[7] The prompt action by the police in Galway ensured that the rebel leaders in the city had little time to bring their men out in rebellion.

A lack of accurate reporting caused a lot of apprehension among Galway's citizens and an atmosphere of siege hung over the city. People were hungry for information and this was fed mostly by rumours.[8] One report, supposedly coming from

Dublin, stated that the Irish flag was flying over all the main buildings in the capital, including the GPO, Dublin Castle and the ancient Houses of Parliament. Apparently thousands of armed Irish Volunteers had seized most of the city, Grafton Street was 'heaped with dead bodies' and a cavalry unit had been ambushed by rifle and machine-gun fire as they galloped through the streets. There was a mixture of truth and gossip in the stories and they spread across Galway city at an alarming rate, striking fear into the hearts of the people.[9]

The Galway police occupied the post office in Eglinton Street as they obviously feared a repeat of the occupation of the GPO in Dublin. One of the youths working there at the time was Joseph Togher, who felt that 'something wonderful had taken place'. He later joined the IRA and became one of the most wanted men in Galway.[10] The fear of rebels occupying the post office in Galway was, according to Thomas Hynes, well founded. He said that this was part of the plan devised by George Nichols; another idea was to take a number of prominent businessmen hostage, including Máirtín Mór McDonogh and Joseph Young. Hynes believed that Nichols was more aware of the Dublin plans than any of the others involved in the Rising in Galway.[11] Other buildings that were to be occupied by the rebels included Alexander Moon's, Maxwell McNamara's, the Bank of Ireland and the National Bank.[12] However, none of these plans could be executed because of the swift action taken by the police and military authorities.

In fact the post office became one of the centres of authority that week as people made their way to there hoping for news.

It was possibly because of this that the following public notice from the military authorities was placed in one of the windows of the post office:

> I, Francis William Hannon, Commander of the Royal Navy, being a competent military authority, do hereby direct that under Article 10 of the Defence of the Realm Act, 1914, Consolidation, all licensed premises in the Urban District of Galway are to be closed forthwith. I further direct that under Article 13 of the aforesaid Regulation all persons within the Urban District of Galway are to remain indoors from the hour of 5 p.m. today 25th April until 8 a.m. on the 26th April. Members of the National Volunteer Force are not included in this order.[13]

All day Tuesday a steady stream of police were pouring into the city. At about 6 p.m. District Inspector Neilan arrived from Oughterard at the head of some seventy policemen from various areas around Connemara. Some of the British naval vessels that had arrived off the west coast began using searchlights to scan areas along the shoreline. There were no national papers or telegrams, which obviously frustrated people waiting for news.[14] A public meeting was held in the city as many people were very fearful, and Galway Urban Council called on the people to support the military in crushing the efforts of these 'disaffected fanatics and mischief makers' who were bent on causing mayhem for the vast majority of law-abiding citizens. They also said that the rebellion should be crushed by every

Barricaded shop of Martin Ward during the Siege of Loughrea.
(*Courtesy of Norman Morgan*)

Crowds of Ward's supporters gather during the Siege of Loughrea.
(*Courtesy of Norman Morgan*)

Moyode House, which was occupied by rebel forces during the 1916 rebellion. (*Courtesy of Galway County Library*)

Galway City Corps, National Volunteers, A Company, 1916. (*Courtesy of Tom Kenny*)

(1). ACTIVE SERVICE AT ANY TIME DURING THE WEEK COMMENCING ON THE 23RD DAY OF APRIL, 1916.

(a) Did you render active service in the week commencing 23rd April, 1916. If so, from what date in that week ? *Yes. From 23rd April to 29th April*

(b) Unit or Units *ClareGalway Coy*

(c) Duration (giving dates) of service. *From April 23rd to April 29th.*

(d) District or Districts in which active service was rendered *ClareGalway. Carnmore. Athenry. Moyode and Limepark*

(e) Officer Commanding in each instance. *N. Kyne Capt. L. Lardner Bgd O.C*

(f) In what way do you claim that your service was active service. *Was a Company Officer. In Action against British Forces.*

(g) Particulars of any military operations or engagements or services rendered during the week. *Engagements at Carnmore, Athenry, Moyode, Limepark*

(h) Absence from duty and cause. *none*

(i) References who can testify as to your statements above :—

NAME.	ADDRESS.
Mr Michael Newell Briarhill. Galway	
Mr Brian Molloy Coolough Galway	
Mr. Laurence Lardner Athenry. Galway.	

(2). CONTINUOUS ACTIVE SERVICE DURING PERIOD COMPRISING—

   (a) period from 1st April, 1916, to 22nd April, 1916, and

   (b) period from 30th April, 1916, to 31st March, 1917.

(a) Unit or Units *ClareGalway Coy.*

(b) Duration (giving dates) of service. *(a) Period from 1st April 1916 to 22nd April (1916)*
(b). Period. From 30th April 1916 to 31st April 1917.

(c) District or Districts in which active service was rendered. *ClareGalway. Carnmore and Surrounding Districts*

(d) Officer Commanding in each instance. *N. Kyne Capt. L. Lardner Bgd O.C.*

(e) In what way do you claim that your service was active service ? *Was a Company Officer. Procured Arms Ammunition, and Equipment for the Rising*

(f) Particulars of any military operations or engagements or services rendered during the period. *Constantly under arms during first Period as above.*
Arrested. Imprisoned, deported, and Interned second Period as above

(g) Absence from duty and cause. *none in 1st Period. In Prison & Interned second*

B (*Period* (B

Pension record mentioning Michael Newell, Brian Molloy and Thomas Courtney. (*Courtesy of the Military Archives*)

John Faller, April 1917.
(*Courtesy of Paul Faller*)

Volunteer Joseph Howley with his
mother.
(*Courtesy of Dr Padraic Keane*)

Volunteer William Newell.
(*Courtesy of the Furey Collection*)

Rebel prisoners being marched to awaiting ships to be transported to internment centres in Britain. It is believed that many of the men in this photograph were from Galway. (*Courtesy of Tom Kenny*)

Constable Stephen Callanan and his wife, Sarah 'Babe' Kennedy, on their wedding day.
(*Courtesy of Luke Silke*)

Volunteer Fred McDermott,
who worked for Galway
County Council.
(*Courtesy of Sean McDermott*)

Volunteer Thomas Coen and his
wife, Kate. He was from Carnaun,
Athenry, and joined the Cussaune
Volunteer Company in 1914.
(*Courtesy of David Morrissey*)

Dr Thomas Walsh.
(*Courtesy of NUIG*)

George Nichols.
(*Courtesy of Galway County Council*)

Captain Éamonn Corbett and Fr Harry Feeney.
(*Courtesy of the Galway Harbour Board*)

Shop Street, the scene of aggression between supporters of the National and Irish Volunteers. (*Courtesy of Kevin Barry*)

The unveiling of the Liam Mellows statue at Eyre Square in 1957. *From left*: Willie Glynn, Patrick Molloy, Pat Newell, Johnny Molloy, John Fahy, Matt Hackett, Jim Furey, Willie Fahy. (*Courtesy of the Furey collection*)

means possible. There were warnings of rebel forces invading the town so people were encouraged to enlist for service as Special Constables. As rumours circulated of rebels amassing around Athenry, there was a general feeling of besiegement among the people in Galway, which only eased when a British warship arrived with some 500 troops to support the garrison at Renmore Barracks.[15]

People and businesses were advised to take their money and valuables and deposit them in the banks as it was felt that should the rebels enter the city these would not be safe from looting. County Inspector Ruttledge, head of the Galway West Riding Police District, placed his forces in the post office and the banks to protect them. Adding to the general feeling of anxiety was the intense search being carried out for suspected rebels throughout the city. The Special Constabulary was set up to help crush the Rising and capture rebels. Ruttledge was also assisted in the search for rebels by members of the National Volunteers, those who had remained loyal to Redmond.[16] These men had reported for duty as early as Tuesday morning, when forty of them turned up at police barracks. All of them were armed with rifles and bayonets as they began patrolling the streets of the city.[17]

It is interesting to note that on 18 March 1916, an issue was raised at a committee meeting of the National Volunteers concerning an excursion to Dublin on Easter Sunday. The secretary recorded that the idea was abandoned because of the costs involved in travelling by train. He mentions that they would have to inform Mr Courtney of their decision, indicating that this man had some part to play in organising the trip. There is a question over who Mr Courtney was. If it was Tom Courtney, why was he involved with the National Volunteers considering his opposition to them? One would have to assume that he was trying to get them out of Galway as Easter Sunday was the original day set for the rebellion. While the Minute Book of National Volunteers in Galway has survived, unfortunately the pages concerning Easter Week 1916 were torn out at some stage. This is not really surprising given the stance the National Volunteers took during the rebellion in Galway, but it means there is no record by the actual men of their actions during that week.[18]

Members of the aristocracy armed with sporting rifles also presented themselves for duty and wished to be included in street patrols. Many of the civil servants from around the city joined the Special Constables. One of them, Constable Edmonds, took up position on top of the Railway Hotel after word came that the rebels were destroying the railway line between Galway and Oranmore. He reported to Ruttledge that he saw a large force of men on a hill close to Merlin Park. Ruttledge contacted the navy for assistance and one of the warships shelled the position, but there were actually no rebels near that area. The military requested more assistance from the government and received word that a force of marines would be sent by sea.[19]

The city had been teeming with people, including holiday-makers there for the Easter weekend, when news of the rebellion was received, and they were afraid to travel until the rebellion was over.[20] One member of a party of English visitors staying in the Railway Hotel (Hotel Meyrick) when the rebellion broke out penned the following words upon hearing the rumour of a rebel army marching on the city:

> We rushed to the cellar, and there we sat,
> For we heard the shouts and the rat, tat, tat,
> For the rebels had risen, and there we were,
> We sat in the cellar, and Oh it was cold,
> With the rats and mice and the green damp mould.
> The shots from the land and the shells from the sea.[21]

Despite the lack of a general rising in Galway, Thomas Courtney, who worked as a postman, certainly had a busy week. Arriving to work at 5.30 a.m. on Tuesday morning he was greeted by armed police at the door of the post office. They also manned the windows and he noticed that among their discarded items were empty stout bottles, which had been left over from the night shift. One of the clerks in the telegraph room told him that there was a rebellion in Dublin. Courtney then went to the sorting office where the acting postmaster was talking to some policemen, and they were also drinking bottles of stout. Courtney wanted to go to Briarhill to warn Brian Molloy and Michael Newell of the police activity in the city and his opportunity came when the acting postmaster, thinking that Courtney had been working the night shift, told him that he could go home. Courtney grabbed a number of letters on his way out, just in case he was stopped leaving the city, as he could pretend he was still on duty delivering the post. He grabbed his bike and cycled towards Eyre Square where a number of armed policemen were standing. The police stopped Courtney and asked if he was delivering the post to Renmore Barracks – when he replied 'yes' they waved him on. Having left Eyre Square he met five soldiers with a military postman on their way to the post office. Courtney thought he was going to be stopped again, but he knew the military postman and, after they greeted each other, Courtney was allowed to continue on his journey unmolested.

According to Courtney, he met with Michael Newell sometime after 6 a.m. and was told that Molloy and Patrick Callanan had gone to Moycullen. Courtney was advised to return to the city as he would be of more benefit to the rebellion relaying information. Before he left, Newell mentioned that arms were to be landed by a submarine off the coast sometime that day. Courtney then made his way to Moycullen, where he eventually located Pádraig Thornton and told him about the boats that were in place to ensure that his men could cross the river safely. Thornton told Courtney that there was little use in an army going anywhere without guns.

Courtney left, annoyed and disheartened, and cycled back to the city, hoping to meet some of the Volunteers, but only saw Micheál Ó Droighneáin in the distance cycling towards him. He didn't want to approach him openly because of the police presence in the streets and, knowing the route that Ó Droighneáin would take when returning home, Courtney pedalled speedily to Sea Road and waited to intercept him there. Having waited for some time he decided to go into the city centre again and as he made his way through Dominick Street he met a friend who told him that Ó Droighneáin had been arrested. Courtney then cycled to Spiddal to inform the Volunteers there. He met a girl with whom he was acquainted, but she was unwilling to take him to the Volunteers. While they were talking, Andy Naughton, the post office mail-car driver, arrived. He knew both Courtney and the girl, a Miss Folan. Courtney explained to Naughton, who was involved with the Spiddal Company, his reasons for being there, and after Naughton spoke with the girl in Irish she agreed to take Courtney to meet the Volunteers. He told them of the events in Galway and the arrest of Ó Droighneáin and also mentioned his disappointing visit to Moycullen, where he felt there would be no mobilisation. The men in Spiddal told Courtney that they were expecting an arms shipment to land and had twenty-five Volunteers watching the coast.

Courtney made his way back to the city and arrived around 8 p.m. to streets full of people all gathered in groups speaking about the Rising in Dublin and the danger lurking on their very doorstep in County Galway. He noticed that a number of young men whom he knew from around the city had joined the Special Constabulary and met a fellow oarsman, Christy Monaghan, who was very annoyed with them. Courtney realised he could trust Monaghan and told him of his involvement with the rebels, after which Monaghan agreed to help him in any way he could.

The word on the street was that the city was prepared for

an attack by the 'Sinn Féin' army, a name which Courtney found strange considering its founder, Arthur Griffith, had spent the weekend in support of MacNeill trying to prevent the rebellion. It was mainly the Irish Volunteers who were out in open rebellion. With little hope of any effective outbreak of rebellion in the city, late on Tuesday night Courtney made his way to Kiloughter and found food and shelter with Mrs Small for the night.[22]

Tuesday had been a day of disappointment for the Galway Volunteers. The city had failed to rise due to the swift capture of its leaders, and while the county companies had seen some action, not all of them had mobilised and the various attacks in which they had been involved had failed. However, the country companies had regrouped under Mellows' leadership and they could only hope that Wednesday would bring greater success.

13

WEDNESDAY'S ACTIONS

At about 5 a.m. on Wednesday morning, Sweeney Newell and the others arrived back in Carnmore with orders from Mellows: they were to march to the Agricultural College near Athenry, join forces with the main army and commandeer horses, carts, food and any other commodities that might be of use to an army on the move. The men assembled and Molloy informed them of the orders, so they began marching towards Carnmore crossroads.

As they neared Carnmore, Molloy and some of the others noticed a girl on a hill in the distance.[1] The girl was Sheila 'Bina' King and she was waving a white apron trying to attract their attention. She was struggling to warn them of impending danger, as a convoy of police and military were coming in their direction.[2] The convoy had assembled in Renmore Barracks earlier that morning and consisted of five or six vehicles carrying police and military personnel under the command of County Inspector George Heard, Captain Sir A. Armstrong and Captain Bodkin.[3] The Castlegar Company, which was about sixty strong, thought at first that it might be Volunteers from Galway city coming to join them, but it soon became apparent that it was the enemy. Molloy ordered his men to take cover behind the nearby stone walls as the convoy continued towards Carnmore, then halted about 100 yards from the rebel positions. The police and military began to advance on foot and, with guns levelled, opened fire. Molloy ordered his men to return fire, but it was difficult as the enemy fire was intense and it was dangerous to leave the protection of the wall.

The attackers advanced as far as the Carnmore crossroads, at which point Constable Patrick Whelan and County Inspector Heard moved closer to the rebels. Heard helped Whelan up onto a four-foot-high wall close to the rebels by holding the collar of his tunic in a secure grip. Whelan then called out for the rebels to surrender and told them that he knew their identities. The rebels opened fire, hitting and mortally wounding Whelan. Michael Newell said that Heard also fell and lay motionless on the ground.[4] However, it was reported in *The Freeman's Journal* that Heard claimed he returned fire immediately and wounded seven rebels.[5]

One report stated that the police had noticed the girl waving the apron, but did not realise that she was warning the rebels until they were about half a mile from the crossroads. It was only then that they saw the rebels ahead of them, halted their vehicles and prepared to advance on foot. Among those at the head of the column were Sergeant John Clarke, Captain Bodkin, Constable Hamilton, County Inspector Heard and Constable Whelan. This report claimed that these men rushed towards the men in view and called on them to surrender, but were taken by surprise by the group of rebels who had taken up positions behind the walls to their left. Suddenly shots rang out and, according to Heard, he dropped down onto the road with the bullets flying over his head. However, Whelan was hit and fell on top of him and, once Heard recovered from the shock of being fired upon, they both crawled along the road to gain some cover against the wall. Whelan was lying on the embankment close to the wall, only a few yards away from Heard, but was unable to move. Heard could see that Whelan was still exposed and bleeding from the head, and said that he then returned fire and could see from his position that some of the rebels were slipping away. Captain Bodkin and other members of the force also began firing, but could not outflank the rebels. As the gunfire slackened, he called for help to get Whelan to the car and take him back for medical assistance. However, Whelan died a short time later.[6] Constable Whelan was from Kilkenny and was over six feet in height. Stationed in Eglinton Street Barracks, he was a young, unmarried man in his twenties and was described as a very good constable.[7]

Some of the rebels later stated that the police and military made an attempt to outflank them during the gun battle, but were forced to retreat. They also said that the shotguns had proved lethal at close range. It was believed that the police and military called off the attack after five or six more of them sustained wounds. They retreated to the safety of their vehicles, which were out of range of the shotguns, and drove off in the direction of Oranmore.[8] However, the *Connacht Tribune* reported that the reason for the military and police retreating from Carnmore was that they were running out of ammunition. To make matters worse they had to run the gauntlet of heavy rebel fire as the convoy drove off.[9]

The following is an extract from the interview mentioning

the death of Constable Whelan: 'Some of the lads regretted the killing of Whelan because they knew him well, and they said that he was a kindly person, but it seems he had his duty to do that morning.' It appears that Whelan had been formerly stationed in a barracks that was located opposite McHugh's pub on the road to Claregalway. Because of this, some of the Volunteers from Claregalway and Castlegar would have known him. It was also rumoured that he was engaged to a girl from Castlegar and it has been suggested that this is how he knew some of the rebels.[10] He is buried in the New Cemetery, Bohermore, where a large Celtic Cross erected by his fellow constables marks his grave.

A report in *The Galway Observer* stated that one of the rebels deserted his company after this encounter. Upon arriving home he told his brother that Mellows was acting 'like a lunatic', discharging shots at random, and that his conduct had a very depressing effect on the men. This is possibly an example of the press wishing to denounce Mellows, as it was a well-known fact that he was not at Carnmore that morning. There is also no record of this account in any of the witness statements explored.[11]

Once the immediate danger to the Volunteers had passed, it was vital to leave that area. Molloy ordered the men to reassemble and, because they felt that the main roads would be dangerous, as there was bound to be a lot of military activity after the gun battle, they decided to go cross-country to reach Mellows at the Agricultural College.[12] A scout was sent ahead to the college and informed Mellows that the Castlegar and Claregalway companies were on the way. He also told him of the clash with the police at Carnmore and said that they had shot a number of them.[13] Molloy and his men reached the college, which was under fire from policemen occupying the railway bridge, between 10 and 11 a.m. The attack was beaten off a short time later and they entered the college grounds bringing the entire active rebel force together.[14] Their strength has been estimated at between 500 and 600 men.

Meanwhile in Kinvara, that same morning, the Volunteers assembled at Clonasee. It seems strange that it was Wednesday before they mobilised in Kinvara given that Pádraic Fahy was supposed to have brought the orders from Mellows on Monday night. Again there is some confusion in the various accounts. Thomas Reidy of the Kinvara Company stated that Fahy was captured before entering the home of Fr O'Meehan and that it was Wednesday before word reached them that the rebellion was under way. This account seems plausible because of the late mobilisation in this area. Interestingly Reidy also claimed that Fr O'Meehan said some months earlier that he believed the RIC would join them once the insurrection began. For this reason he had advised the Volunteers to be respectful towards them, which seems a bit naïve; events over the previous days had proved his theory totally incorrect.[15]

Once the Kinvara Volunteers heard about the situation in Dublin and east Galway they assembled and were addressed by Fr O'Meehan. During his speech he said that it was very likely that some of them would die in the rebellion and asked if any of them wished to leave without going into action. All stayed and received a general absolution. He then told them to march into Kinvara to collect all the weapons available, which they did. After this they encountered an RIC patrol outside the town and fire was exchanged between the parties. The police retreated and thus ended the action, without anyone on either side being killed or wounded. The Kinvara men then made an attempt to join up with the main rebel army on Wednesday evening, but at Ballinderreen a dispatch arrived advising them to return to Kinvara and remain there until they received definite orders. Michael Hynes recalls that the rebels received some support from the people in Kinvara as most of them were housed and fed in the town that night, before word arrived the following day that the rebellion had ended.[16]

However, according to the acting brigade scout, Thomas McInerney, on Thursday the Kinvara Company began marching towards Moyode without having orders to do so. When he was informed of this, McInerney sent a dispatch ordering them to return to Kinvara and not to move without orders, as he had information that British forces were closing in on Moyode. The plan for this area now was for the Gort, Kiltartan, Ballycahalan, Ballinderreen and Kinvara companies to stand to and hold their own areas.[17] The rebellion in this area was not very effective, and the Rising in north Galway, if one can refer to it as that, never really amounted to much.

In Tuam, news of the rebellion had reached the police on Monday. District Inspector Comerford, who was in charge, immediately placed his men on alert. However, he did not receive any instructions and was unsure of how to handle the situation initially. It seems that he contacted Sir Matthew Nathan, the under-secretary for Ireland, but he too was unsure of what the procedure was for a rebellion. This left Comerford in a more or less isolated position, with no definite orders, so he proceeded with his own plan of action. He ordered all police in outlying districts to abandon their positions, collect arms and ammunition, and make their way to Tuam. His reasoning for this was that these outlying areas were too isolated and vulnerable to attack. His plan was simple but effective and he now had a force of over 100 well-armed men in control of a large population centre.

Comerford then assessed the situation and began sending armed patrols out along the various roads leading into Tuam. Roadblocks were set up and all vehicles entering the town were searched. There was much anxiety among the police as there were rumours of heavy fighting around Galway and rumours that gun boats had entered the bay. Another rumour in circulation said a large force of rebels was marching from Dunmore and their objective was to occupy Tuam. Comerford placed some twenty-five men in ambush positions along the Dunmore Road and stood on the road himself in full view of anyone approaching. Sometime later three vehicles came into view. Comerford shouted for them to halt, but his command was ignored. He then called on his men to fire, and although they pulled the triggers, the guns failed to go off as the police had forgotten to release the safety catches on their carbines. Nevertheless, this had the desired effect as the rebels, about ten in number, stepped out of the vehicles and surrendered. It seems that the rebels' plan was to seize a train, wait for more Volunteers and then proceed to Athenry, where they would join the men under Mellows' command. Instead, they were taken into custody and thus ended the Rising in Tuam.[18]

According to Volunteer Patrick Dunlevy, who was a member, the Tuam Company made three attempts to mobilise. It met in Connolly's forge on the Galway Road on the nights of Easter Sunday, Monday and Tuesday. However, it received no clear orders and disbanded each time. He confirmed that a train was secured by a man named Sam Brown from Tuam. Dunlevy's part in the Rising ended when he was making his way home on Tuesday night with another Volunteer, Joseph Cummins. Dunlevy and his companion ran into an RIC ambush and were captured. When they arrived at the barracks in Tuam, they found five of their compatriots already there.[19] Others arrested in Tuam that same night were Thomas Kilgarriff, William McGill, Michael Roynane, John Conway, C. J. Kennedy, James Ryan and M. S. Walsh.

District Inspector Comerford made contact with the military in Galway and was instructed to transport his prisoners there, which he did later that week. Almost the entire population of the town supported Comerford and were against the rebellion.[20] As in other areas of the county, rumours flooded the streets and some businesses closed out of fear. The rail service was also suspended, but resumed towards the end of the week.[21]

It was later stated by John Costello, one of the Volunteers in north Galway, that the men had been waiting for orders from Athenry for days before the rebellion. He said the reason for the failure of the Rising in the north of the county was that these orders never came.[22]

14

GALWAY CITY – SHELLING AND ARRESTS

In the early hours of Wednesday, Thomas Courtney cycled across to the old village of Ballybane and as he approached it he heard the sound of motor vehicles in the distance. They were coming in his direction so he hid behind a stone wall. As they passed him by, he could see that they were military vehicles. He was curious about where they were going and decided to follow them. However, his bicycle was no match for the speed of the convoy and he quickly lost sight of them. Then, as he passed Briarhill, he heard shooting coming from the direction of Carnmore. He continued cycling, inquisitive about the gunfire, but he was also aiming to join up with the Castlegar unit and knew that they were somewhere ahead of him. By the time he reached Carnmore, both the rebels and the military had moved on. He saw a pool of blood on the road but the people there could tell him nothing of what had happened.

He headed for Athenry, but after a few miles decided to turn back to Carnmore, where this time he met with a Volunteer who was waiting for him and was able to tell him what had happened in the fight with the police. They went for breakfast and the Volunteer informed him that there were several others waiting for him on different roads, as Molloy knew that Courtney would follow and needed to be intercepted. He told Courtney that the orders from Molloy were that he was to return to Galway city and report on police and military activity and whether the arms had been landed.

Courtney was to stay in contact with the Volunteer from a position just outside the city and this man would relay any information back to Molloy and Mellows. The roads leading into Galway were now well patrolled by police and soldiers, and all carts and civilian vehicles coming into the city were being searched at roadblocks. In some places the military had mounted machine-gun posts. The streets were awash with rumours of the rebel army advancing on the city and there was also talk of the Germans landing, which was of great concern. Courtney made his way home to Newcastle, where Andy Naughton was waiting for him. Naughton told Courtney that he believed a German submarine had surfaced off the coast near Ballinahown, but the Volunteers did not signal the sub at the time as they were unsure whether it was German. Courtney then cycled to Spiddal to investigate and discovered that the craft spotted had been identified by a man who had served in the naval reserves as British.[1]

The arrests in the city continued on Wednesday as the British captured other suspected rebels, including Tom Flanagan and John Faller.[2] Two members of the academic staff of University College Galway had also been arrested in the police and military swoop: one was Dr Thomas Walsh, who served as professor of pathology, and the other was Valentine Steinberger, professor of modern languages, who had served on the university staff since 1886. County Inspector Heard and a number of armed constables arrested Steinberger while he was tending to the garden of his home at Belmore in Salthill. He was in his seventies at the time and was very distressed when the police took him away. Informers had told the police that Steinberger had been signalling German ships from his home, which overlooked Galway Bay. Another man, Con O'Leary, a student at the university, was also arrested. However, O'Leary was a prominent member of the Sinn Féin branch at the university, so there was a good reason why he was taken into custody.

Both Steinberger and O'Leary were taken to Eglinton Street Barracks and en route they were subjected to much hostility and abuse from the crowds lining the streets.[3] They soon joined the others on the *Guillemot*. They were transferred the following day, along with Micheál Ó Droighneáin, George Nichols, Frank Hardiman, Seamus Carter and Pádraic Ó Máille, to HMS *Laburnum*, which arrived in Galway that morning, as the British had decided to keep all the prisoners together. According to Frank Hardiman, the HMS *Laburnum* sailed out into the bay and began shelling supposed rebel positions at about 3 p.m. He also noted that the results of the shelling were being reported by observers on the roof of the Railway Hotel.[4] Micheál Ó Droighneáin later said that at least fourteen shells were fired in the direction of Castlegar, and when he asked one of the sailors what the targets were, the seaman simply replied that they were firing at 'a meeting of rebels'.[5]

One source states that the gunboat fired a shell in the direction of Moyode Castle, which landed in a field near the

Ballybrit Racecourse some twenty-five miles wide of its target.[6] It was also reported that some shells were fired in the direction of Cooper's Cave near Castlegar. This district would have been a possible target given that so many of the rebels were from this area. None of the houses in the district had been damaged and no one was injured as the shells had landed in open fields.

On Wednesday night Thomas Courtney met three friends, who were involved in the boat club. They were Special Constables and he felt that one in particular was suspicious of him from the tone of the conversation. Although he wanted to get away from them, Courtney did not want to arouse their suspicion further and so allowed two of them to walk with him to his home. While they were talking about fishing, this man continued to centre the conversation on the Rising, asking Courtney if he knew any of the lads from the country who were involved. Luckily for Courtney they must have left him at his house, because later that night he met with the Volunteer from Carnmore just outside the city to give him what information he had. Courtney had to avoid the roads and made his way across some fields in darkness, but his movements were detected by the military guarding the approaches to the city and he was challenged to stop. Upon hearing the shouts he ran and, although shots were fired in his direction, he managed to escape and keep the rendezvous with the Volunteer. Lines of communication had been established between Galway and Moyode and Volunteers were posted at various points to relay information. While Courtney was playing a most dangerous role moving in and out of the city, his courage never failed him and he was determined to keep this line of communication open, even when Mellows moved further south. However, he had to remain at liberty to carry on his intelligence work and thus he applied for and received a doctor's certificate stating that he was ill. He sent it to the manager in the post office without raising much suspicion.[7]

On Thursday morning the prisoners on HMS *Laburnum* were allowed on deck. According to Hardiman, it was a 'perfect day' as they admired the wonderful scenery and wished that they could go ashore. The sea was calm as they watched HMS *Gloucester*, which was acting as escort to a troop ship on its journey to the port, enter Galway Bay. HMS *Laburnum* then 'put about' and began making its way towards Galway port also. On the way it came across a Galway hooker laden with turf. The boat had sailed from Carraroe in Connemara with its cargo and was on its way to a sale in Ardrahan. The officer on deck called to the man in the hooker to 'heave to' but got no reply. The man apparently didn't understand the order and continued on his journey. It was obvious that the officer suspected that weapons were hidden beneath the turf and so he ordered the gunners to fire a shot across the bow of the hooker. This time the man complied with the command to stop.

A boat was lowered from HMS *Laburnum* and a short time later one of the British sailors boarded the hooker. The plan was to tow the hooker into port where it could be searched properly. The sailor fastened a rope to the mast of the vessel, surprising the prisoners on deck, as the rope should have been

147

tied to the bow of the boat. Hardiman, who was watching proceedings intently, later remembered thinking that any ten- or twelve-year-old from Galway with even a basic knowledge of sailing would not have done this. Even he knew that this was fraught with danger. The ship then began to tow the hooker but once the strain was applied to the rope, the boat capsized, sending the turf and the men into the water. The *Laburnum's* small boat went to their rescue and picked up the two men who were hanging on to the mast. The ship then returned to Galway port, arriving shortly after the other vessels.[8] When the troop ship docked, a battalion of Royal Marines and Munster Fusiliers disembarked, assembled on the dock side and marched to Renmore Barracks with a large supply of guns and ammunition.[9]

Other ships that arrived in Galway Bay that Thursday morning included the HMS *Snowdrop* and HMS *Birmingham*. One source states that it was the HMS *Birmingham* that had fired shells inland on Wednesday. However, this could not have been the case as the ship did not arrive until Thursday. Moreover there are testimonies by some of the prisoners who were on board the HMS *Laburnum* that this ship was the source of the shelling.[10]

The shelling near Castlegar had been unnerving for the people living in the area and on Thursday morning some women from this part of the countryside arrived in the city. It seems that a member of the local gentry told them that the British were going to shell the villages of Castlegar, Kiltulla and Carnmore, but this didn't happen as the rebels were moving south and away from the city. These women met Thomas Courtney by accident and he told them that he did not believe there would be any more shelling. Courtney had made his way to the docks after the shelling and met with Thomas Murray and a sailor named Stark. He asked Stark why the big guns were shelling areas close to the city. Stark laughed at the idea of 'big guns', saying that they were only four-inch shells and that the heavy weapons would shake the town. Courtney then asked them to go for a drink, the idea being to acquire more information. They went to Walsh's pub at the docks, where Courtney learned that Commander Hannon, Leslie Edmonds of the Congested Districts Board and a senior navy officer had produced a map with possible target areas should the rebels advance on the city. They were then joined in the pub by some other sailors; one of them a gunner. During the conversation this man mentioned he could drop a shell into a five-square-foot target if he wished. The shells fired already were to give the rebels a false sense of security, thinking that gunners couldn't hit their targets or were unable to determine their range. Courtney was playing a dangerous game, pretending to be of a nervous disposition and drawing out more information from these men. They did notice, however, that although Courtney had asked them to go for a drink, he was only drinking lemonade. He left them a short time later and noticed that the troops who had been stationed on the roads leading into the city had been withdrawn. He now realised why: if the rebels did move on the city they might well think it was unguarded, but the large naval guns would play havoc on their ranks, so he went directly to Castlegar to give the information to his contact there.[11]

While the public houses were supposed to be closed, the fact that Courtney was in a position to invite the sailors for a drink shows that some remained open. Another indication that the pubs were doing business was the fact that as the week progressed they ran out of Guinness, which did not help the rebel cause as far as the customers were concerned.[12]

Courtney was frustrated with the situation and still battling away, trying to get the rebellion under way in the city. He was also tired from lack of sleep and all the cycling between Briarhill and Spiddal. There was no doubt that he needed help to continue gathering and relaying information and, as he knew some members of the Galway Company were still at liberty, he called on the captain to request his assistance in getting a message to Castlegar. The officer refused and when Courtney asked if any of his men could take the information, the captain called him a fool. Courtney then got his brother to ask three Volunteers whom he knew to call to his house later that evening, but none of them turned up and on Thursday evening he saw one of them actively avoid him. What Courtney did not realise was that his movements were being reported to the British authorities.[13]

15

MOYODE

By Wednesday the numbers of Volunteers at the Agricultural College and Model Farm had increased dramatically. Some of the areas represented included Oranmore, Maree, Clarenbridge, Craughwell, Castlegar, Claregalway, Cregmore, Kilconiron, Rockfield, Newcastle, Cussaun, Athenry and Derrydonnell. A scout arrived from Athenry and informed the rebels that a contingent of police had left the town and were going to attack their position from the south-west. Captain Éamonn Corbett called on six of the men with rifles to accompany him as he tried to intercept the constabulary. He wanted to make a surprise attack on the police before they could reach the college grounds and as soon as he spotted them he gave the order to open fire. The police returned fire, but retreated soon afterwards and quickly headed back towards the town. Some of the Volunteers from the Athenry Company set off with the intention of cutting the RIC party off from behind, but before they could do so, the RIC had retreated. It was the second retreat by the police at the college in two days. It seems that there had been an RIC hut in the college grounds, which was garrisoned by a sergeant and three or four constables, but they had made a hasty retreat when the Volunteers first arrived.[1]

While Éamonn Corbett is called a captain by Martin Newell, according to another source he was vice-commandant of the Volunteers gathered at the college. The ranks of some of the Volunteers leaders differ between various witness statements, causing some confusion. For the sake of clarity the following were the senior officers' ranks recorded while they were at the Agricultural College: Liam Mellows was supreme commander, Larry Lardner brigade commandant, Alf Monahan and Éamonn Corbett both vice-commandants, Matt Niland adjutant and Seán Broderick quartermaster.[2]

Shortly after Corbett returned from his attack on the police, the Volunteers held a council of war. Along with the senior officers, Fr Feeney, Tom Ruane, Dick Murphy, Stephen Jordan, Brian Molloy and Patrick Callanan attended this meeting. Ruane suggested that they should break into smaller groups and take on the enemy as they found them, but no one agreed with this plan and it was decided that they should stay together and move to Moyode Castle. Following the meeting Mellows asked Patrick Callanan and William Newell, a brother of Michael Newell, to go to Moycullen with orders for Pádraig Thornton and his company to join them at Moyode. Before leaving, Mellows also told Callanan that he expected the southern counties of Clare and Limerick to mobilise soon and he had no intention of surrendering.[3] The reason Mellows believed that this would happen was that a meeting of the Limerick, Clare and Galway brigade delegates had taken place on Palm Sunday to discuss the Rising, at which Larry Lardner, Éamonn Corbett and Fr Feeney had represented Galway.[4]

After Callanan left, Mellows assembled the men and the Volunteers marched away to Moyode, a distance of about four miles.[5] The mansion at Moyode was owned by the Persse family, but was unoccupied at the time because of a land dispute. Despite the failure to secure any of the towns, the Volunteers had freed some 600 square miles of Ireland from British rule and Mellows' plan was to unite all the forces in Galway and then march south, rising the country to armed rebellion as he went.[6] Mellows believed the Connemara companies would be of great value to him once all the Volunteers had come together and that more objectives could be achieved. However, when Callanan and Newell reached Moycullen, Thornton could not be found, so they decided to follow Mellows to Moyode. On the way they met Fr Moran, the parish priest of Claregalway, who gave them two Webley revolvers. When they reached Bushfield, about seven miles from Moyode, they were joined by a number of other rebels including Thomas Furey, Roger Furey and Pat Flanagan. They decided to set up an outpost there and send word to Moyode of any British troops entering the area.[7]

Moyode was a hive of activity, with each company drilling and practising harnessing horses and carts, and loading and unloading all means of transport as fast as possible in case they had to leave in a hurry. Children visited the Volunteers' stronghold with 'exciting news' about anything they thought was going on in the locality; and of course there were the never-ending rumours. As each company was responsible for its own food, foraging parties were sent out to scour the countryside for supplies. Scouts were coming and going on reconnaissance missions and before they left camp Fr Feeney heard their confession and gave them general absolution. Others were sent out in search of supplies and in one instance some of the rebels seized a bullock and it was slaughtered for food. Beef stew, onions and potatoes were on the menu that day for the men. Despite the reason they were all at Moyode, there was a great sense of excitement and adventure in the camp.[8]

One of the Volunteers, James Barrett, later said that when commandeering provisions, including tea, sugar and tobacco, they issued shopkeepers and farmers with receipts to ensure payment if the rebels won, and they chose only wealthy shop-keepers so that the loss would not be too great for them if they lost.[9] The cooking was done by the women of Cumann na mBan from Rockfield, who had been with the men from the beginning, including Julia Broderick, Bridie Hegarty, Kath-leen and Ciss Clery, Anne and Nellie Walshe, Julia Morrissey, Mary Corbett, Kate Glynn, Julia Forde, Bridie Lane, Bridie Walsh, Gretta Walsh, Tess Walsh, Bridget Kelly, Margaret Greally and Bridie Morrissey. Bridie had six brothers taking part in the rebellion.

Later on Wednesday Mellows received information that some members of the UIL in Craughwell, who had initially been against the rebellion, were now in favour of the action taken, so he sent Martin Newell and Darby Deely to Craughwell to meet with them and gain their support. However, they met a friend from the village who warned them to stay away from Craughwell as they would be arrested on sight, and told them that some members of the UIL, rather than having a change of heart, were in fact collaborating with the police.

On Wednesday night a dance was held in the drawing-room of the Moyode mansion for the girls of Cumann na mBan and the Volunteers, possibly to raise spirits. However, the young men and women had to be careful as the dance took place under the watchful eye of Fr Feeney.[10]

On Thursday morning Mellows asked Stephen Jordan and a number of other Volunteers to accompany him on a reconnaissance mission. They called to several houses in the district enquiring about police and military movements. They also went to New Inn and found that the barracks there had been evacuated, with the exception of two women. One of the women seemed very nervous when the rebels arrived and she told Mellows that there were no policemen in the building. However, as they attempted to go upstairs, she admitted that her husband was a sergeant in the force and was in one of the upstairs rooms, very ill. Seeing that she was worried, Mellows assured her that they would not harm the man; they just wished to ask him a few questions. Jordan and Mellows then questioned the sergeant about the strength and movements of the military and police. The policeman was surprised and relieved by Mellows' politeness and answered, giving him the few details of which he was aware. As with other outlying stations, he said that they had been ordered to go to Loughrea. Mellows and the others then left the barracks and returned to Moyode. Shortly after returning, Stephen Jordan and a number of other men were sent out on a foraging mission and found a good supply of potatoes in a local farmyard belonging to a man named Joseph King. While they were loading the potatoes onto a cart they were interrupted by a large police patrol that came into view, moving in their direction. The rebels climbed onto the roof of a shed and opened fire on the patrol. The gunfire could be heard in Moyode and Mellows deployed a number of the men in two cars to support Jordan. He also went himself, but by the time they got there the gun battle was over as the police had retreated.[11]

That evening a meeting of the officers was held to discuss the situation as there was continued uncertainty and the rumours were having an adverse effect on the men. The sound of naval artillery fire the previous day had also damaged the morale of the men. The rebels seemed isolated and, worse still, there was no definite information available. It was decided to allow the men without arms to disband and return to their homes. Armed men were told that if they wished to go, then it was only a matter of handing over their weapons to men who wished to stay. This decision reduced the force by about 200 men.[12] Another source stated that many of the rank and file who mobilised on Easter Tuesday morning had believed they were simply going to take part in a route march, and when they realised that they were now engaged in open rebellion about 200 went home, but returned the following morning. This could have been confused with the disbandment of the unarmed rebels.[13] According to Martin Newell, the men who did not wish to continue with the fight were given the option to leave by Alf Monahan, but as they left, Matt Niland stood waving a tricolour in a bid to remind them of what the Rising was all about. He said that most of those who left that evening returned the following morning.[14] This is possibly where the confusion between the sources occurred. After all, the rebels were well aware that a Rising was going to take place as there had been plenty of warnings issued over the previous months. The only problem was in communications as to when it would happen. Whatever the truth of the matter, it seems that those who remained got little sleep as there were a number of roll calls throughout the night.[15]

The rebels must have wondered why there were no communications reaching them from the city. Any hope of information from Galway was lost on Thursday when Thomas Courtney was taken into custody that evening. Courtney was walking through Shop Street when he spotted two Special Constables coming towards him. Knowing who they were, and in an effort to avoid having to speak with them, he turned to look into the window of Naughton's Shop. They passed by, but as he was about to continue walking towards Eyre Square two policemen fell in with him. One said, 'You are wanted in the barracks … You have been to too many dances in the country I think.'

Courtney agreed to go with them to the barracks and the policeman told him he could walk ahead of them if he wished. Although the policeman was very polite, it was a nerve-racking time for Courtney and upon entering the barracks he noticed two Volunteer prisoners, one of them a man named Conroy from his own company. He then observed one of the policemen who had allowed him to pass by on Eyre Square on Tuesday morning thinking he was going to Renmore Barracks.

Conroy acknowledged Courtney, leaving him unsure of how to react. The police sergeant on duty asked Conroy if they knew each other and he replied saying, 'I know him well, he is a post-boy.' The sergeant accepted this and carried on with his duty. The following minutes seemed like an eternity for Courtney as he waited for the next move by the police. He was then taken to another room and questioned by a police officer, who asked him if he knew the Newell brothers. He said he knew a number of families named Newell from his postal rounds. Just then Conroy was brought into the room and the officer looked directly at him and asked if he was in the Volunteers and if he knew Courtney. He answered both questions in the affirmative. He was then asked if Courtney was in the Volunteer movement. Conroy replied, 'No, he is the postman' and was then taken away again.

The officer continued to question Courtney, asking if he knew Michael Newell and what rank he held in the Volunteers. Courtney said he was acquainted with Newell, but only as a blacksmith. The officer then asked if he knew Brian Molloy. Courtney replied saying he was the son of a farmer. The officer asked, 'Don't you know he was drilling the Volunteers?' When Courtney replied saying that he never saw him involved in this activity, the mood of the police officer completely changed. He looked at a document in front of him and said in a raised voice, 'Now Courtney, I want the truth.' He began to remind Courtney of his movements over several nights in the lead-up to and during the rebellion. It seems that when Courtney was leaving the city on his nationalist activities he would say that he was going to a dance in the country if quizzed. Courtney told the officer that he liked dancing and had organised such events for the Temperance Club of which he was captain.

The policeman then looked again at the paper on his desk and asked Courtney to account for his movements in the city over the previous few days. He was able to tell him that, although he had not marched with the Volunteers on St Patrick's Day, he was in their company that night. It was a shocking revelation for Courtney, as they seemed to have his movements pinned down to exact times and dates. However, Courtney managed to bluff his way through these questions. The police officer continued by saying, 'I don't believe you are telling me the truth', adding 'your movements are suspicious and also your association with those murderers of policemen'. He then said that the postmaster, Mr Plummer, had given Courtney an excellent character reference and it was because of this he was going to set him free. He warned him to go directly home and also said he believed Courtney had fallen in with bad company and told him to stay away from these people. As he was about to leave, Conroy was brought back into the room and the police officer said loudly, 'Conroy, you have lied to me. This man admits to being an officer in the Volunteers.' Courtney looked at Conroy, who continued to stare directly ahead and replied, 'I have told you the truth and if he said he is an officer in the Volunteers, he is telling lies or he is mad.' Conroy's quick thinking and response impressed Courtney.

After Courtney left the barracks he began making his way home. He met two Special Constables who were former friends from the boat club and felt they were surprised to see him out. They asked where he was going and, angry now, Courtney told them to 'go to hell'. He then met Christy Monaghan, who warned him that the Special Constables were watching his every move. With the help of Monaghan and another man, Paddy Heffernan, Courtney began compiling a list of the Special Constables and their addresses in Galway city. He knew for sure now that the police had a lot of information about him and he was determined to have revenge. He left home that night, going on the run, and was given shelter over the following week in Menlo, Kiloughter and Carrabrowne.[16]

Meanwhile, back in Moyode, Tom Kenny had come with information that a train loaded with soldiers and artillery had arrived in Ballinasloe and was advancing in their direction. Mellows was determined to make a stand and have the west remembered for one memorable battle, regardless of the loss of life. However, following a meeting with his officers, it was clear that they preferred to disband. Mellows refused and tried to transfer his command to Commandant Larry Lardner, who would not accept this position. Mellows then sent out a number of motorcars that had been commandeered earlier to try to locate any enemy positions, and asked Stephen Jordan to accompany him in a bid to find out for certain if the British were indeed advancing. All the scouts reported back that there was no troop movement in the area.

On Friday morning Fr Thomas Fahy called to Moyode. As there was no word from Galway, he agreed to cycle to the city for news. While he was away it became known that policemen from the northern counties of Ireland were arriving in County Galway. They were already arresting some of the disbanded Volunteers who had been caught making their way home.[17] British troops had also arrived on Thursday morning in Loughrea – members of the Derbyshire Regiment and the Sherwood Foresters – and they had horse-drawn artillery with them. They were billeted in an old brewery in Barracks Street.[18] Several meetings were held on Friday between the Volunteer officers and news was received that the British were going to mount a large-scale attack on Moyode. It was believed that British troops were on the way from Loughrea and a large force of police, which had been assembled in Athenry, would support them. It was also reported that a battalion of marines was marching from Galway city. This would amount to a huge armed military force and it was believed that all their efforts would now be concentrated on the rebel stronghold at Moyode.[19] To make matters worse, the rebel command received word that 900 troops had arrived by train at Attymon and they were also preparing to march on Moyode. The reports had been sent by some of the scouts, so as far as everyone was concerned they were reliable. Moyode would have to be abandoned as it could not be held against a sustained and brutal attack. The rebel leadership decided to move further south through County Clare and fight their way to Limerick if necessary.[20]

16

THE REBELS DISBAND

At about 6 p.m. on Friday evening the Volunteers lined up by company and marched out of Moyode. There were cars loaded with men, followed by horses and carts carrying provisions. Scouts were sent ahead to report on any military activity. It seems that some of them were not fully aware of their next destination at that time.[1] They bypassed Craughwell and this caused an argument between Mellows and Tom Kenny, who was in favour of attacking the police barracks there. At the time a number of National Volunteers had entered the barracks to support the constabulary. Kenny became extremely annoyed over the order to avoid Craughwell and considered this a serious lack of action on the part of Mellows. It seems that there was no real communication or contact between the two men following this incident.[2]

The men marched on and the route took them through Shanclough, past Creag Castle and Grannagh until they finally reached Limepark. This was another unoccupied mansion and it became the final headquarters for the rebel army.[3] Martin Newell recalled that when the rebel column arrived in a place called Coxtown, about a mile from Limepark, they were joined by two priests, Fr Fahy and Fr Martin O'Farrell.[4] In contrast, Michael Kelly recorded that the priests caught up with the rebels at Monksfield.[5] However, according to Fr Fahy himself, he caught up with them on the road to Limepark. He also stated that the bishop of Galway and many of the clergy were fully supportive of Fr Feeney's connection with the rebels. This would indicate that they were in support of the rebel action, which seems a bit strange given that the authorities and most of the people in the city were totally against the uprising.[6] Upon reaching Limepark, the men who were not placed on sentry duty went to the outhouses to try to grab some sleep.[7]

Mellows, Fr Fahy and the senior officers went into Limepark house for a meeting. Mike Athy, Frank Hynes and Dick Murphy were also present. Fr Fahy informed Mellows and the others that he had received information that Dublin was in flames, but the Rising was more or less over. He said that British troops were marching from Athlone and Ballinasloe and advised them that they had no effective resistance against such a superior force. The only real option open to them was to disband. It seems that Mellows had not slept in three days and dozed off while Fr Fahy was talking. He awoke a few minutes later and heard the general opinion of the senior officers, who were discussing the disbandment of the Volunteers.[8] Mellows apologised for having slept during the meeting and explained how he had got little sleep over the previous nights. He was not in favour of disbanding the men under his command and said, 'I brought the men out to fight, not run away.' Mellows believed that if they disbanded at this stage the men would be like rabbits in the fields, caught without a chance to defend themselves. He then said that he was going to get some sleep before the British arrived and 'fight while I am able and then they can do what they like to me'.[9]

However, having spoken with Fr Fahy, the leaders were under no illusion about their situation.[10] The company captains were called into the meeting and asked to give their opinion on the path forward. Brian Molloy said that as far as the Castlegar Company was concerned they were willing to carry on.[11] Fr Fahy again spoke and advised the officers against wasted bloodshed and lives lost needlessly now that Dublin was on the verge of surrender. It was then agreed by those present to disband the men, but to tell them to secure their weapons in a safe place as they may require them again. Mellows would not disband the Volunteers himself, but allowed Fr Fahy to do it. Thus, after so much enthusiasm, confusion and excitement a week earlier, the rebellion in Galway ended in disappointment for many. It seems that Alf Monahan suggested fighting a guerrilla war from the Aughty Mountains, but this plan of action was not accepted by any of the others.[12]

The men in the outhouses were awakened by the blasts of a whistle and told to assemble in front of the house where Mellows and Fr Fahy were standing just outside the main door. As soon as they were all lined up Fr Fahy addressed them and told them that their position was untenable, that resistance was futile and that to continue in rebellion would lead to an avoidable 'holocaust'. He advised anyone who was contemplating carrying on with the Rising that it was a fruitless sacrifice and would mean that Galway would have nothing to offer in the nature of a future rebellion force. He told them that the Volunteer movement was far more useful alive than dead.[13] He then warned that once Dublin surrendered, British forces would concentrate all their efforts on Galway.[14] This news could not have been new to the men, because Fr O'Farrell had already warned them upon arrival at Limepark that they would all be killed.

Fr Fahy then said that the Sherwood Foresters had been ordered not to take prisoners. He explained that Mellows would not disband the men himself and it was because of this that he was speaking to them. As he looked out from the steps of the old mansion, the moonlight gave some brightness to the gathering before him. He then noticed that there was one woman remaining, Julia Morrissey; she had refused to leave earlier with the other women. Fr Fahy praised the men for the stand they had taken for their country. He said that they had shown the world that the spirit of freedom was very much alive in Ireland. Their courage would be remembered down through the generations. He advised them that a huge military and police force was converging on their position as he spoke and stressed that the best option, and the one that made most sense, was to disband and place their weapons in a secure location and prepare to fight another day.[15]

Some of the men wept openly after hearing the news of the disbandment, as this was not the end or result they had expected. They had trained hard in the years before 1916 and were willing to put their lives on the line for their country. While they lacked proper weaponry, they certainly were not lacking when it came to courage. Some tossed their weapons on the ground in frustration, but were told to pick them up again. Mellows went around and shook hands with them, offering words of encouragement. He said farewell and shook hands with Frank Hynes, one of the officers from Athenry. But Hynes said that he was going to stay with him regardless of the outcome. Mellows said 'God bless you' as he caught him with both hands.[16]

By late on Friday evening Patrick Callanan, who was still at Bushfield, had not received any orders from Mellows. He knew that the men had moved south and at 3 a.m. on Saturday morning decided to take his men and follow the main force. On the way he met a number of rebels making their way home. They told him that they had been disbanded, thus also ending his rebellion.[17]

All hope of freedom seemed to disappear as the remnants of the Army of the Republic streamed along the road from Limepark. Some were on bicycles, others on sidecars, but most of them were walking. Many of the men were unsure of the road home. The night had slipped into total darkness as cloud cover obscured the moonlight. According to some of the rebels the searchlights of the British warships in Galway Bay swept across the night skyline from time to time. It reminded them of the long and powerful arm of Britain that would soon reach out to seize and punish those who had dared challenge the Empire. Most of the men followed the byroads and even travelled cross-country to avoid being captured. Some discarded their weapons and equipment just in case they encountered the enemy. It was reported that in the weeks following the rebellion, haversacks, caps, bandoliers and sometimes guns were found by locals. The men were dispirited, tired and hungry; some found temporary shelter where they rested for a time before continuing their journey home.[18]

The Castlegar Company stayed more or less together and arrived back in Briarhill late on Saturday night. On Sunday most of the company came together as they were still unsure of their next move, but the police arrived and they escaped cross-country towards Lough Corrib. However, most of them were captured the following day. Michael Newell and Brian Molloy managed to evade capture and went on the run together, but by the end of the week they too were in captivity.[19]

The failure of Clare and Limerick to rise was a great disap-pointment to Mellows. Some say that he was holding out for as long as possible in the hope that the rebels from these counties would join him. Their failure to do so left east and south Gal-way isolated and given these circumstances there was very little the rebels could have done long-term.[20] They had released their five police prisoners before disbanding – Constables Manning, Malone, Donovan, McDermott and Walsh, who later reported that they had been well treated and fed by the rebels. Before the police were released, there was reluctance on behalf of the rebel leadership to set the men free as they would be in a position to identify them, but they got an assurance from the prisoners that they would not inform their colleagues and would not identify their captors. It seems that they kept their promise.[21] Despite this, there was soon a huge convoy of military vehicles combing the surrounding countryside in search of rebels and this conti-nued over the following days.[22]

While it was disbandment in Galway, it was surrender in Dublin. According to Peg Conlon, surrender must have been considered as early as Wednesday. On that morning, along with Nora Foley, another member of Cumann na mBan, she made her way to the GPO and met with Pearse and Connolly. She felt that from the tone of the conversation with Connolly, there was already a feeling of defeat. Heavy artillery was pounding the rebel headquarters and the women left heartbroken. Both tried to reach their husbands who were fighting at Church Street, but failed to get through the barricaded streets.[23] By Friday most of Sackville Street was destroyed and the rebel headquarters in the GPO, which had been heavily bombarded by British artillery, was ablaze. The rebels were forced to evacuate this position and withdrew from the burning building before it fell in around them. They moved to buildings in Moore Street and there a new headquarters was set up. However, the evacuation was not without casualties, as The O'Rahilly and a number of others were killed by machine-gun fire.

The following morning, Saturday, Pearse, Clarke, Mac-Diarmada, Plunkett and Connolly, who had been wounded, held a meeting to discuss their position and decided to try to negotiate surrender terms with the British. The guns fell silent at 12.45 p.m. when the flag of surrender was held out in a bullet-swept Moore Street. A few minutes later Nurse Elizabeth O'Farrell stepped into the street and began walking towards the military positions. She made her way up the street to the barricade, where she informed the military officer in command that Commandant Pearse wished to discuss surrender terms with Brigadier-General Lowe. However, Lowe would only accept an unconditional surrender. O'Farrell returned to the rebel leaders and informed them of the British demand. Another meeting of the war council was held and, as their position was hopeless and there would be no support arriving from the country, it was felt that to continue was futile. The rebels had over the past few days given an excellent account of themselves as soldiers, but now it was over, so they decided to surrender on British terms.

Following the surrender the Volunteers assembled outside their position and marched to Parnell Street where, under the shadow of the Parnell Monument, they surrendered their arms. The signed surrender orders were then sent out to the other rebel-held positions around Dublin. The 1916 Easter Rebellion was officially over. The courts martial of the rebel leaders began almost immediately, followed in quick succession by their executions.[24]

17

REBELS ON THE RUN

When the last of the Galway Volunteers had left Limepark, there were three officers remaining with Mellows: Frank Hynes, Peter Howley and Alf Monahan. Two of them, Hynes and Monahan, agreed to go on the run with Mellows and were willing to accept the consequences. It seems that it was Hynes' decision to remain with Mellows at Limepark that changed the leader's mind from self-sacrifice to escape. Mellows did not wish to be responsible for the death of Hynes, a married man with young children. Peter Howley, who was the captain of the Ardrahan Company at this stage, lived nearby and his home was their first stop, where they were treated to a welcome home-cooked meal.[1] It seems that Mellows was good friends with Howley's father and they spent some time chatting. A short time later, Mellows, Hynes and Monahan made their way across scrubland near Peterswell because the Howley homestead was not the safest place for the rebels to hide out, as they were well known to the military authorities. Another location needed to be found quickly and so it was decided to go to the home of Patsy Corless, who was a friend and supporter of the rebels. The plan was for the men to rest there and Howley would join them later that night.

However, sometime after the rebel leaders left, a twelve-vehicle motor-convoy of police and military arrived and arrested three of the Howley brothers: Peter, Michael and William. They were brought to Limepark house and forced to walk in before the soldiers just in case there were still some rebels there. If there was any shooting the Howley brothers would be first in the line of fire.[2] According to the *Connacht Tribune*, when the military and police arrived at Limepark, they surrounded the estate and approached the place with caution. They fired a number of shots into the buildings awaiting a response, but it soon became apparent that Limepark was deserted. They discovered explosives and equipment left behind by the rebels.[3] Once it was established that the house was vacant, the brothers were taken to Gort Barracks and later to Renmore Barracks in Galway. They weren't allowed to speak with each other and Peter was singled out and placed under armed guard until he was transferred to a prison ship.[4] Their fourth brother, Patrick, was captured a few days later.

Frank Hynes provided a detailed account of what happened over the next few days in his witness statement. When Mellows and the others reached the home of Patsy Corless, he had a great welcome for them as he was a member of the Ballycahalan Volunteers and was happy to be of service to them. They slept there for almost twenty-four hours and then went to another safe house, owned by William Blanch. While they were there, a lady visitor arrived and began talking about the Rising. The fugitives remained hidden in a back room, but they could hear the conversation. They heard her say that Liam Mellows was supposed to have escaped dressed as a woman, which brought a smile to their faces.

A short time later a number of men arrived but remained outside the house. Nevertheless, Mellows and the others could hear them talking. One of them began commenting about the police who were searching in a valley below. He said that this was a terrible business and added that he had always known that Mellows was 'no good'. Mellows also got a laugh out of this when he later told Hynes that this man was always the first to greet him whenever they met.

That night, Monday, they went further up the mountain and found an unoccupied cattle shed where they sheltered. The straw was damp, but they stayed there until the following Friday. Blanch kept vigil for the police and military during the day and did his best at night too. He also brought them food, consisting of 'boiled cabbage stuffed into a jam jar' and sometimes potatoes. A local farmer owned the shed and he became frightened when he discovered that there were rebels sheltering there. His contribution to their safety was to tell them every night that the police would be searching the area in the morning and he hoped that by morning they would have left, so was disappointed throughout the week. However, on Friday morning they began making their way towards Scariff in County Clare, where Mellows had an uncle he felt might be able to help them.

The following day they reached a wooded area with a stream running through the trees and although the water was cold, it was most welcome as they washed for the first time in a fortnight. When darkness fell they ventured out onto the road, but were unsure of where they were and having walked a number of miles they came across a house. Alf Monahan said that he would check out the place: he knocked on the door and a very tall man answered. Monahan asked for directions to Scariff, but the man told him he'd never make it in the dark and invited him in despite having a house full of children. When Alf revealed he was not alone, the man offered to walk a way with them instead. They knew that they were in Clare by the man's accent and he suspected that they were on the run so asked if they were rebels. When they told him that they had taken part in the rebellion, he said that the soldiers were searching the country for them. He was worried about them as he said that they would be shot if they were caught. He gave them directions steering them clear of the main roads. They continued walking until evening, but could not find a suitable place to shelter. There was a slight drizzle that night and they had to sleep in the open with only their coats for warmth. It was a disturbed sleep given the circumstances, but they obviously kept their sense of humour. As dawn approached Mellows asked Hynes how he was feeling. He replied, 'I am shivering with the cold.' Mellows laughed and said, 'Remember … many are cold, but few are frozen.'

The morning was dry as the rain had cleared, but having checked their map they discovered that they were not on the right road for Scariff. They were extremely hungry and a search of the haversack only produced one cold boiled potato, which was bad in the centre. They saw smoke rising in the distance; it was a farmhouse. A young woman, who was not very welcoming, answered the knock on the door. Nevertheless, she agreed to make tea for them and gave them homemade bread and duck eggs. They wanted to pay her before leaving, but she refused to take any money.

They were soon on their way again, this time walking in sunshine. They took to the hills rather than the roads and found an area of soft heather where they lay down to rest as they had very little sleep the previous night. Hynes woke a number of hours later and began to pray, something they did regularly. After a few minutes he saw a man in the distance walking towards them. When the man reached their position he sat down on a rock and they got into conversation. He was Michael Maloney from the village of Balloughtra, which was located about three miles on the Galway side of Tulla, and he was out looking for some horses. Frank tried to tell him that they were 'cattle jobbers', but the man replied that he suspected they were 'Sinn Féiners'. The others awoke and when they admitted that they were rebels, Maloney told them that he was acquainted with a number of people in Dublin who were friends of Mellows and then admitted that he was a captain in a local company of Volunteers. They told him that they were on the way to Scariff, but he warned them that soldiers were combing the countryside for rebels. He then told them to stay where they were and he would bring them some food and supplies. He returned a few hours later with a basket full of food and some newspapers.

While that meal was very welcome, they were upset reading about the executions. Mellows was particularly sad as he had been close friends with the Dublin leaders. Maloney enlisted the help of another young man named Tom Hogan and they found shelter for Mellows, Hynes and Monahan in an old stable that had a fireplace. They also brought them bedclothes, which were as welcome as the food. Maloney told them that there were some 900 British troops in the Tulla area searching for rebels. It is interesting to note that the police in this area would not support the military in the search because of the attitude of their commanding officer, and after two weeks the military departed without having found any fugitives. Hynes stated in his witness statement that it looked as if God had a special hand in guiding them to the only district where there were no arrests. There is no doubt that Mellows and his companions had stumbled into perhaps the safest place in the west of Ireland.

They stayed there for some time, lighting fires at night to warm their new home as the smoke might attract attention during the day. As time passed they began to feel a greater degree of safety and over the following few months they enjoyed their time in the mountains. However, it was a life without much excitement. At one stage, Mellows felt that Hynes should try to contact his wife and let her know that he was safe. Mellows also decided that he would send a note to a lady friend in Athenry, which may confirm the story of him having a girlfriend in the town. Maloney agreed to take the messages to Athenry hidden in the bowl of a pipe and covered with tobacco. However, he was stopped and searched by the military on his way to the Athenry fair and because he was nervous he lit the pipe during the search. The notes were destroyed, but at least no incriminating evidence was found and Maloney was allowed to go on his way.

Towards the end of September the three men received word that a place had been secured for Mellows to leave the country on a ship bound for the United States. Although he did not want to leave, Mellows was told by the senior officers who were now running the Volunteers that he had no choice in the matter. It was the IRB Supreme Council that wanted Mellows to leave the country as they felt that he was much more valuable to them in the United States than on the run in Ireland. He had to dye his hair before leaving his mountain refuge.[5] When the time came for him to leave, a man named Seán McNamara brought him to Ennis where he was given shelter in the home of a priest, Fr Crowe. He had secured a nun's habit from the Convent of Mercy in Ennis for Mellows, who escaped in early October, making his way to Liverpool. This city was not safe either and Mellows was almost captured on one occasion. However, he managed to evade capture and escaped from England with the help of friends and supporters. He was taken on board an America-bound ship, first working as a stoker and later as a deckhand.[6]

It had been rumoured that Mellows was hiding out in a convent near Kinvara and the building was raided, causing a great deal of concern to the nuns and local clergy. General Maxwell had to write a letter to the local bishop explaining the reason that such action was taken. Of course the fugitives were delighted as the authorities were concentrating their search in the wrong locations.[7]

Monahan and Hynes were lonely after Mellows left for the United States but remained another month in their hideout in the mountains before they moved on themselves. They were taken to a location near Nenagh in County Tipperary, to the family home of a priest named Fr Kennedy. Monahan was then moved to another location. A short time later, Hynes had to move again, when he received word that police knew of his whereabouts. He was taken to the home of another priest, Fr Culligan, whom Hynes later described as 'a rebel at heart'. He was able to send letters home to his wife, although a personal visit was out of the question. His home was raided continually and it seems that each time the police or military arrived they warned his wife that they were going to kill Hynes once he was apprehended. Someone whom Fr Culligan described as a 'spy' became aware that Hynes was staying at his house, and Fr Culligan threatened to shoot the man if he informed the police. However, it was too dangerous to take a chance and so Hynes moved again. This was the life of rebels on the run, not sure who to trust and placing their lives in the hands of a stranger. Over the following months Hynes and Monahan again met and spent time together. Hynes eventually reached Dublin, where he met Michael Collins and was later sent to Cork.[8] By this time the hunt for the 1916 rebels was over and they were becoming heroes in the eyes of many people. This set the scene for a new phase in the war to free Ireland.

Éamonn Corbett also went on the run and managed to evade capture despite the best efforts of the military. He escaped to the United States in August 1916 where he continued to work for the Irish cause.[9] Patrick Callanan managed to escape to the United States with him.[10]

When Mellows arrived in New York in mid-December he found members of the IRB awaiting him and they escorted him to his boarding house at 141 West 97th Street. He received a great welcome as Callanan and Corbett were among the rebels waiting for him, so it was a long night of catching up and stories.[11]

Tom Kenny had also escaped to the United States in the weeks following the rebellion. In a letter to his wife, Kenny mentioned that he was engaged in public meetings and various other gatherings, making his uncompromising intentions clear: 'the day is not too far away when we shall be united in the dear old land of shackles and slavery ever removed from our midst, baptised with the blood of our best'. While it was reported to the authorities that Kenny had made his way to the United States, the police were unsure of this rumour and continued to watch his house. They paid special attention to his wife and mother when they were going out for any reason. It was said that the police were also watching anyone they suspected who came within a ten-mile radius of his forge. The police said that Kenny possessed all the qualities of a 'mob orator' and they needed to apprehend him, if he was still in the country, or, depending on the situation, if he ever returned to Ireland.[12]

Mellows was in good company and was seen by many in America as one of the last surviving senior officers of the Volunteers, so he was greatly welcomed. Shortly after arriving in

New York, he was taken to meet John Devoy, who represented Clan na Gael, the American counterpart to the IRB. While in America, Mellows continued to promote the Irish cause and became involved in a number of nationalist organisations. He also began writing for *Gaelic American* and his first article was an account of the Rising in Galway; it appeared on 17 January 1917 and was signed 'A Volunteer Officer'. This article resulted in a verbal attack by Kenny, who almost accused Mellows of cowardice because of the incident at Craughwell, when he had refused to attack the barracks. However, Kenny was forced to retract his words after Mellows publicly explained his decision and pointed out that it could well have been a disaster considering the National Volunteers had mobilised against them and had occupied the barracks with the police. Mellows at that time did not wish to spill the blood of former comrades, although he had obviously changed his mind by the time the Civil War broke out.[13]

Éamonn Corbett returned to Ireland in 1918 and was arrested and sent to Arbour Hill Prison. He was later sent to Lincoln Prison on a charge of attempted murder of a police constable. This charge dated back to the rebellion, when he led the group of rebels against the police outside the Agricultural College. Corbett went on hunger strike and was released in October 1919. Following the War of Independence, he became chairman of Galway County Council. He died in 1945.[14]

18

REBEL ROUND-UP

The round-up of rebels was intense and all the roads leading into Galway city were closely watched. The disbanded men who had returned home rather than going on the run did not go back to their normal routine of work, as they were unsure of how much the police knew about their activities. Because they were worried about being arrested, some of them cycled directly to the homes of neighbours in the hope of receiving information about military activity in their area. Over 200 police were drafted in from the north of Ireland and while they were not familiar with the areas around the county, the local police assisted them. They combed the countryside with a persistence never witnessed before, with three lorries leaving the city each day touring the roads to Athenry, Clarenbridge and many other areas, and they rarely returned without rebel prisoners or suspects. Terror tactics were common: the homes of some suspected rebels were destroyed and some suspected supporters had their homes torn apart during searches for weapons. Within weeks many arrests had been made and some eighty-six shotguns and seven rifles seized. It seems that members of Cumann na mBan were not arrested in Galway, but they were subjected to numerous house searches and severe interrogation.

A special train for prisoners had to be introduced because of the amount of men being arrested. During one journey to Dublin the train stopped in Athlone just opposite a train carrying troops. Some of the soldiers began shouting at the rebels. One of them, sixteen-year-old Tommy Bindon, who had served with the Clarenbridge Company, was dragged from the train with the help of the guards and kicked along the platform, before he was eventually forced back onto the train. While this was an isolated incident, it was nonetheless an example of the general hostility towards the rebels. Some of the prisoners later reported that the further away from Galway they were, the better the treatment they received. Many had bitter memories of being pelted with 'filth' as they were marched through the streets of the city.[1]

The local newspapers carried lists of the names of those arrested in the weeks following the rebellion and in many cases they also gave details of the localities. On Saturday 6 May 1916 over 200 prisoners were taken from Galway Jail under a heavy military (Royal Marines) and police escort and moved to the railway station. The streets of the town were crowded with people anxious to catch a glimpse of the rebels and a lot of jeers and abuse were hurled at them. A special train was waiting to take the prisoners to Dublin to relieve the pressure on Galway Jail, which was overcrowded because of the number of arrests. The situation was such that Renmore Barracks was also being used to accommodate prisoners.[2] When speaking of the rebellion sometime later, Lieutenant-Colonel Henry Jourdain, officer commanding at Renmore, said, 'It was evident that the recruiting fervour and the war on the whole obscured its importance, and the people were generally in the dark, and not on the side of the scattered rebels in the province. The news blackout was complete for the vital week, and then it was over, bar the round-up.'[3] He was obviously of the opinion that the war overshadowed the rebellion; however, this changed in a short time.

The following Wednesday another fifty prisoners were sent to Dublin and it was the same again on Friday. While there was little or no sympathy for the men, it was noted that the prisoners marched in military formation and were in step with each other.[4] For the prisoners, this was the first stage of a journey to Britain. The voyage across the Irish Sea was extremely dangerous as German U-boats were patrolling the seas around the coast. In seems that all military personnel were issued with lifebelts, but the prisoners had none. In some cases the prisoners had to wait some thirty hours for rations of food and water.[5]

While most of the rebels were taken to Dublin by train, some were transported by sea. On the evening of Thursday 27 April 1916, Micheál Ó Droighneáin, George Nichols, Pádraic Ó Máille, Seamus Carter and Frank Hardiman were told to write a letter to their families requesting additional clothing. The prisoners immediately suspected that their days on board HMS *Laburnum* in Galway Bay were numbered. The following morning they were all transferred by launch to HMS *Gloucester*. Once on board the *Gloucester*, they were searched, including the man from the Galway hooker (it is not known if there were guns hidden beneath the turf). All the prisoners were lined up on deck, and as their names were called out, a charge of treason was read out for each individual by a naval officer. He warned them that if a guilty verdict was passed on them they would be put to death, and if they tried to escape they would be shot. That evening they were among twenty-one prisoners transferred to HMS *Snowdrop* before it began its journey to Cobh. They were bundled down through a manhole into two cells below deck. Frank Hardiman later said that he believed that the cells were only intended for two prisoners, not ten or eleven. To make matters worse the portholes were locked shut and there was little ventilation – the only fresh air available was through the manhole. The sentries ignored their calls for attention. Professor Steinberger shouted 'this is murder' on a number of occasions, but despite his age no mercy was shown. They were forced to remain there for around eight hours and were then allowed on deck, but only for about five minutes.

Upon arrival at Cobh, they were transferred to the HMS *Albion*, a large man-of-war, where they were held for a number of days. The prisoners' accommodation was on the floor just below the deck and the little food allocated to them was of very poor quality. They had to eat with their hands from a dish placed on the floor as there was no furniture and they were not allowed knives or forks. Every morning the prisoners were given a bucket of water between them for washing. They occupied themselves by having mock trials, with judge and jury presiding over supposed charges of crimes. Conditions improved after a number of days, but they were unaware of what was going on in the outside world. One night they heard an argument between some of the sailors, and it seems that one of the crew members was defending the rebel action saying that they had as much right to arm themselves as Carson's men in the north.

A week later, they were transferred to HMS *Adventure* and that night it sailed out of Cobh as a gale was making its presence felt. It was a rough voyage, but they landed safely at Dún Laoghaire the following morning. Once they disembarked, the prisoners were detained in the local RIC station while awaiting transport to Richmond Barracks.[6]

Micheál Ó Droighneáin later recalled that upon arrival at Richmond they were placed in a room with no furniture; worse still the windows were broken so it was difficult to stay warm and the only way to sleep was to sit huddled up against the wall. After three days all the prisoners were assembled in the barracks square and told that they were going to be transported to England. Ó Droighneáin met Seán MacDiarmada while in the square and MacDiarmada said to him, 'I don't think they will send me across'. He was correct and was separated from them a short time later.[7]

The rebels were marched through streets thronged with people on the way to the North Wall and were then escorted onto a cattle boat for transportation to England. Conditions were so dreadful on board that one of the officers apologised to some of the prisoners. The rebels had to spend the crossing perched on the cattle rails rather than sit or stand on the filthy floor.[8] Having docked in Holyhead they were taken to London by train. Their destination in the British capital was Wandsworth Prison, where they were placed in solitary confinement for the first few days. Ó Droighneáin later remembered meeting Arthur Griffith in Wandsworth.

Religion was important to the men and Ó Droighneáin led the prisoners in the rosary, which they recited in Irish every day. A poignant memory he had of this was when one of the wardens asked them if they would offer up a rosary for his son who had been killed on the Western Front.[9] Some of the rebels themselves had family members fighting on the Western Front, for example John Kennedy-Lydon from Cahercrin. He was with Larry Lardner and Liam Mellows from the start of the rebellion and following the disbandment went on the run, but was captured. His brother, Patrick, died of wounds in November 1918, while serving with the 3rd New Zealand Rifles. Their sister, Sarah 'Babe' Kennedy-Lydon, was married to an RIC constable named Stephen Callanan and he was stationed in Craughwell during the rebellion. Had Mellows attacked the police station in Craughwell as Tom Kenny requested, John could have ended up in a gun battle with his brother-in-law. Stephen and Sarah later settled on a farm in Ballymanagh, Craughwell and were well respected by the community.[10]

The following account of conditions in Wandsworth Prison comes from the witness statement of Frank Hardiman:

> We were kept in solitary confinement and not allowed to speak or mix with each other. Neither were we allowed to exercise for some days until the convicts had prepared the exercise yard, cindered and rolled it. The food we got was awful, and the filthy

tins we got it in were most revolting, but we were starving and glad to get anything. After about two weeks we were reduced to skeletons. Things were so bad that on marching to Mass one of the prisoners broke ranks and made a dive for a dirty crust of bread on the ground.[11]

After seven weeks in Wandsworth, Hardiman, Ó Droighneáin and many of the other prisoners were transferred to the North Camp in Frongoch as the South Camp was already full. Ó Droighneáin, being an excellent Gaelic speaker, began giving Irish classes to the prisoners.[12]

Pádraic Ó Máille was also sent to Frongoch and there is a story of a young Welsh girl falling in love with him. She obviously worked at the camp and is supposed to have helped him escape disguised as a priest. However, he was rearrested and sent to Wandsworth Prison, where he remained until he was released under the general amnesty in 1917.[13]

Two of the most wanted men from the Castlegar Company, Brian Molloy and Michael Newell, almost escaped detection. However, on the Friday evening following the disbandment of the rebels at Limepark, they made their way to the house of a friend in Coolough as they needed a change of clothes and something to eat before making their way to Connemara, where they felt they would be safer. Shortly after they arrived police surrounded the house and they were forced to surrender. They were taken to Galway Jail.[14] Newell was then sent to Richmond Barracks and later to Wandsworth Prison. After this he was transferred to Frongoch, along with a large group of other prisoners, by train. During the journey they were delayed in a station, possibly Nottingham, for over an hour while waiting for a troop train to pass. They were ordered to line up on the platform and were guarded by armed soldiers with fixed bayonets. While they were standing there a hostile crowd gathered and began shouting abuse and spitting at them. One of the soldiers guarding the rebels struck three people in the crowd with the butt of his rifle, knocking them to the ground. The soldier was obviously Irish as he then shouted, 'Up Carraroe, Up Connemara'. His name was John Keane, a native of Carraroe in Connemara, and he was later brought up on assault charges.[15]

Shortly after arriving in Frongoch, Newell was called to appear before the Sankey Commission at Wormwood Scrubs Prison. He was questioned about his activities during the rebellion and the killing of Constable Whelan at Carnmore. Having given as few details as possible, he was returned to Frongoch without being charged.[16]

Sweeney Newell went to work as usual at the family forge on the Monday following the disbandment, and a short time later police surrounded the forge and took him prisoner. He was taken to Eglinton Street Barracks that night and the following day he was imprisoned in Galway Jail. On Saturday of that week, Newell was taken to Arbour Hill Barracks in Dublin. He later said that in the early morning he could hear the volley of shots as the firing squads executed the rebellion's leaders. He also remembered seeing their bodies being brought into the yard for burial. Having been questioned in Richmond

Barracks, he was sent to Stafford Jail in England and then to Frongoch. He also appeared before the Sankey Commission and, like his brother, was returned there after questioning. While at Frongoch he refused to remove any refuse belonging to the camp guards so was placed in solitary confinement, the punishment for all rebel prisoners who refused to do so.[17]

On Monday morning just two weeks after the rebellion, Brian Molloy was singled out for special treatment, as he was believed to have been responsible for the death of Constable Whelan. He was removed from Galway Jail handcuffed to a policeman and taken by train to Richmond Barracks. A few days later he was charged with waging war against His Majesty's forces and tried by general court martial. During the trial he was asked if he was in command of the Castlegar Volunteers. Having replied that he was, he was then asked if he was present at Carnmore when the policeman was killed. Again he replied 'yes'; although he had not shot Whelan, being in command, he took responsibility for the action of his men. Molloy was then sentenced to death. However, the sentence was afterwards commuted to ten years' penal servitude in Mountjoy Jail. Molloy was forced to dress as a convict and was placed in solitary confinement. A week later, he was given civilian clothing and was transferred to Dartmoor Prison in England. Again he was placed in solitary confinement, but occupied himself by sewing sandbags, which was a practice in the prison. After two weeks he was allowed one hour of exercise in the prison yard. The remainder of the day was spent sewing coal bags in a shed with other rebel prisoners. However, they were not allowed to talk.

In October 1916 Molloy and a number of other prisoners were transferred to Lewes Prison, where conditions were much better. In May 1917 the rebels demanded prisoner-of-war status, which was refused. They demonstrated their anger by breaking the windows in the cells. Molloy was then transferred with a number of others to the Isle of Wight. The day after his arrival they were told that they would have to work as common criminals. Molloy refused on the basis that he was a political prisoner and was brought before the governor of the prison. His continued refusal to work cost him two days in the punishment cells on bread and water. In August 1917 he was transferred to Maidstone Prison, from where he was released the following day. Those released with him were all given 5s each and made their way back to Ireland. The sight of the land for which they had fought had a huge effect on the former prisoners. Many of them broke out in cheers of joy.[18] Molloy later told his son that they were almost overwhelmed with emotion. There was a great sense of victory among them also as they now tasted this freedom of expression with pride.

Tom Ruane escaped immediate capture and made his way to Moycullen, where he took a boat and rowed out to one of the islands on Lough Corrib. The police searched extensively for him, but were unable to apprehend him. However, while shopping in Galway city, his wife had her handbag snatched by the police and it contained a letter from Ruane with his contact details. He was arrested a short time later and sent to Frongoch, where he spent ten months. After his release, he continued his involvement in the republican movement and was arrested again in 1918 and sent to Wormwood Scrubs for a time.

The names and descriptions of some of the men on the run were published in police bulletins. One of them, Nicholas Kyne, an officer with the Claregalway Company, was a close friend of Tom Ruane. He was charged with 'having on the 25th April 1916 and subsequent dates at Carnmore and Oranmore, committed various acts of rebellion'. All around Claregalway, as in other areas, the homes of suspected rebels were searched by the police and military in a bid to find arms or incriminating documents, and many houses were damaged. In one week alone some 270 rebels, including those suspected of being involved in the rebellion, were arrested and sent to Richmond Barracks in Dublin to await court martial.[19]

Larry Lardner also went on the run and evaded capture until 1918. After his arrest he served three months in a Belfast prison. Upon his release, Lardner was rearrested immediately and deported to England where he served twelve months in Lincoln Prison. While in prison he became closely acquainted with Éamon de Valera and is believed to have assisted him in his escape from that prison.[20]

Following their disbandment, Stephen Jordan and Dick Murphy went on the run together. They stayed in various locations around the county, moving from one safe house to another over the following weeks. It was June before they were eventually captured near Tuam and they were first sent to Galway Jail before being transported to Richmond Barracks. They were both to face the ordeal of a court martial, but the night before their judgment, orders were received from England that all trials were to cease. Nevertheless, they ended up in Frongoch with the others.[21]

Martin Newell was captured on 12 May 1916 and taken to Moyvilla RIC Barracks. Later that same day he was sent to Richmond Barracks and after a week Newell, along with many other rebel prisoners, was marched to the North Wall in Dublin and loaded onto a cattle boat. Some of these men were sent to Barlinnie Detention Barracks in Glasgow and others to Perth. Although they were unaware of their destination at the time, spirits were high among the prisoners. Newell and a number of others were placed in solitary confinement for four or five weeks in Glasgow before being transferred to Frongoch. Over time many of the prisoners were taken in batches to London to appear before the Sankey Commission. While in London they were housed in Wormwood Scrubs Prison. The questions put to Newell followed a pattern experienced by many of the prisoners: 'Did you take part in the rebellion? Were you armed? Who did you serve under? Why did you take part?' and 'Is that all you have to say for yourself?'[22]

Professor Steinberger was among the prisoners transferred to Richmond Barracks by sea. He was then sent to Wandsworth. After an investigation was carried out, it was quickly realised that the accusations against him were false. A lamp movement from the window of his house was simply emitted as the man was going to bed. He was released on 22 May 1916 on the orders of the under-secretary of Ireland after he became aware of the stupidity of the arrest. Professor Steinberger returned home, and it seems that he was not overly affected by his ordeal in prison. However, he died on 3 November 1916 from pneumonia. Large crowds of people attended his funeral from St Joseph's church to the New Cemetery in Bohermore. A large body of students from the university attended, some of whom acted as pallbearers. In addition to his colleagues and staff from the university, there was a large attendance from the civil and commercial leaders in the city. It was rumoured that many of those who lined up to lament the death of Professor Steinberger had been part of the hostile crowd who shouted abuse at him just a few months earlier. One of his sons had been serving with the Royal Navy and was away at war when his father was arrested.

Dr Thomas Walsh, who was also arrested in the swoop of April 1916, was also released, possibly at the time of the general amnesty. He resumed his position at the university and remained there until his retirement in 1946.[23]

19

FRONGOCH

Frongoch was an internment camp in north Wales where over 1,800 Irishmen were placed following the 1916 Rising. It had housed German prisoners of war before the Irish displaced them. One Galway man later said that Frongoch was a bleak place where the food was 'bad, white turnips, turnip soup, skilly, bread and tea – all in small quantities'. The buildings were as 'cold as the grave' during bad weather.[1] There were of course other detention centres and prisons used, but Frongoch was the main place of internment for the Irish rebels. It was divided into two sections, the North and South Camps. The North Camp was built on a height and consisted of a series of wooden huts. The South Camp was a dismal-looking place, which had formerly been a distillery and was infested with rats scurrying over and under the beds at night, constantly disrupting sleep. Both camps were surrounded with barbed-wire fencing.

Having arrived at Frongoch Railway Station the prisoners were marched to the internment camp where Commandant-Colonel F. A. Heygate Lambert addressed them. He read the rules of the camp and warned prisoners that anyone caught try-ing to escape would be shot with buckshot. His speeches were the same for all the prisoners when they arrived and in time they gave him the nickname 'Buckshot'.

Once settled, the prisoners organised themselves, and those

who had trades such as cobblers, tailors and barbers were kept busy. Stephen Jordan from Athenry was placed in charge of the cobblers. Dr Thomas Walsh from Galway city was appointed as medical officer for one of the camps. The prisoners formed a camp general council to deal with civilian matters and a military council which more or less ran the camp.[2] At least five Galway men served on these councils: John Faller, Frank Hardiman, Dr Walsh, Pádraic Ó Máille and George Nichols. John Faller, whose jewellery premises in Williamsgate Street, Galway, included an optician's office, was also appointed as optician for the prisoners. The council was formed on 11 June 1916, just two days after the camp was opened to Irish prisoners, which shows just how organised they became in a short time.

Education was also important and there was a particular interest in learning the Irish language, so a branch of the Gaelic League was set up in the camp to support men wishing to read and write in their native tongue. Certain events were also celebrated, such as the anniversary of Wolfe Tone, when a concert was held to honour their hero, a rebel of another era. Some twenty different acts were performed, involving songs, poems and musical entertainment. Pádraic Ó Máille's job was to address the audience in Irish.

The prisoners in Frongoch began playing Gaelic football almost immediately and developed a pitch for themselves, which they called Croke Park. Hurling was not permitted as the camp commanders viewed hurleys as potential weapons. The matches were extremely competitive and one of the main organisers was Dick Fitzgerald from Killarney, who had been captain of the Kerry team in two All-Ireland victories, 1913 and 1914. Track-and-field events were also organised and there seems to have been no shortage of competitors. There was also entertainment in the form of a written bulletin entitled 'Frongoch Humour', which lifted the spirits of the men; Dick Murphy from Athenry was a regular contributor.

Another form of exercise involved route marches, but these were introduced as a supposed punishment by the camp authorities after the men refused to clean up for the soldiers stationed at the camp because they saw themselves as prisoners of war and not criminals. The marches took place about three times a week and were approximately six miles long. There were various routes chosen through the Welsh countryside and the men marched in military formation. A British Army officer and a number of guards accompanied them. Some of the prisoners in the camp had war pipes, which were often played during the route marches.[3]

While some of the British officers were able for the marching pace of the prisoners, the older men were not, and as the prisoners became aware of this they began to march much faster to put pressure on their guards. The more they were called upon to slow down, the quicker they marched. Placing a sergeant in front of the column eventually prevented this and he set the marching pace. Over time the route marches were seen as being too enjoyable for the men and thus a different form of punishment had to be introduced. Because of their continued refusal to clean out the soldier's ash-pits, the prisoners were accused of insubordination and some were sent to detention cells and deprived of all privileges. However, these men received their quota in tobacco and cigarettes thrown in through their cell windows when the camp guards were otherwise occupied.[4]

As winter approached, the Welsh countryside began to look bleak, and the thought of having to spend Christmas in Frongoch was even bleaker for the prisoners.[5] The River Tryweryn ran close to the camps and brought a degree of pleasure to the Galway prisoners, as it reminded them of home. Frank Hardiman later recorded: 'To most Galway men, so accustomed to seeing water such as the sea, lake or river, when away from home the absence [of] water is felt – so that to look on this little river occasionally was a pleasure and restful to the eyes.' The change in weather conditions made matters worse and the rain seemed to fall in torrents, making everything look even more miserable. However, December brought a heavy blanket of snow that covered the countryside, giving it a 'picturesque appearance'.[6] Then rumours started to spread around the camp that there was a possibility that the prisoners might be let home by Christmas, which brought a degree of hope.

On 21 December 1916 it was announced in the House of Commons that the Irish prisoners being held in Frongoch and Reading Prison were to be released unconditionally. Special trains were organised to take the prisoners to Holyhead ensuring that many of them would be home for Christmas. The official day for the amnesty was 23 December.[7] It seems that a few weeks before the announcement, John Redmond had told the House of Commons that the best gift they could give to the Irish people was the release of all the prisoners.[8]

The men returning from Frongoch arrived in a country that had utterly changed in a matter of months. A renewed longing for freedom had spread across Ireland, bringing with it a deep respect for those who turned out in rebellion during 1916. They could not have envisaged this when they were marched away amid ridicule and abuse, all of which was hurled at them in plentiful measure.[9]

Overall there are mixed feelings and reports from those interned in Frongoch. When speaking of it some years ago, the late Michael Diskin, director of the Town Hall Theatre in Galway, said, 'Frongoch remains a rare Welsh intervention in the lexicon of Irish historiography. But Frongoch in our minds is always a prison camp, in theory a symbol of defeat, but also a turning point, a victory of sorts, a Dunkirk if you will.' Frongoch had a positive effect on the revolutionary movement, as the men interned there became acquainted with each other. To many historians it was a place of rebirth for a revolution that began in 1916 and culminated in the War of Independence. Tim Healy, an MP, described it as the Sandhurst of the Irish Republican Army. Frongoch has been described as the 'Cauldron of Re-Birth', 'Recruitment Centre for Irish Nationalists' and Sean O'Mahony called his book about the camp *University of Revolution*. While many of those imprisoned there would not have been considered very dangerous upon arrival, they were certainly staunch republicans by the time they left. Michael Collins, Richard Mulcahy, Dick McKee and some of the other leading rebels took full advantage of their time as prisoners there, organising and planning the next stage of the fight for Irish freedom. Rebel songs were sung openly in the camps and on the route marches – it was there that *The Soldier's Song*, now the Irish national anthem, became popular. All of this was done under the watchful eyes of the British. Some people believe that the rebels could not have achieved their later victory had they not been imprisoned together, as it gave them the opportunity to build up strong ties with like-minded men from across the country.[10]

The following is a list of 521 Galway men who were arrested and sent to Frongoch and other prisons and detention centres after the rebellion, as well as ten who were arrested but released. It is not a definitive list, as a complete record is not available, but it does record the names of Galway men who are known at this point in time to have been incarcerated; others may surface later. The men are listed under towns and village names, but bear in mind that these include surrounding areas. Where (2) or (3) is included in the body of the list of prisoners it means that there were two or three men with the same name arrested. This list was compiled from a number of sources and records, which are mentioned in the relevant endnote:

Aran Islands (3): Brian Joyce, John O'Brien, Micheál Ó Mullane.

Ardrahan (8): John Coen, Patrick Howley, Martin Keighery, Michael Sylver, Patrick Sylver, Martin Tanniam, Martin Thompson, William Thompson.

Athenry (145): Christopher Barrett, James Barrett, Michael Barrett, Patrick Burke, Stephen Burke, William Burke, Michael Burns, Pat Cahaleen, Michael Cahill, William Cahill, T. Callinan (2), Chris

Caulfield, James Cleary, John Cleary, Joseph Cleary, Thomas Cleary, Thomas B. Cleary, Thomas Coen, Patrick Colohan, Joseph Commins, Michael Commons, William Commons, Thomas Connell, John Connolly, Patrick Connolly, Robert Connolly, Joseph Connor, Joseph Coreen, Martin Costello, Michael Costello, Martin Crowley, M. J. Cullen, John Cullinan, Michael Cuniffe, F. Curran, Matthew Daly, Patrick Daly, J. Doherty, Patrick Donnellan, M. Dooley, J. Dooley, P. Doyle, William Duffy, Michael Dunleavy, Joseph Earl, Thomas Egan, George Fahey, John Fahey, Peter Fahey, A. Fahy, Laurence Fahy, Patrick Fahy, Thomas Fahy, J. Farrell, Michael Farrell, William Feeney, Michael Freeney, Jeremiah Galvin, John Gardiner, Patrick Gilligan, John Gilvin, John Grealish, Thomas Grealish, Michael Hession, Michael H. Hanniffy, Daniel Hassett, Michael Healy (2), Patrick Healy, Patrick Henehan, Peter Henehan, Patrick Higgins, William Higgins, Martin Hynes, Patrick Jordan, Stephen Jordan, Michael Joyce, Michael Kane, Patrick Kane, James Keane, Michael Keane, Daniel Kearns, John Kearns, John Keating, Joseph Keating, Michael Keating, Joseph Kelly, Michael Kelly (2), William Kelly (2), Martin Kennedy, Patrick Kennedy (2), John Kennedy-Lydon, Patrick Kenny, James Lally, Thomas Lally, John Lawless, Patrick Lawless, Patrick Lynskey, Peter Mahon, Peadar McKeown, Michael Molloy, Martin Moloney, Gilbert Morrissey, J. Morrissey, Martin Morrissey, Patrick Morrissey (2), Richard Morrissey, Tom Morrissey, Thomas Mullen, T. Mullins, John Murphy (2), M. Murphy, Michael Murphy, Richard Murphy, Patrick Naughton, Michael Nestor, James Nolan, Patrick Noone, Patrick O'Connor, Francis O'Reilly, M. Quinn, Bryan Rohan, John Rooney, Joseph Rooney, Martin Rooney, Martin Ruane, John Ryan, T. Shaughnessy, Mick Treacy, John Waldron, John Walsh, Martin Walsh, Michael Walsh, Patrick Walsh, Thomas Walsh, Walter Walsh, James Ward, Joseph Whyte, Patrick Whyte.

Attymon (1): John Mitchel.

Ballinasloe (2): James Connor, Bryan Roughan.

Belclare (1): Patrick Cummins.

Connemara (2): Pádraic Ó Máille, Michael Thornton.

Carnmore (18): Willie Carr, John Collins, Ned Cummins, John Connelly, William Flaherty, James Grealish (Peter), James Grealish (Roger), Martin Paddy Grealish, Mairtin Watt Grealish, Patrick Grealish, John Hughes, Jack Lally, Mike Lally, Peter Lally, Tom Lally, John Walsh, Patrick Walsh, Stephen Walsh.

Castlegar (19): Martin Carr, Thomas 'Baby' Duggan, James Feeney, Michael Farrell, Michael Flannery (2), John Hanley, Brian Molloy, John Molloy, James Newell, Thomas 'Sweeney' Newell, William Newell, Matthew Ronan, Michael Ruffley, John Ryan, Michael Ryan, Thomas Silke, Michael Tallon, Martin Wall.

Claregalway (38): Michael Blake, Martin Casserly, Peter Casserly, William Cody, John J. Collins, John Concannon, Patrick Concannon, William Corcoran, Thady Corkett, Patrick Cummins, Dan Duggan, Henry Duggan (Liam), Henry Duggan (Seán), Willie Duggan, Martin Fahey, Patrick Feeney, George Glynn, Michael Glynn, Patrick Grealish, Patrick Hughes (2), Pat Kelly, Martin Kyne, Nicholas Kyne, Michael Lally, John Merrin, John Molloy, John Moran, Michael Murphy, Philip Murphy (2), Tom Murphy, Patrick O'Brien, Charles Quinn, Thomas Ruane, Tom Ruane, Tom Hession, Martin Samways.

Clarenbridge (13): John Connoll, John Corcoran, Edward Cummins, J. Egan, Patrick Fahy, George Fleming, Joseph Fleming, Michael Fleming Sr, Michael Fleming Jr, Patrick Fleming, William Hussey, Denis Keane, Michael O'Leary.

Craughwell (48): Michael Barrett, Patrick Barrett, Peter Barrett, John Browne, Thomas Colohan, Michael Conway, Dominick Cooney, Dominick Corbett, John Corbett, Patrick Corbett, Peter Corbett, Thomas Corbett, P. Coy, Tom Cullinan, Jeremiah Deely, Patrick Dempsey, Patrick Fahey (2), Thomas Fahey, John Fahy, Patrick Fahy, Michael Ford, John Forde, Michael Furey, Patrick Golding, Hugh Greaney, James Hanniffy, Michael Hynes, Patrick Hynes, Thomas Hynes, James Kelly, Patrick Kelly, John Kennedy, John Mannion, Tim Mannion, Martin McEvoy, Thomas McNamara, George Moloney, John Moloney (2), Martin Moran, Edward Newell, Martin Newell, John Quinn, John Rooney, Martin Rooney, Michael Shaughnessy, Patrick Walsh.

Curragrean–Merlin Park (1): Patrick Grealish.

Dinish Island (1): Stephen Larkin.

Doughiska (6): Mick Burke, Tom Burke, James Fahey, Mick Fahey, Tom O'Connor, Thomas Somerley.

Dunmore (3): Thomas Kilgarriff, William McGill, Michael Ronayne.

Galway city (12): Seamus Carter, John P. Faller, Thomas Flanagan, Michael Flanagan, Frank Hardiman, S. MacArthur, P. L. Madden, George Nichols, Bart Nolan, Con O'Leary, C. O'Seary, Thomas Walsh.

Gort (21): Thomas Burke, John Coen, Martin Coen, Michael Cunniffe, Thomas Cunniffe, Martin Egan, Michael Egan, Michael Fahy, Daniel Kelleher, James Kelleher, John Kelleher, Martin Kelleher, John Loughrey (2), John Joe Nelly, Bryan O'Connor, John O'Fahy, P. J. Piggott, Peter Roughan, Thomas Stephenson, Michael Trayers.

Killeenan (3): Dominick Cahill, James Coen, Bernard Grealish.

Kilcolgan (15): John Bindon, Thomas Bindon, Thomas Brennan, T. Ford, P. Forde, P. Joyce, P. Kilkelly, T. Kilkelly, Martin Neilan, Thomas Neilan, John O'Dea, Michael O'Dea, Patrick O'Dea, Thomas O'Dea, T. Stephenson.

Kiltulla (17): John Connolly, Thomas Doyle, Patrick Forde, John Gilligan, Dennis Halloran, Michael Kelly, John King, Patrick King (2), Patrick Mahon, Michael Mannion, Bart Mulryan, John Mulryan, William Mulryan (2), John Wall, Michael Walsh.

Kinvara (19): Patrick Burke (2), Peter Burke, J. Callinan, Patrick Fahy, John Glynn, Patrick Hanbury, Michael Hanlon, Martin Hynes, John Kilkelly, Michael Kilkelly, Patrick Kilkelly, Stephen Leech, Thomas McInerney, Michael O'Conlon, David O'Hanlon, William Quinn, John Whelan, James Whelan.

Loughrea (32): Patrick Conniffe, Charles Coughlan (3), Patrick Coy, Michael Delahunty, John Fahy, Joseph Fahy, Patrick Fahy, Thomas Fahy, Tom Fahy, Bernard Fallon, Joseph Flaherty, James J. Flynn, Laurence Garvey, Joseph Gilchrist, Thomas J. Green, Martin Greene, John Kearns, Joe Kearns, Charles Kelleher, Christopher Kelleher, Patrick Martin, Patrick Martyn, Patrick McGinge, Patrick McTigue, M. Melody, Edward Roche, Patrick Sweeney (2), Peadar Sweeney, Richard Wilson.

Monivea (9): Patrick Donnellan, James Gardiner, James Glynn, Peter Lawless, Michael Molloy, John Moloney, Martin Murphy, Thomas Tully, Walter Walsh.

Moylough (1): James Haverty.

New Inn (2): John Craven, Michael Melody.

Oranmore (54): James Burke, Joe Burke, Martin Burke, William Burke

(2), James Burns, John Burns, Michael Burns, Patrick Burns, William Burns, Christopher Carrick, John Carrick, T. Connolly, J. Cooley, Edmond Corcoran, Willie Corcoran, Patrick Couley, Martin Costello, Michael Costello, Patrick Costello, Thomas Cunniffe, J. Egan, Michael Fahy, James Flanagan, Patrick Flanagan, Pat Flanahan, Michael Freeney, Patsy Furey, Tommy Furey, Tom Furey, Thomas Fury, Peter Grealy, Patrick Harte, William Harte, Martin Hawkins, T. Hawkins, Thomas Hawkins, Mike Hehir, Mike Higgins, Patrick Holland, Joseph Howley, Thomas Hynes, William Hynes, Patrick Keane, Francis Kearney, Jim Loughlin, John Monaghan, John Mulligan, Michael O'Rouke, Martin O'Toole, Mike O'Toole, Michael Ryder, Michael Ruane, Michael Walsh.

Peterswell (6): William Burke, Peter Howley, William Howley, Michael Howley, Patrick Howley, Thomas Kelley.

Rosshill (1): Thomas Duggan.

Tawin Island (1): Thomas Holland.

Tuam (4): Joseph Cummins, Gerald Feeney, John Ford, Liam T. Langley.

Turloughmore (1): Augustus O'Brien.

Address Unknown (14): Edward Burke, Thomas Connolly, Edward Conroy, James Coy, Michael Coy, Richard Haverty, D. Hynes, John Hynes, Michael Kilkelly, Patrick Kilkelly, M. Kyne, Martin McGlynn, Michael McGlynn, John Molloy.

Arrested and Released (10): T. Carney, Thomas Corcoran, Patrick Corless, T. Flanagan, J. Holloran, M. Hynes, William Hynes, J. Kennedy, J. P. Martin, Valentine Steinberger.[11]

20

LOYAL TO THE CROWN?

During its long history Galway had remained loyal to two kings in times of war, and in a sense, it now added a third. During the Cromwellian wars of the mid-seventeenth century it pledged its allegiance in military terms to Charles I. Just over forty years later, Galway displayed the same loyalty to James II in the Jacobite-Williamite war. In 1914 it pledged its loyalty to Britain in the war for the freedom of small nations as it was sometimes called in Ireland. While many Irish people would not wish to be associated with the word loyalism, this is in fact what it was – loyalty to the British government.

After the Rising the authorities were quick to point out the sheer number of Irishmen who had enlisted for military service in Europe. On 6 May 1916 the *Connacht Tribune* reported a figure of up to 400,000 Irishmen fighting in the trenches. It was making a comparison with the estimated 700 men who turned out in rebellion in Galway. They reported that the nationalists loyal to Britain made up the vast majority of Volunteers, while the Sinn Féiners, like the unionists in Galway, were a mere handful. The report also stated that these nationalists were as loyal to Britain as the British themselves.[1]

When looking at the rebellion in Galway one would have to admit that it was in reality a rural insurrection rather than an urban fight. In the city during Easter Week many members of the National Volunteers took to the streets in support of the police and military. Members of the public who joined the Special Constabulary, a group specially formed to crush the rebels and their cause, also supported the police. Yet just a few years later, many politicians and people who had shown open hostility towards the rebels and their cause in 1916 displayed disdain towards the young men they had encouraged to go to the killing fields of Flanders and Northern France through propaganda and other means. One witness later stated that the reason they had supported the British was because they were informed that the rebels were against John Redmond and the Irish Party. However, this explanation could simply be an excuse for people who found themselves living in an Ireland that had changed dramatically in the post-rebellion years.[2]

After the Rising broke out, a large public meeting was organised by Galway Urban Council, which called on the people to help the police and military to crush the rebellion. They promoted the enrolment of young men into the Special Constabulary in support of the police so that there would be a large enough force to repulse any rebels who might enter the city. While there was much anxiety when the warships began shelling what they believed at the time to be rebel positions, there was also great enthusiasm for this among the inhabitants of Galway. Some felt besieged by the revolutionary forces, while others thought of it as a type of civil war. What was very apparent in the city during the rebellion was that even nationalists on the council were in fear of the rebels. This fear seems to have been widespread, and what may be viewed as surprising today is the fact that the people of the town felt a great sense of relief when British forces arrived.[3]

On Tuesday during the week of the rebellion, Brid from Waterlane made comments regarding the loyalty of the people in the city: 'Some of the ordinary citizens of Galway who were loyal to the British got together all of the policemen and firemen they could find to go against the Volunteers.' She mentioned that her father was very angry because of this. However, although Galway city had remained loyal, it was not exempt from homes being searched in the aftermath of the Rising. On 20 May the area around Eyre Square was blocked off by the military while all the houses were searched.[4]

The following letter from a Galway city man who was a Special Constable is an example of the support and loyalty members of the general public felt towards the British authorities:

> Sir – I doubt if the public generally realise how much it is indebted to the magnificent conduct of the Royal Irish Constabulary during the present crisis. The devotion to duty of this splendid body of men has been simply superb. They have been under arms literally night and day since Easter Monday, not having an opportunity of taking off their clothes for the past six or seven days, and only catching an odd hour's sleep when and where they could, still armed and ready for a call to duty at any moment. We can never repay them. Their officers have displayed untiring zeal and energy, showing the greatest pluck under fire, under trying circumstances. Those who have followed the situation carefully know that the daring and bril-

liant little raid on Carnmore (although we unfortunately lost one poor fellow there) was a masterpiece of strategy. From that moment I believe the Sinn Féiners were unnerved and the town was safe. Although the city owes a deep debt of gratitude to the RIC, I think this fact should be brought home to everyone.

Lewis A. Tolputt,
Taylor's Hill, Galway, May 1916.[5]

Thomas Courtney later described Galway city as being the most 'shoneen' town in Ireland. The word 'shoneen' is meant as an insulting term for those embracing British traditions and behaviours and ignoring Gaelic customs. As a youngster in 1903, Courtney had been amazed at the reception that King Edward VII and Queen Alexandra received when they visited the city. He had never seen as many flags, Union Jacks, banners and decorations. One in particular that grabbed his attention announced 'God Save Our Glorious King'. Courtney held this opinion of Galway even in later periods.[6]

Despite this accusation, an interesting situation arose in the schoolyards of the city in the weeks following the rebellion. School children whose parents supported the rebels wore green, white and orange badges to school, while those whose families supported the government, who were in the majority, wore red, white and blue badges. Fights broke out between these children, as they tried to rip the badges off the clothing of their opponents. The only solution for the schools was to declare a ban on the wearing of both badges.[7] This, perhaps, shows that the picture of complete loyalty in the city was not as black and white as it has sometimes been painted.

In the county the rebellion was mainly contained in east and parts of south Galway. It has been estimated that there were over 1,500 National Volunteers in East Galway at the time of the rebellion and they vastly outnumbered the Irish Volunteers under Mellows. Redmond was in New York when the rebellion broke out, but he was quick to send his criticism of the action taken by the Irish Volunteers. Although he had issued orders to the National Volunteers to place themselves at the disposal of the British military, there was widespread reluctance to do so. With the exception of Loughrea and Craughwell, the National Volunteers in other areas of County Galway did not wish to become involved in action against their former comrades.

The Loughrea branch of the National Volunteers was under the command of William Duffy, a member of the Irish Party, an MP and a strong supporter of the government and the war effort. It was believed by many people that the Rising was a prelude to a German invasion of Ireland, so, as far as Duffy was concerned, the rebels were legitimate targets for the men under his command.[8] There had been warnings of such an invasion from the outset of the war and this had convinced many young men to enlist in the army. In fact during one of the Loughrea recruiting meetings, people were warned that their homes and farmlands were already mapped out for the Turks once Germany had won the war. Similar warnings were given at other recruiting meetings around the county, with people being told that the Germans had plans of their own regarding land in Ireland.[9] During the week of the rebellion there was much speculation about the German connection. One rumour that caused a lot of concern was that thousands of German troops had landed on the Connemara coast and were marching through County Galway. This was later given as a reason for the expression of loyalty in the city.

In Craughwell during Easter Week the people and authorities expected the rebels to attack the police barracks in the village. According to one report there was a great sense of worry and anxiety about the place, forcing the police to remain confined to barracks. The National Volunteers abandoned their work in the fields to meet to discuss the situation. A reporter from *The Tuam Herald* recorded in rather florid style that these brave men knew the call of duty, which they obeyed, and many of them tore themselves away from a fond wife whose kisses were still upon their lips as they prepared for action. Others left aged and worried parents who, with tears in their eyes, blessed their sons as they went to fight for such a noble cause rather than be slaves to rebels. Over 100 of them gathered their arms in preparation to defend the village as it was said that 'very little mercy would be shown to some of them if those lunatics got into the village'. The account went on to say that these 'fearless men' left their homes with grim determination and were prepared to sacrifice their lives and strike a blow against an element they had been fighting for years. The reporter accused the rebels of cowardice because they had avoided Craughwell knowing the National Volunteers were protecting the village.[10]

While this report is rather dramatic, it is a good example of the mindset of the general public at the time of the rebellion. The report's conclusion leaves no doubt about the general loyalty to the government and not to the rebel cause:

> Well may poor Ireland weep, the cup has been dashed from her lips by her degenerate sons, and a strain placed upon her history which time cannot efface. Still the action of the National Volunteers all over Ireland, and especially that of the men of Craughwell (which was considered a hell upon earth by the men who knew it not) should have a far-reaching effect in lessening that strain which was the outcome of German intrigue and German money. Why should poor Ireland suffer for the action of a handful of men? Nine-tenths of her population have been loyal subjects and thousands of her sons are today fighting with the English army and covering themselves with glory. They have fought England's battles in the past and will continue to fight them wherever the cause of justice is at stake if she will only prove her sympathies towards Ireland in this her hour of trial.[11]

It was reported that Pope Benedict XV gave instructions to all Irish bishops to strongly advise the clergy and the Catholic people of Ireland to 'maintain perfect loyalty towards England'. This was bound to have influenced the general public.[12]

The situation in Loughrea and Craughwell was reflected in many other Galway towns, with much opposition to the insurrection. It was reported from Tuam that the people were in total opposition to the rebellion. In fact it has been said that its district inspector had the support of the entire civilian population.[13] In June 1916 a reporter from the *Tuam Herald* stated that a feature of the Rising in Galway was the fact that the north constituency remained almost exempt from the revolutionary movement, which was attributed to the strength of the national organisation that had given its loyalty to Redmond and the Irish Party.[14]

Even in Athenry, which was often considered a rebel stronghold, the Union Jack flew proudly over the town hall. It seems the British purposely did this as a way of saying that victory was a certainty, as the town hall had been the rebel headquarters when the rebellion broke out.[15]

Following the rebellion, Loughrea and Craughwell were singled out and acknowledged by the government as places that remained totally loyal. One report stated that the people of Loughrea were 'especially loyal and did everything they could to assist the military and police'.[16] The Loughrea Board of Guardians spoke out about the blindness and folly of their fellow countrymen and said that it was a deplorable action for Irishmen to take. The board stated that they would remain true to the constitutional leadership and felt that the Loughrea district had reacted splendidly in the recent trouble.[17]

The rapid change in the political climate following the execution of the rebellion's leaders caught many of those who had shown loyalty to the British by surprise. William Duffy in Loughrea, who had clearly nailed his colours to the mast by ordering his men to crush the rebellion, suddenly became very careful on the matter, referring to the rebels as 'misguided

fellow-countrymen'. He obviously saw the shift in public opinion coming as support for the rebels began to materialise at
national level. He began calling for clemency for those involved
and was careful not to advertise his stance during Easter Week,
as he did not want his words at that time of the rebellion to be
misinterpreted as loyalty to Britain. Duffy was trying to ensure
that his loyalty was seen instead as support for Redmond. He
started to praise the courage of the men who had taken part in
the rebellion and even visited some of the deportees in England
and secured the release of some prisoners. This was a complete
U-turn for the man who would have used weapons against
these men had the opportunity arisen during the rebellion.[18]

The people of Loughrea had also changed their views
on the rebels, and the men they had described as fanatics a
short time before were now heroes. The runaway nationalist
train was careering down the track and everyone wanted
a chance to jump on board. It is important to mention that
while the majority of people in Loughrea had remained 'loyal'
to Redmond, some men from the area had joined up with the
rebel forces during the rebellion. Following the disbandment
at Limepark, at least twenty-nine men from the Loughrea
area were arrested and deported, including Patrick Coy, and
one of the charges brought against him was carrying a prayer
book for the purpose of swearing men into the Volunteers. It
is interesting that he had shown the prayer book to a friend
sometime earlier and jokingly said, 'You might as well join us.'
It seems that there were informers at work, as Volunteers in
other areas also discovered having been arrested.[19] Another

two prisoners from Loughrea, Peter Sweeney and Joseph Flaherty, were both town councillors. Sweeney wrote the following while incarcerated in Reading Prison: 'Liberty is a divine right. Liberty is the first and best decree of heaven, the charter of our Birth-right which human institutions can never cancel without tearing down the first and best decree of the omnipotent creator.' Such words were a sure indication of what lay ahead for Ireland.[20]

21

CONDEMNATION
OF THE REBELS

The condemnation of the rebels that followed in the immediate wake of the rebellion came from many areas. On 26 April 1916 Galway Urban Council called a public meeting in the town hall to discuss the rebellion and to voice their opinion on the situation. The chairman of the council, Martin McDonagh, opened the meeting and asked that the resolutions regarding the crisis be read. He stated that the members of the council and those attending utterly deplored the action taken by the ill-advised rebels. The council regretted the uprising, particularly at a time when Irish soldiers were bringing so much glory to the Empire on the battlefronts of Europe. It was said that the actions of this small group of men on their own soil shocked and outraged the general public and every Irishman and woman had the right to be proud of their soldiers fighting in the war. The audience was reminded that Irish regiments were at the core of the hardest fighting of the war and so had suffered more than others. The audience erupted in applause, which they did every few comments. McDonagh asked what these misguided people had hoped to gain from such 'silly proceedings' and went on to condemn the occupation of public buildings in Dublin. He reminded those attending that the English flag was in reality made up of three flags, which included the crosses of St

George, St Andrew and St Patrick. He claimed that the Union Jack was really an Irish flag when Irishmen fought under its shadow, and it was these same men who helped it fly so high. There were a number of other speakers, but they all simply echoed McDonagh. One opinion that they had in common was the fact that they all condemned the rebellion.[1]

At another meeting the Galway city branch of the UIL also condemned the rebellion in the strongest possible terms: 'We the members of the Galway City Branch United Irish League hereby place on record our abhorrence at, and condemnation of the recent insane, wicked and criminal rebellion in Ireland'. The UIL also claimed that the overwhelming majority of people in the country were against such action. The league members were extremely annoyed with the Volunteers and said that the public had not even the slightest sympathy for the rebels. They also regretted the uprising because it resulted in the loss of many valuable lives and caused so much destruction of property. But while they condemned the rebels, they also requested an amnesty for them, as they felt that their leaders had misled many of these people. They also blamed Edward Carson in the north of Ireland and the British government for allowing the formation and arming of the UVF, as the nationalists' answer to this situation was the establishment of the Irish Volunteers, which ultimately led to the rebellion. They appealed to all nationalists who supported the idea of self-government for Ireland to rally around the UIL.[2] Given the rise of the Volunteers and Sinn Féin before the rebellion, and the loss of faith in the Irish Party, it is perhaps surprising to find that the UIL still had fifty-one branches with a membership of 4,248 by Easter 1916.[3]

Margaret Scott from Galway was trapped in Dublin during the rebellion. She was the daughter of the editor of *The Galway Observer*, and the wife of Richard 'Dick' Smith, who worked in the Galway Cinema Theatre. Margaret was wounded during the fighting and was very clear in her condemnation of the rebels. After two weeks she made her way to Kilkenny, from where she wrote the following letter to her father, outlining her situation during the Rising:

Dear Father,

I arrived here [Kilkenny] yesterday [Tuesday] alive, thank goodness, after a fortnight's terrible experience. I was to have left Dublin on Easter Monday, when the war broke out. Dick was here, went up to the train; no trains, no papers, no nothing. He didn't know what to do, he was only after posting on £1 on Saturday night and I got it just in time. When they heard all about the riot Major Humphries sent a man to call on me to see if I was alright, but no more than that. We thought Kilkenny was the same, so we were in a terrible state. Anyway, on Tuesday, the second day, I went down to Sackville Street, watching the looters, when bang goes a bullet right into the side of my head, another inch and I was killed, as it went near my skull. So I was taken to Jervis Street Hospital, and it went in so far, that after trying his best to get it out, he [the doctor] had to open my head with a scissors. Such pain I never went through.

Then I was to call back on Thursday, but the whole place

was blockaded, and I went to the Mater Hospital. Well, I thought myself bad, but the sights I saw there were worse. I had a bandaged head till Saturday and Dick got a letter from me after posting it three days before, so he registered another £1 for me to come at once. I spent the £1, and after all we were starving, no gas, coal, no nothing. We had to boil the kettle on papers. Well, to read the papers, it's nothing, but to experience it, it is something of a dose. Bullets flying in all directions, into the rooms etc. The noise of the cannons was terrible. There is no Sackville Street there now. It took them a week to bury the dead. I was going down Sackville Street on Thursday night last [a week after the rebellion] with another girl, so there was a drunken fellow followed us, a Sinn Féinner [*sic*], I suppose. He demanded to know where we were going, so the girl said, 'What business is it of yours', so with that pointing a pistol, he said 'Do you see that'. So with that we took to our heels.

There is a crowd of Sinn Féinners after going up the street [in Kilkenny] with a heavy escort, and one man, rather stout was held [linked] by two soldiers; we thought he was trying to resist from going; and just two minutes later he dropped dead a few doors from his own house. I think only for the military in Dublin we would all have been killed or starved, as the Sinn Féinners were taking every bit of food that there was to be got. Dare anyone look crooked at them, while they had their guns, but it was short work. God help them; they couldn't last a week. The cannons frightened the life out of them. So I hope now they are all in a warm spot, and that they will stay there. No more now.

I remain Yours, Mag.[4]

While Seán O'Neill from Tuam said, 'By the end of this memorable week came the news of the surrender and many hearts were sad', he admitted that these were the rebels' feelings, not those of the general public. He recalled that most of the newspapers denounced the 'appalling and dastardly outrage' by the rebels and many priests condemned them, calling them anarchists, atheists and traitors.[5]

The following extracts from *The Tuam Herald* obviously reflect the mood of the day, otherwise one cannot see them being published. The *Herald* voiced extremely strong opinions in its condemnation not just of the rebellion, but also of James Larkin and James Connolly, recalling the Dublin Lockout and placing at least some of the blame for the Rising on the ICA. The loyalty of the Irish people to Britain was also made clear in the article. Full credit and support for General John Maxwell and the British troops were given in no uncertain terms. Moreover, it is worth noting the support it voiced for the National Volunteers and their colleagues fighting on the Western Front. This in turn indicates that there was still support for the war effort and the British government in the immediate aftermath of the rebellion. The report was also critical of the authorities for allowing the Volunteer movement to spread:

> The awful tragedy of the past ten days is now happily closed –
> the melancholy exhibition of midsummer madness by a small
> but desperate section of the Irish people, has been cured in a bath
> of blood, and the lunacy of the Sinn Féiners which has been the
> cause of the loss of countless lives and the destruction of untold

commercial wealth has got a lesson to sober and steady it for all time. A monument to their desperate doings has been erected by them in Sackville Street, and one of the finest streets in Europe is, in part, a mass of ruins, their handiwork, and the outcome of this latest and we trust last exhibition of intolerance, ignorance and stupidity. The Germans, it is clear, organised this insurrection … The action of the Irish Executive in allowing this formidable and demonstrably illegal organisation to grow and spread, to defy the authorities, to flaunt its rebel flag in their faces, as it did last St Patrick's day, is unpardonable … The day that wretched wobbler, Lord Aberdeen, with misplaced zeal commenced the fatal policy of placation and surrender to Larkin and his gang, was the beginning of the labour trouble in Dublin that came to a horrid head on Easter Monday when the same Larkin's Citizen Army, under his lieutenant, James Connolly – forming the brazen face and backbone of this conspiracy, lending to it all its fierceness, all its fury, and all its murderous mischievousness – made a pandemonium of a city so long cursed by their pestiferous influence and presence.

… This obviously illegal body some twelve months ago seceded from the real Volunteer movement. They took divergent and different paths – one became lawless and disloyal, the other, the National movement, was directed by constitutionalists and was moving on constitutional lines. It was a truly loyal and patriotic body of men. It sent thousands of recruits to the Army and showed its true spirit last week in Craughwell and Loughrea, in this county, to their credit be it said, and all over the country, the National Volunteers helped the police and maintained public order. The moment of seditious secession of the Sinn Féiners when they hoisted the flag of rebellion, subsequently to be translated last week into bloody action, that moment they should have been disarmed and the organisation proclaimed illegal. They, however, were allowed to remain and grow strong, to become a menace to society, a danger to the State, a terrorising and troublesome organisation with no reason for their existence, nothing that honest men could understand to justify their existence ... The city and country was overrun with them and deluged with newspapers and pamphlets of the most treasonable character. These seditious rags were sold openly in the streets and vended in shops. Its revolt has now, thanks to General Maxwell, been crushed, but crushed at a terrible cost. Over 150 brave soldiers and officers and some 20 policemen, countless unknown harmless citizens who were accidently shot, some 200 rebels themselves shot in action, thirteen already shot by military court-martial, some hundreds of others sentenced to varying terms of imprisonment, the ruin of some 200 fine businesses.

... The ring leaders have properly been executed. While not wishing to disparage the dead, we must still say that we are really surprised that such men with such reputations and such records as they had could have been able to find and influence so many foolish adherents. It is sad to find such credulity in the Irish character, such trust in traitors who are soft-tongued, tricky and plausible ... Ireland was saved by the Irish nation as a whole rising up and showing its loyalty and its good sense so bravely and consciously. Ireland was saved by its own sons from its degenerate sons and rebels. In that work of salvation the people welcomed the co-operation of the English Army. It received the English soldiers as friends and creditably and well they did their difficult work. Whatever may be said of the suicidal folly of the Sinn Féiners and the Larkin gang, history must bear willing and emphatic testimony to the proven and sound loyalty of the Irish people as a whole, the splendid and heroic conduct of the soldiers and police and the citizens of every rank. Ireland was sorely tried but she has nobly proved her loyalty, her good sense, her fortitude and her bravery.[6]

The Loughrea town commissioners were quick to condemn the rebellion, stating that they deeply deplored the action of these fanatics who called themselves Irishmen. They expressed their utter revulsion and said that there was no doubt that German agents had exploited this. The commissioners were horrified by the loss of life and the wanton destruction of property, and sympathised with the leadership of the Irish Party and John Redmond after a lifetime of service to the nation. A resolution condemning the rebellion was proposed by Martin Ward and Thomas Smyth, who made no secret of their hostility and bitterness towards the rebels. It was issued after the first wave of executions – had they waited a little longer, they may not have been as strong in their condemnation as the leaders of the rebellion continued to face the firing squads.[7]

Condemnation for the Rising came from many quarters, including the Galway Harbour commissioners and University College Galway. The senior staff at the university stated that they had learned with horror of the recent attempt by irresponsible individuals to use arms against the government of the country. They expressed their profound sorrow at the loss of life which resulted from this disgraceful act.[8]

The local authorities were also concerned about their image as the London newspapers were reporting that the situation in Ireland was good, with the exception of fighting in Dublin and Galway. On 3 May 1916 Galway County Council held a meeting during which they added their names to the list condemning the rebellion. The following resolution was read and passed unanimously:

> That the Galway County Council desires to express its condemnation of the recent disturbances of social order brought about by irresponsible persons whereby great damage has been done to the material prosperity of Ireland, and numbers of simple uneducated peasants have been cajoled and threatened into open defiance of the Law. We resent most of all the outrages upon the honour and dignity of Ireland and the attempt which has been made to dishonour her pledge solemnly given by her responsible Leader, Mr Redmond. We rejoice that this dastardly attempt has failed, and that the people of Ireland have shown by their conduct in this crisis that Ireland is determined that her word shall be faithfully kept. We tender to Mr Redmond the fullest assurances of our sympathy and support in the present trying circumstances.[9]

Support for John Redmond was unanimous from all quarters

and in his condemnation of the rebellion, Redmond made reference to those Americans who supported the insurgents:

The misguided and insane young men who have taken part in this movement in Ireland have risked, and some of them lost, their lives. But what am I to say to those men who have sent them into this insane and anti-patriotic movement while they have remained in the safe remoteness of American cities? I might add that this movement was set in motion by this same class of men at the very moment when America is demanding reparation for the blood of innocent American men, women and children shed by the Germans, and thus they are guilty of double treason – treason to the generous land that received them, as well as the land that gave them birth. Is it not an additional horror that on the very day when we hear that men of the Dublin Fusiliers have been killed by Irishmen on the streets of Dublin, we receive the news how the men of the 16th Division – our own Irish Brigade and of the same Dublin Fusiliers – had dashed forward and by their unconquerable bravery retaken the trenches that the Germans had won at Hulluch. Was there ever such a picture of the tragedy which a small section of the Irish faction had so often inflicted on the fairest hopes and bravest deeds of Ireland? As to the final result, I do not believe that this wicked and insane movement will achieve its ends. The German plot has failed. The majority of the Irish people retain their calmness, fortitude and unity. They abhor this attack on their interests, their rights, their hopes, their principles. Home Rule has not been destroyed; it remains indestructible.[10]

Although completely against the rebellion, Redmond requested that Prime Minister Asquith stop the executions of the leaders immediately. However, Asquith refused to interfere with Sir John Maxwell, saying that he had been sent to Ireland to suppress a dangerous insurrection and it was his duty to extract the necessary penalties against those who had organised and led the rebels onto the streets. As far as Asquith was concerned, Maxwell was doing his duty responsibly and to the satisfaction of the government. He also told Redmond that Maxwell was in direct contact with the government regarding the executions and his general instructions were 'to sanction the infliction of the extreme penalty as sparingly as possible, and only in cases of responsible persons who were guilty in the first degree'. When pressed to cease the executions, Asquith replied, 'I cannot give any such undertaking.' He warned that the safety of the entire United Kingdom and peace in Ireland was at stake if the strongest action was not taken against the rebels and their leadership. He went on to say that a desperate plot was hatched and executed when both Ireland and Britain were fighting for their very lives against a foreign enemy, Germany. This enemy supported the Irish rebels and attempted to arm them. This rebel conspiracy had been growing and spreading for years. Asquith felt that a great majority of the Irish people supported government policy and this included nationalists as well as unionists. He continued, saying that Ireland could not be destroyed by ten days of fighting; it would rise and be a better country. In a long and drawn-out debate in the House of Commons, Asquith concluded by saying that he felt all Irishmen would support the period of martial law.

He added, 'We have learned by bitter experience that the sword of the soldier is a far better guarantee of justice and liberty than the peace of politicians.'[11]

The condemnation from so many people and organisations in Ireland must surely have had an influence on Asquith and his government. Asquith seemed positive of Irish support despite the dragooning measures taken by General Maxwell. While the executions continued, Maxwell placed a ban on all parades and political meetings. When this ban was extended to all football, hurling and athletics, unless authorised permission had been granted from the local police, the tide really began to turn.[12]

Seán O'Neill described the change from condemnation to acceptance in dramatic and bitter terms. He said that initially it was 'painful' to have to listen to the 'slavish, unchristian' remarks, which he compared to the case of Joan of Arc of former times, as they cried out for the blood of the 'heretics' who dared challenge England. 'The '"Bastiles" of Dublin were too good' for the rebels. The people wanted their 'pound of flesh' and like the mob 'who howled for the Blood of Christ, nothing else would satisfy but rich red blood'. Then came the executions and 'still more executions to appease the thirst of that execrable Empire England! What an appalling and unnecessary slaughter of men and boys in their teens – the cream of our own small nation, and which no other great power could stand equal if merit alone was to be the basic test for such a judgment.' However, O'Neill notes that in the short space of a week or two the newspapers were publishing photographs of 'those poets and dreamers, literary men, artists, authors and sculptors' and now those who had condemned them 'were sorry at heart'. A great surge of pity and admiration seemed to sweep across the country. The change in opinion now brought 'a glow of pride' to the hearts of those associated with the movement 'to know of the noble qualities and genius possessed by those heroic men and women who … made the Rising possible'. The very people condemned 'a short time ago were now becoming heroes'.[13]

22

THE AFTERMATH
OF THE REBELLION

On 6 May 1916 it was announced that the insurrection in Galway had been quelled and tranquillity prevailed everywhere. The first train had left Galway Station after an eight-day suspension of services. It was crowded with holiday-makers who had been stranded in Galway since Easter Monday travelling back to Dublin.[1] Some weeks later, with their duty completed, the Royal Marines marched to Galway docks where a ship awaited them for the journey back to England. They were accompanied by the band of the Connaught Rangers and many civilians followed to give them a 'fitting send-off'. This support for the military was not really surprising considering some local newspapers were calling the uprising 'Germany's Rebellion'.[2] As these emergency troops left Galway, life in Renmore Barracks returned to normal and the daily routine of preparing troops for the war in Europe continued.[3]

Business in Galway city returned to normality as newspapers replaced rumours. News of the continued executions in the capital fuelled anxiety among many people. Others were anxious to see investigations into the causes of the uprising getting under way. In his evidence to the Royal Commission, which followed soon after the rebellion, District Inspector Ruttledge stated that the rebel encounter at Carnmore took place on Thursday morning. This seems strange given that an inquest into the death of Constable Whelan was opened on the Wednesday evening after the shooting and one would imagine that he should have been aware of this. It seems that over time the inspector had made meticulous notes of so-called Sinn Féin branches, but many of these were probably Volunteer companies. His accuracy is also called into question by the fact that he recorded the distance from Gort to Galway as nine and a half miles – it is actually about twenty-six miles. Ruttledge mentioned that the rebel army marched on Galway city on Wednesday and were repulsed by warships in the bay. However, the rebels were marching in the opposite direction at that stage. The only time there was a chance of an advance on Galway was on Tuesday, when they attacked Oranmore, and even then the arrival of the police outside the village by train forced them to retreat to Athenry. Ruttledge was also incorrect about the time of Mellows' arrival in County Galway. Because of this, the information he gave to the Royal Commission is doubtful and unreliable.[4]

In the aftermath of the uprising, many people felt that if the arms from the *Aud* had been landed and had reached Galway as planned, the story of the Rising in the west would have been very different. Ruttledge expressed this belief also and said that if the arms had been landed and the rebellion had not been plagued by confusing dispatches and lack of vital information, they would not have been able to overcome the rebels.[5]

Many of the leading rebels in Galway thought that arms were going to be landed off the coast of Connemara, but there is little or no evidence for this at a national level. This was something that Thomas Courtney had been concerned about throughout Easter Week. Courtney returned home from being on the run when he was sure that the police weren't looking for him, and secured another medical certificate from his very understanding general practitioner, Dr Arthur Colohan. He needed this upon returning to work and hoped no questions would be asked. Although he was a little concerned about the reception he might receive at the post office, little notice was taken of him. In fact, the head postman, James Walsh, put him on a shorter route delivering the post that week because he felt that Courtney looked unwell.

However, one of the managers, a known loyalist, approached him on his first evening back at work with a wage packet saying, 'I have got to pay you for stabbing the boys [on the Western Front] in the back.' When Courtney asked him what he meant by this comment, he replied, 'I know you are up to your neck in this Sinn Fein Rising' and continued, 'I really should go to the police.' Courtney then told him to go ahead and inform the police like all the other 'good loyalists'. This angered the manager and he admitted that while he was a loyalist, he was 'also an Irishman, just as good as you are'. He then told Courtney that a week earlier a woman had come into the post office and asked to speak with the postmaster. As the man was away at the time, the manager was asked to meet with her. She told him that Courtney was one of the main instigators of the rebellion around the countryside. When the manager asked why she didn't go to the police herself, she replied by saying she was afraid that her house would be burned down and she said that Courtney had a lot of young people spying for him. The woman had compiled a written statement and handed it to the manager, but refused to sign the document. Courtney was surprised and shocked at this revelation and realised that he owed the manager a debt of gratitude for not informing the police. He thanked him for this and added that he would always think of him as a good Irishman. A few weeks later the manager destroyed the incriminating document.

Courtney called on the families of his friends in Castlegar while they were in prison. He also helped with prisoner support, which involved organising dances to raise funds for the families of men in the internment camps. Gretta Newell, a sister of Michael Newell and a noted Irish dancer, also helped by giving dance performances. Courtney still felt animosity towards the men who had signed up as Special Constables during the rebellion, as he believed that they were responsible for many of the arrests in Galway, including his own experience. The police were aware of his movements, but the senior staff at the post office had protected him so the only way that the police could have known so much about him was through information given. He was determined to get even with them but was unsure of what action to take. An opportunity presented itself when the military authorities sent recruiting forms to the post office for distribution. Courtney took a batch of them and filled in the name and addresses of the Special Constables he knew and sent them off to the military. As far as the recruiting officers were concerned these men had enlisted and this resulted in many of them being sent to the Front, despite objections and denials of any knowledge of the recruiting forms. He also filled in the names and details of some friends of the Galway Recruiting Committee.[6]

The Rising was not just news in Ireland. Many foreign papers had reported on it and continued to do so in the aftermath. For example, while it disagreed with the action taken by the rebels, the *New York Daily Post* laid the responsibility for the Rising firmly at the door of the British government because of government policy. The report reminded members of parliament that ever since the days of Cromwell there had been bands of Irishmen ready to risk all for a chance to strike a blow against England. There was a constant smouldering desire by the Irish to be free of British rule and this was caused by a lack of statesmanship on behalf of the government. This, they said, was true of all generations and it was proof of England's folly with regard to their administration of Ireland. The fact that the rebellion took place was testimony of the government's mismanagement. However, the paper also stated that the rebellion was idiotic and doomed to failure. Regardless of the feeling of many rebels that Britain's difficulty was Ireland's opportunity, the Empire had never had so many soldiers at its disposal.[7]

The Rising also brought the issue of Home Rule to the fore once again. Many people felt that the implementation of Home Rule, suspended in 1914, would be affected by the insurrection. However, even before the Rising it was clear that Home Rule was going to be extremely difficult to implement.

After all, Edward Carson, the leading unionist in Ulster, and his followers were prepared to bring the country to civil war if there was an attempt to enforce the bill in that part of the country. Many of his followers had signed the Solemn League and Covenant against Home Rule and some did so in their own blood. Then there was also the so-called mutiny by the British officers in the Curragh military camp in County Kildare in 1914, involving some fifty-eight British officers who said they would refuse to enforce Home Rule in Ulster. This would have caused an extremely serious situation had the war not overtaken the issue. One cannot imagine the British accepting insubordination by their military, or even the threat of such action, but the officers were not even reprimanded for their defiance and this must have been seen by many as evidence that Home Rule would never be implemented. Those who thought that the bill would be introduced were seen as naïve by a lot of people, and still are.[8]

Many in Ireland believed that the government had no intention of honouring the promise of Irish Home Rule. Despite the massive Irish losses on the battlefields of Europe, Ireland was alone in its fight for freedom. In the end the Galway men and other Volunteers who had turned out in 1916 would rise again, but this time in a much deadlier manner.[9] The idea of pitched battles with the British was replaced by a more secretive method of action. Many people believe that the idea of continuing hostilities using guerrilla warfare was born in Frongoch. The adoption of this tactic in Ireland created the first crack in the armour of the British Empire and this type of warfare was adopted by many nationalist armies across the world in the years that followed.[10]

In July 1916 a requiem mass was celebrated in the Augustinian church in Galway for those who had died in the rebellion. This was one of the indications of a definite shift in public opinion as the summer progressed, with support for the rebellion growing. By autumn the rebellion was beginning to find its place in history as simply the latest in a series of justified uprisings.[11] Nationalist poems were starting to appear in newspapers and were being recited in public. The following are two examples: the first written by a priest, Fr Levington in New York; the second, by Albert C. White, was published in August 1916 in *The Tuam Herald*, which just three months earlier had been so scathing about the Rising:

The Rising of 1916

Not for the cause of faithless France
Nor for the Russian Bear's advance
Was done their glorious deed
Against grim foe at home they rose
In manly patriots pride
And though that birth was crushed to earth
For Ireland's rights they died.
Not by far off Dardanelles,
Nor shining Tigris banks
Nor mid the din of many yells
Went down their bleeding ranks
O'er sainted ground with glory crowned
Rolled on the battle tide

And proudly, brave, their homes to save
On Ireland's soil they died.[12]

*

On the Irishmen Executed in Dublin

Pray every man in his abode,
And let the church bells toll,
For those who did not know the road,
But only saw the goal.

Let there be weeping in the land,
And charity of mind,
For those who did not understand,
Because their love was blind.

Their errant schemes that we condemn,
All perished at a touch,
But much should be forgiven them,
Because they loved so much.

Let no harsh tongue applaud their fate,
Of their clean names decry,
The men who had not strength to wait,
But only strength to die.

Come all ye to their requiem,
Who gave all men could give,
And be ye slow to follow them,
And hasty to forgive.

And let each man in his abode,
Pray for each dead man's soul,
Of those who did not know the road,
But only saw the goal.[13]

Those who published accounts of condemnation in dramatic and strong tones in the immediate aftermath of the rebellion certainly changed their opinions radically in the months that followed. They now saw Galway as a place charged with an atmosphere of electricity because of the threat of conscription. The newspapers were saying that the government had been losing the confidence and respect of the Irish people every day. Stories of Carson asking the British government to have the Irish Volunteers disarmed before the rebellion started to be circulated as another reason for the uprising. A report in *The Connacht Tribune* stated, 'Out of this nerve-trying atmosphere sprang on the morning of Easter Monday bank holiday [24 April] a small, but formidable, armed body of Irish Volunteers and by their side marched the members of the Citizen Army. In a twinkling, the General Post Office, Sackville Street, the Four Courts on the Quays, the Royal College of Surgeons, Jacob's biscuit factory, and the major buildings were in their possession.' The report went on to describe Patrick Pearse as a brilliant scholar and Thomas MacDonagh as a poet of genius. It did not wish to discuss the executions because they had dragged on so painfully day after day and shocked and horrified the entire country. The report also said that an object of the rebellion was to sow seeds of ill-will between Ireland

and an Empire that didn't have the courage or statesmanship to grant legislative freedom. The question of Home Rule was raised yet again, but no confidence could be taken in the words of a government that could not be trusted. In Galway, it said, many of those arrested were innocent of insurrection, so many felt the government had contributed to a later increase in the rebel force through these arrests and internment without trial.[14]

The government was obviously concerned about the changing attitudes in Ireland and in April 1917 all commemoration ceremonies were banned on the first anniversary of the rebellion. However, the efforts of the British authorities to enforce this ban were ineffective and the national flag of Ireland was flown proudly over the buildings occupied by the rebels a year earlier. Some 20,000 people thronged into the streets of Dublin for the anniversary.[15] The British had again misread the situation in Ireland and it seems fair to say that the more something is banned in Ireland the more attractive it becomes to the Irish.

By May 1917 more poems in favour of the rebellion were being recorded and the people who had fought in 1916 were no longer seen as traitors, but rather had emerged as national heroes. The following version of the poem 'Who Fears to Speak of Easter Week?' appeared in *The East Galway Democrat* in 1917 and differs from the usual adaptation, criticising those who jumped on the bandwagon of the Rising after the fact:

> Who Fears to Speak of Easter Week?
> When all the fighting's done?
> Who's sure to flaunt the Sinn Féin flag?
> When danger there is none?

Who will not boast of Ashbourne fight.
Or yet of Boland's Mill
'Tis fine to pose as fighting men.
When all the guns are still.

Who Fears to Speak of Easter Week?
Or Sinn Féin's catch-cries shout,
Oh! Surely not the valiant men
Who failed to turn out.
The men who wisely shirked the fray
In fatal Easter Week,
No! Though they were afraid to fight
They do not fear to speak.

Who Fears to Speak of Easter Week?
Sure talk was ever cheap,
And 'tis not always they who sow
Who are the men to reap.
Oh! ye who brag so loudly now
And sing 'Who Fears to Speak?'
Pray tell us! Tell us! Where were you
In tragic Easter Week?[16]

These words would undoubtedly have struck a cord with Liam Mellows, who at this stage was still in America promoting the cause of Irish freedom. On St Patrick's Day 1918 he spoke at a rally in the United States and during the proceedings a 'James Connolly Club' was formed. James Larkin chaired the meeting to promote socialist education among the Irish, one of the main tenets of the 1916 Proclamation. During his speech

Mellows said, 'We demand the absolute independence of Ireland, economic as well as political. We are not fighting to free Ireland from the foreign tyrant in order to place her under the thumbs of domestic tyrants.' While his words certainly reflected James Connolly's principles, he does not seem to have had much contact with people involved in socialism.

In December 1918 Mellows learned of the shattering defeat of the Irish Parliamentary Party by Sinn Féin and was also made aware that he had been elected to two constituencies: East Galway and Meath. In August 1920 he received word that his father had died, which influenced his decision to return to Ireland, and he arrived in Dublin on 20 October that year. The War of Independence was raging and Mellows found himself being elected to the IRA Army Council.[17]

Mellows took the anti-Treaty side during the Civil War and was among those who occupied the Four Courts in 1922 under the lead of Commandant Patrick O'Brien. Following the fall of the Four Courts, he was taken prisoner.[18] On 8 December 1922 Mellows was executed by Free State forces along with Rory O'Connor, Richard Barrett and Joseph McKelvey. The executions were in reprisal for the fatal shooting of Seán Hales (Dáil Deputy) in Dublin the previous day.[19] He was not made aware of his fate until after 3 a.m. and faced death with exceptional courage. He wrote a letter to his mother explaining his situation and stated, 'The greatest human honour that can be paid to an Irishman' was to die for Ireland. Following confession and communion he was led out to face the firing squad. According to one account the first volley of shots rang out, but Mellows was only wounded and, having raised himself on one knee, he said to the men of the firing party, 'You'll have to shoot straight boys.'[20] There was much sadness and anger in Galway as news spread of his execution. Many people were shocked that the man who had led the rebellion in the west was executed not by an English firing squad, but an Irish one.

Liam Mellows is still remembered in Galway and has become a folk hero to many people. In the years after his death he was honoured on a number of occasions: in 1934, one of the greatest sporting organisations in Galway was formed under the name Liam Mellows Hurling Club; in 1954 Renmore Barracks was officially renamed 'Dún Uí Mhaoilíosa' after Mellows, the irony of this decision being that it was from these barracks that so many troops were sent to hunt him down in the months following the rebellion. His old motorbike was restored some years ago and placed in the museum at Dún Uí Mhaoilíosa by the Howley family near Peterswell, as they had been its custodians for many years. This family suffered a number of attacks by the Black and Tans during the War of Independence and had their home burned to the ground.[21] On 18 August 1957, Bishop of Galway Dr Michael Browne unveiled the Liam Mellows statue on Eyre Square and this has since become one of the most iconic landmarks in Galway. The sculptor was Donal Ó Murchadha and the Mellows Memorial Committee under the chairmanship of Martin 'Matt' Niland of Kilcolgan erected it. On Easter Sunday annually various nationalist groups gather at the statue in memory of those who fought in the rebellion.[22] One man involved in this commemoration over the past sixty years is Tom Joe Furey, whose family took part in the 1916 rebellion under Mellows, and he also made the ceremonial wreath for many years – a duty he has now passed on to his son Declan.

In January 2006 President Mary McAleese delivered a speech at University College Cork. She spoke very personally about the year 1916, with the massive casualties and loss of life on the Western Front. However, she focused mainly on the Easter Rising and spoke of the ideals and beliefs of the men, who, against overwhelming odds, fought for the freedom of their own small nation on their own home soil. She concluded by saying:

> I am humbled, excited and grateful to live in one of the world's most respected, admired and successful democracies, a country with an identifiably distinctive voice in Europe and in the world, an Irish republic, a sovereign independent state to use the words of the Proclamation. We are where freedom has brought us. A tough journey but more than vindicated by our contemporary context. Like every nation that had to wrench its freedom from the reluctant grip of empire we have our idealistic and heroic founding fathers and mothers, our Davids and Goliaths. The small band who proclaimed the Rising inhabited a sea of death, an unspeakable time of the most profligate worldwide waste of human life. Yet their deaths rise far above the clamour – their voices insistent still.[23]

Epilogue

Looking back at the Easter Rising from the comfort of the twenty-first century it is difficult to envisage the country under British rule. Regardless of personal politics one has to acknowledge the courage of the men, who, in the face of overwhelming odds, decided to try to take control of their own country. While Galway did not demonstrate the same blood sacrifice as Dublin, its people were not lacking in courage. Most historians would say that the uprising in Galway lacked direction, planning and ambition, and the idea of simply turning out in armed rebellion without any clear objectives seems naïve and almost pointless. Moreover, the fact that the rebellion in north and west Galway failed to materialise, and the lack of arms for those who did turn out, greatly reduced any chance of success in the Galway area. Then there were the dreadful difficulties with communications, not just between Dublin and Galway, but also amongst the local companies. The aborted attacks on police stations must have been disheartening for the poorly armed rebels, but in the actions that occurred almost by accident the Volunteers displayed considerable bravery. One must remember that many of them were without proper arms and some had only pikes, and they must have been aware that their rebellious actions could mean death on the field of battle or before a firing squad. Yet they stood by their ideals and in doing so showed unquestionable gallantry and commitment to Ireland.

While some might say that the rebellion in Galway had all the hallmarks of failure from a military standpoint, it certainly could have been different had circumstances been in the rebels' favour. The same, of course, could be said of the Dublin uprising. The Rising remains one of those events that tantalises the modern observer with what could have been: what if John Redmond had not gained access to the Irish Volunteers and the organisation had remained under the control of the IRB? What if the Great War had not occurred and there had been no split in the Volunteers, leaving a force of some 120,000 men? What if the *Aud* had delivered her arms and there had been no countermanding orders? What would the outcome have been? If history had followed this path it is tempting to think that the result, if not a complete military victory, might have forced the British government to the conference table. The question could be also asked: what would have happened if the executions hadn't taken place? Whatever might have happened, destiny has led the country to where it is today.

There was nobility and extreme courage among the entire rebel army. Reading the last words of the executed leaders, one cannot help but be moved by the honour and integrity of these men. The following are extracts from the letters of the seven signatories. Thomas MacDonagh, in a letter to his wife, stated, 'I still hope and pray that my acts may have for consummation her lasting freedom and happiness ... I am ready to die, and I thank God that I die in so holy a cause. My country will reward my deed richly.' He also said of his family, 'I have devoted myself too much to national work and too little to the making of money to leave them in competence.'

James Connolly's daughter, Nora, remembered the last time she saw her father and mother together and he said, 'Wasn't it a full life, Lily, and isn't it a good end? ... Look Lily, please don't cry. You will unman me.' She continued, 'I was trying to control myself too. ... One thing he said to Mama I remember, "The Socialists will never understand why I am here. They will all forget I am an Irishman".' One could well say that the labour movement have forgotten him and his ideals.

Joseph Plunkett married his sweetheart Grace Gifford just before his execution. The following account was given by her sister, Mrs Sidney Czira: 'Father Eugene McCarthy, the prison chaplain, read the marriage service by the light of a candle (the gas supply having failed). Two soldier witnesses shifted their rifles from hand to hand as they assisted at the ceremony. Immediately afterwards the newly married couple were separated ... They met only once again. ... Soldiers with fixed bayonets stood while she spoke to her husband in his cell. "Your ten minutes are up", said the officer in charge, glancing at his watch, and they parted for ever.'

Éamonn Ceannt, writing to his wife, showed pure courage in the face of death, saying, 'Not wife, but widow before these lines reach you. I am here without hope of this world and without fear, calmly awaiting the end ... You will be – you are – the wife of one of the Leaders of the Revolution. Sweeter still, you are my little child, my dearest pet, my sweetheart of the hawthorn hedges and summers eves. I remember all and I banish all that I may be strong and die bravely.'

Patrick Pearse's final words to his mother included, 'I am happy except for the great grief of parting from you. This is the death I should have asked for if God had given me the choice of all deaths – to die a soldier's death for Ireland and for freedom. We have done right. People will say hard things of us now, but later on they will praise us.'

Thomas Clarke died confident that Ireland would ultimately win its freedom: 'I and my fellow signatories believe we have struck the most successful blow for Freedom. The next blow, which we have no doubt Ireland will strike, will win through. In this belief we die happy.'

Seán MacDiarmada wrote the following in his letter to the old Fenian John Daly: 'Just a wee note to bid you goodbye. I expect in a few hours to join Tom and the others in a better world. I have been sentenced to a soldier's death – to be shot tomorrow morning. I have nothing to say about this, only that I look on it as part of the day's work. We die that the Irish nation may live. Our blood will re-baptise and reinvigorate the old land.'[1]

What can one say of the legacy of these men who sacrificed all for their belief in an independent Ireland? The men who turned out in Galway were prepared to follow that same path of sacrifice. Standing at Eyre Square at the Easter Commemoration in 2010, a woman near me was very upset and said, 'They died for nothing.' I spoke with her for some time and could understand her words and her dismay at what had happened to the country in recent years between the banks and the politicians over 'pure greed' as she saw it. She had been a 'true nationalist' all of her life and found it difficult to comprehend the actions of the people in power. It was appalling for her that these same people were attending commemorations for the men of 1916, who were made accountable for their actions, yet today's leaders do not seem to be held accountable for anything. Realising her anger and frustration, I said to her, 'I fully sympathise with your feelings, but feel very strongly that now, more than ever, we must remember and honour them.' This is certainly not the Ireland that the men of 1916 died for, but it is up to the people to bring the country forward. I spoke with a number of people following the commemoration to see if the woman's feelings were isolated and discovered that most of them were of the same opinion.

A country should never remain stagnant and its leaders must continue to strive to make changes for the betterment of its people; every generation must share this responsibility and burden, and make continued improvements. There are an abundance of possibilities, which call for dedication and action across the wide spectrum of life. The Irish Volunteers of the past gave their lives, time and commitment freely to ensure a better country for future generations. The 'Irish Volunteers' of today are the people who dedicate their time to the communities in which they live without expecting anything in return. They do this across the world of sports, music, art, drama and many other aspects of Irish life. Hundreds of thousands of children and young people across Ireland benefit greatly from these 'Volunteers' every day and their contribution cannot be measured, as they provide these services for free to improve the lives of the people and the amelioration of the country. This is the real legacy of the men of 1916 and one of which they would be justly proud.

Let each successive generation blaze new trails wherever possible so that Ireland can continue to grow and make its presence felt on the world stage. Ireland was deprived of these opportunities for many centuries and yearned for justice and honest government. This country needs total honesty, integrity, truth and wisdom in government. The leaders of 1916 cannot be honoured properly until these qualities are restored to all who enter the corridors of power. These men fought not just for Irish freedom but also for the common good of the people. Remember the words of the Proclamation: 'In this supreme hour the Irish nation must, by its valour and discipline, and by the readiness of its children to sacrifice themselves for the common good, prove itself worthy of the august destiny to which it is called'. As the lady at Eyre Square said, it is difficult to comprehend that type of dedication and honour when one looks at successive governments in Ireland today. The men who led the 1916 rebellion sacrificed their lives for the country; the tragedy for Ireland is that today's leaders wouldn't even sacrifice expenses. Perhaps the last letters of those executed for Ireland should be placed on the walls of Dáil Éireann to remind those in power of the ideals for which the founding fathers of this country paid the highest price.

The last words on this subject one must leave to the leader

of the rebellion in Galway, Liam Mellows. When speaking of the men who served under him in Galway, Mellows stated: 'Many of them are poor – almost all are. Most of them are unheard of, yet their work for Ireland deserves to be known. It will never be, in our day anyway, in all probability, but it is to them the thanks of future generations of the Irish people will be due. They gave all in silence, seeking no reward and getting none … Dreamers, fanatics, intransigents, fools, yes, but un-conquerable and sublime'.[2]

Appendix

Commemoration

The following is a brief overview of the 1916 rebellion commemorations that have occurred in Galway city and county over the years. Many people assume that it was 1966 before any serious commemoration of the 1916 rebellion took place, but honouring these people began earlier in Galway. In 1955 the local authorities decided to name the avenues in the new housing estate of Mervue in honour of the leaders of the rebellion and other nationalists. This was followed on the fiftieth anniversary with huge commemoration events throughout Galway city and county. On Easter Sunday 1966 the streets of Galway were thronged with people who turned out to both view and take part in this historic event. It was described as a 'dignified but stirring ceremonial' and the most representative parade through the city in many years. Almost every organisation was represented, with the army taking a leading role in proceedings. Siobhán McKenna acted as master of ceremonies and her duties included reading the Proclamation in both Irish and English in the shadow of the statue of Liam Mellows on Eyre Square. The Mayor of Galway, Councillor Brendan Holland, raised the national flag to the sound of a drum roll. The Bishop of Galway, Dr Michael Browne, led the people in a decade of the rosary. The mayor, on behalf of Galway Corporation and the people of Galway, then laid wreaths at the statue; Colonel P. Ó Ceirin representing the Irish Army and Seán Turke, a former member of the old IRA, represented the Liam Mellows Hurling Club.

There were week-long commemorations, which included a twenty-one-gun salute in South Park on the Saturday and pontifical high mass on Monday.[1] As part of the commemoration the railway station was named in honour of Commandant Éamonn Ceannt and a plaque in his memory was unveiled by Josephine McNamara (née O'Keefe), who was living in Mervue at the time. She was a former member of Cumann na mBan who had served with the 4th Battalion of Irish Volunteers under Ceannt at the South Dublin Union in 1916. Éamon de Valera had asked her to perform the ceremony. A reception was held that evening in the Great Southern Hotel for all those involved in the commemoration. Sadly Josephine collapsed during the event, having suffered a brain haemorrhage, and died later that night.[2]

Another event organised was the '1916 Commemoration Exhibition' hosted by St Patrick's School in Lombard Street, which proved a huge success and attracted people throughout the week.[3] A 1916 memorial plaque was also unveiled in Dún Uí Mhaoilíosa (Renmore Barracks) that week, followed by a detailed and graphic account of the barracks. Lectures on the rebellion were given by a group of army officers and some of the 1916 veterans attended. While Castlegar was really part of the city celebrations, it did have its own unique addition to commemorate the men from the village. Pádraig Ó Fathaigh composed the following poem-song, 'The Boys of Castlegar', for the anniversary. It is sung to the air of *The Felons of Our Land*:

The Boys of Castlegar

'Tis joyous Spring, the wild birds sing,
the rain has ceased to fall,
And Dawn's bright ray acclaims the day
when came Liam Mellows call;
Then loud resounds the slogan sound
proclaiming Freedom's war.
And Brian Molloy has heard the cry ring
out through Castlegar.

The elders grey, the youngsters gay,
deserters there are none,
The lad would like an antique pike,
his dad that rusty gun,
The champion sowers, the stalwart
mowers prepare for strenuous war,
As Brian Molloy arrays with joy
the Boys of Castlegar.

Although they knew no aid came through,
the 'Aud' rocks 'neath the waves,
Yet they would be, they must be free,
if only in their graves.
Young Baby Duggan, and the
Newells and many a hurling star,
Resolved to die with Brian Molloy
and the Boys of Castlegar.

They marched to meet the City boys,
till reaching Carnmore,
Down soldiers trim, and peelers grim,
and Specials on them bore,

The cry of 'Yield' rings through the field
above the din of war,
'We'd rather die,' says Brian Molloy,
'we're the Boys from Castlegar'.

The RIC began to flee
when Specials all had fled;
Their leader lay stretched on the clay
pretending he was dead,
His comrades bold in death lay
cold with many a bruise and scar.
No more to spy on Brian Molloy
and the Boys from Castlegar.

In Carnmore there gaily soars
the Banner of Sinn Féin,
And of the bragging British braves
no vestige now remains.
On to Moyode the victors strode
without a stain or scare.
Where hailed with joy was Brian Molloy
and the Boys from Castlegar.

From Monivea to Loughrea
are rebels to the crown,
No dastard foe his face dare show from
Gort to Galway town,
And we were free as bird or bee till
closed the Easter war,
The 'Hue and Cry' bans Brian Molloy,
the Boy of Castlegar.

Though poor they fare, and chill the air,
his mind was free from care,
Till bitter spies with honeyed lies
had lured him from his lair,
Then peelers came from every side,
on bicycles and car,
And to Mountjoy dragged Brian Molloy,
the Boy from Castlegar.

The sentence death, although revoked
'tis long he must endure,
The hunger's pain, the fog, the rain,
and the rigors of Dartmoor,
There came a change, they loosed his chains,
and in a jaunting car,
Mid shouts of joy brave Brian Molloy
comes home to Castlegar.

The spirit wave the Rising raised,
a deluge swept the land,
Which murder gangs and Black and Tans
were powerless to withstand,
Should bigots strike this land to rive
or freedom's pathway bar.
We've many a boy like Brian Molloy
and the Boys of Castlegar.[4]

Areas in the county also organised their own commemorative events. On 11 April 1966 the commemoration ceremony began in Athenry with a mass celebrated in memory of those who fought in 1916. This was followed by a parade through the streets of the town, which included veterans of the old IRA and Cumann na mBan, and was led by two schoolboy bands, one from Athenry and the other from Loughrea. Alf Monahan in the boys' national school in Athenry unveiled a memorial bust of Liam Mellows. Stephen Jordan presented the school with the national flag in the hope that future generations would be aware of the fight for freedom. A platform was set up at the school and the Proclamation was read in Irish by Donal Ó Ceinnide and in English by Kitty Lardner, the daughter of Larry Lardner. Monsignor Thomas Fahy gave an address explaining the course of events that occurred in Galway during Easter Week 1916 and said time had proved that the men of 1916 were among the greatest in the history of Ireland. He said that the rebellion was regarded as 'folly and madness' in the eyes of the world and indeed by many Irish people initially. However, they were left in wonder about it in a very short time. He continued, 'Providence favoured the rebellion from the start', and said that one could see, fifty years on, how glorious its success was. Monsignor Fahy stated that lesser men would have fought on, but Pearse and Clarke decided to surrender to save the lives of others and forfeit their own. These men believed that through their deaths they would gain the ultimate support of the people of Ireland. He stressed that Galway had played a significant part in the rebellion and added that, if these men had not turned out, the British could easily have passed the Rising off as an isolated Dublin event. Following the speeches, a bugler sounded the last post. As part of the commemoration the Agricultural College in Athenry was officially named in honour of Liam Mellows. Many of those who had served there in 1916 attended the event.[5] The park in Athenry where the Irish Volunteers assembled was later renamed as the Kenny Memorial Park.[6] This was in honour of Thomas Kenny.

Commemoration celebrations were held in Ballymoe on 8 May 1966 to acknowledge Éamonn Ceannt. The commemoration committee included Joe O'Shaughnessy, Martin Hanly, Michael Gaffey and Michael Keane. The ceremony opened with President Éamon de Valera inspecting a Guard of Honour of the old IRA and the 6th Irish Battalion was also part of the parade. A mass was celebrated by Fr J. Smith in St Croan's church, where Éamonn Ceannt had been baptised over eighty years earlier. The state was well represented, with Minister for Justice Brian Lenihan, Senator Mark Killilea, leader of the opposition Liam Cosgrave, the commissioner of An Garda Síochána and Mayor of Galway Councillor Brendan Holland all attending. Members of the Ceannt family also attended, including Ceannt's only son Rónán and his grand-nieces Mary and the late Joan Gallagher. Following a mass, the James Connolly Pipe Band and a colour party of the old IRA led the congregation to the garda station, formerly the old RIC barracks, where Ceannt was born on 21 September 1881 (his father, James, was a constable in the RIC at the time). Once all the guests were seated, Colonel W. H. Byrne, OC of the Western Command, unveiled a plaque honouring the executed leader. Éamonn T. Ceannt, grand-nephew of Éamonn Ceannt, then addressed the gathering on behalf of the family and the Proclamation was read by Richard Walsh. A salute to the flag, the last post and reveille were sounded, followed by the national anthem. A private reception was also held for the official guests at which the president gave a short talk about his old comrade-in-arms.[7]

On 17 April 1966 the Oranmore ceremonies began with a Guard of Honour by troops from Dún Uí Mhaoilíosa during 11 a.m. mass, followed by a parade from the Presentation School to the Joseph Howley monument in the village. Members of the surrounding GAA clubs, such as Oranmore, Maree and Ballinacourty, also took part. A girl from the local school read the Proclamation, the idea being that this would include the younger generation in the event. The last post and reveille was sounded and the crowd then walked to the local cemetery where wreaths where laid at the graves of Commandant Joseph Howley, Joseph Athy and Patrick Cloonan, three men who lost their lives in the War of Independence. Later that same day a plaque was unveiled on the old manor house by Fr J. Larkin, parish priest of Peterswell, and Matt Niland delivered an oration at the ceremony organised by the Gort Battalion of the old IRA.[8] Ballinasloe also honoured the men of 1916 and during a meeting of the local branch of Sinn Féin a number of issues were raised regarding the commemoration celebrations. Its members felt the country should set its sights on finishing the job started by the men of 1916 and go all out for a thirty-two-county Ireland.[9]

The 1916 jubilee celebrations were held in Tuam on 1 May 1966, where some twenty-five organisations accompanied by five bands assembled for the event. They gathered in the square in Tuam and marched to the Cathedral of the Assumption for noon mass. After mass the various groups again assembled and paraded along the Dublin and Athenry roads before turning at Tubberjarlath and marching back to the car park on Bishop Street. They stopped at the cemetery and recited a decade of the rosary before laying a wreath on the grave of Michael Moran, an old republican. A platform was erected in the car park and a guard of honour of the old IRA stood in front of the stage. There the Proclamation was read and the last post was sounded. The national anthem completed these proceedings and the national flag was raised. The people of the town were requested to decorate their houses with the national colours for the event.[10]

Each event around the county was followed by a local priest leading the people in a decade of the rosary. In Athenry Fr Terence Hynes, son of Frank Hynes, led the people in prayer. One of the men taken hostage by the rebels at Clarenbridge on the morning of the rebellion was Constable Donovan, as he was on the way home to see his wife who had just given birth to a baby that morning. A local poet later celebrated both events in a poem entitled 'When Donovan's Kid Was Born'. In 1966 it was performed by eighty-six-year-old Margaret Greally, who had been one of the Cumann na mBan girls with the rebels during the rebellion:

When Donovan's Kid Was Born

On an April morning 1916,
on a day remembered well,

When the blackbirds warbled
merrily over woody vale and dell,
Along the roads and through the
fields and over the hill and crag,
The Galway boys were marching
and rallying to the flag,
They carry shotguns in their hands,
prepared to do or die,
To face their well-trained enemies
they'd have another try,
What matter if they're ten to one
they'll treat those foes with scorn,
For 'twas Ireland first and Ireland last,
When Donovan's kid was born.

Now Donovan came along the
road avisiting the town,
He prided in his helmet and the
Harp beneath the Crown,
'Hands up' a voice commanded him,
Now this was not good news,
And Donovan's joyful heart at
once went down into his shoes,
He quickly raised up both his hands,
though he couldn't believe his ears,
'Twas treason this curt command
of the Irish Volunteers,
We brought him to the village then
to see his comrades there,
And the Bridge was just as lively

as at the Pattern Race or Fair,
There were bottles of lemonade
and fizz, and bread and beer galore,
But you couldn't coax the Bobbies
to come outside the door,
The police were armed to the teeth,
but too cowardly to fight,
We held possession of the town 'neath
the Orange, Green and White,
Their lassies jeered the cowards and
the Lion and Unicorn,
And the Bobbies will never forget the day,
When Donovan's kid was born.

Their little army starts to march
and all in splendid glee,
The rear brought up of prisoners
of the gallant RIC
And on through county Galway
and on towards county Clare,
With the Bobbies out before us you
might say fun was rare,
We held mansions and demesnes,
but the RIC stayed shy,
They ran away like mountain goats
when the Volunteers drew nigh,
Over rocks and stones and over
walls and hedges of whitethorn,
'Twas a glorious day for Ireland,
faith, When Donovan's kid was born.

Though beaten in the struggle, boys,
we're not one bit dismayed,
We're proud of our dear country
boys and the gallant fight they made,
And our Colleens too, were also true
to our Dark Rosaleen,
And raised aloft the banner of
the Orange, White and Green,
Then hurrah boys lets lift our voice in song,
And praise the band who took their
stand against tyranny and wrong,
Who smashed Conscription in
the land on Easter Tuesday morn,
And buried the Union Jack to hell,
When Donovan's kid was born.[11]

NOTES

1 Rebellious Behaviour

1   Thomas Kenny, *Galway: Politics and Society, 1910–23* (2011), p. 13.
2   Pat Finnegan, *Loughrea 'That Den of Infamy': The Land War in Co. Galway, 1879–82* (2014), pp. 62–3.
3   David Ryan, 'The Trial and Execution of Anthony Daly', *The District of Loughrea*, Volume I: 1791–1918 (2003), pp. 91–3, 95, 98.
4   Interview: Christy Burke, 2 December 1998.
5   Finnegan, *Loughrea 'That Den of Infamy'*, pp. 11, 17, 50, 56–7, 60–1, 95.
6   Seán O'Sullivan, 'Popular Perceptions of the Royal Irish Constabulary during the Land War in Galway', *Journal of the Galway Family History Society*, Vol. V, 1998, p. 143.
7   William Henry, *Hidden Galway: Gallows, Garrisons and Guttersnipes* (2011), pp. 159–63.
8   M. J. Shiel and D. Roche (eds), *A Forgotten Campaign and Aspects of the Heritage of South-East Galway* (1986), pp. 22–3, 25.
9   'Riotous Proceedings in Galway', *The Galway Express*, 18 September 1886.
10 Shiel and Roche (eds), *A Forgotten Campaign*, p. 29.

2 A Garrison Town

1   'Renmore Barracks – Foundation', *Galway Independent*, 16 April 2014.
2   'St David's Day', *The Galway Express*, 1 March 1890.
3   'Riot in William Street', *The Galway Express*, 31 December 1881.
4   'The Disgraceful Riots in Galway', *The Galway Express*, 2 April 1887.
5   'Disorderly Conduct by Soldiers', *The Galway Express*, 2 June 1888.
6   'The Queen's Birthday', *The Galway Express*, 5 June 1888.
7   'The Fatal Riot Between Soldiers and Civilians', *The Galway Express*, 28 September 1889.
8   'The Police Attacked by the Military', *The Galway Express*, 15 November 1890.
9   'Trouble & Strife', *Galway Independent*, 30 April 2014.

3 The Spread of Resistance

1   Finnegan, *Loughrea 'That Den of Infamy'*, pp. 64–5.

2   William Henry, *Supreme Sacrifice: The Story of Éamonn Ceannt 1881–1916* (2005), p. 43.

3   Finnegan, *Loughrea 'That Den of Infamy'*, pp. 67, 72.

4   Shiel and Roche (eds), *A Forgotten Campaign*, pp. 1, 108.

5   T. Gorman *et al.*, *Clanricarde Country and the Land Campaign* (1987), pp. 30–1.

6   'Brutal Outrage', *The Galway Express*, 2 April 1887.

7   Carol O'Regan and Audrey Lacy, *Abbeyknockmoy: A Time to Remember*, (n.d.), p. 102.

8   Eugene Duggan, *The Ploughman on the Pound Note: Farmer Politics in County Galway during the Twentieth Century* (2004), pp. 9–14.

9   *Ibid.*, pp. 27, 32–3.

4 Independent Future

1   'Siege of Loughrea', *Galway Independent*, 26 September 2012.

2   Noel McDonnell, 'The Ward Eviction 1906', *The District of Loughrea*, Vol. I: 1791–1918 (2003), pp. 552–3.

3   'The Loughrea Siege Ends', *Galway Independent*, 3 October 2012.

4   McDonnell, 'The Ward Eviction 1906', pp. 551, 557.

5   'The Significance of the Galway Revolt', *Connacht Tribune*, 2 April 1966.

6   Kenny, *Galway*, p. 13.

7   'Reign of Terror at Craughwell: Tom Kenny and the McGoldrick Murder of 1909', *18th–19th Century Social Perspectives*, Issue 1, Vol. 18, January–February 2010.

8   Martin Newell, BMH WS 1562, pp. 4–5.

9   Kenny, *Galway*, p. 13.

10 Duggan, *The Ploughman on the Pound Note*, p. 30.

11 Kenny, *Galway*, pp. 13–14.

12 Henry, *Supreme Sacrifice,* pp. 25–7.

5 The Irish Volunteer Force

1   Henry, *Supreme Sacrifice*, pp. 30–2.
2   'The Significance of the Galway Revolt', *Connacht Tribune*, 2 April 1966.
3   Kenny, *Galway*, p. 14.
4   Frank Hardiman, BMH WS 406, pp. 1–2.
5   *Ibid.*, p. 1.
6   'I.R.B. Centre', *Connacht Tribune*, 16 April 1966.
7   Kathleen Villiers-Tuthill, *Beyond The Twelve Bens: A History of Clifden and District 1860–1923* (1990), pp. 186, 191–2.
8   Peter McDonnell, BMH WS 1612, pp. 1–2.
9   Micheál Ó Droighneáin, BMH WS 374, pp. 1–2.
10 'Pearse As I Remember Him', *The Mantle*, Vol. 9–10, No. 33, Spring 1966–1969, p. 7.
11 *Ibid.*, pp. 7–8.
12 Henry, *Supreme Sacrifice*, p. 22.
13 Micheál Ó Droighneáin, BMH WS 374, pp. 1–2.
14 Patrick Callanan, BMH WS 347, p. 1.
15 'The Significance of the Galway Revolt', *Connacht Tribune*, 2 April 1966.
16 Patrick Callanan, BMH WS 347, pp. 1, 3.
17 'The Significance of the Galway Revolt', *Connacht Tribune*, 2 April 1966.
18 'A Memory of Ardrahan 50 Years Ago', *Connacht Tribune*, 2 April 1966.
19 Peter Howley, BMH WS 1379, pp. 1–2.
20 Brian Molloy, BMH WS 345, p. 1.
21 Thomas (Sweeney) Newell, BMH WS 572, p. 1.
22 John A. Claffey, *Glimpses of Tuam since the Famine* (1997), pp. 192–5, 197.
23 Adrian Frazier, *George Moore, 1852–1933* (2000), pp. 433–4.
24 Martin Newell, BMH WS 1562, pp. 4–5.
25 Claffey, *Glimpses of Tuam since the Famine*, pp. 195–6.
26 Stephen Jordan, BMH WS 346, p. 3.

6 A Divided Force

1   'The Galway Rising', *The Tuam Herald*, 3 June 1916.

2   Henry, *Supreme Sacrifice*, p. 35.

3   Claffey, *Glimpses of Tuam since the Famine*, pp. 195–6, 198.

4   J. Forde, 'The Irish Party and Sinn Féin in Loughrea', *The District of Loughrea*, Vol. I: 1791–1918 (2003), p. 580.

5   Frank Hardiman, BMH WS 406, p. 2.

6   Minute Book: Irish National Volunteers, Galway: 1914–1916.

7   Forde, 'The Irish Party and Sinn Féin in Loughrea', p. 579.

8   Duggan, *The Ploughman on the Pound Note*, p. 31.

9   Claffey, *Glimpses of Tuam since the Famine*, pp. 198–9.

10 Forde, 'The Irish Party and Sinn Féin in Loughrea', pp. 581–3.

11 Kenny, *Galway*, pp. 15–16.

12 Thomas Courtney, BMH WS 447, pp. 2–3.

13 Thomas Hynes, BMH WS 714, pp. 1–3.

14 Claffey, *Glimpses of Tuam since the Famine*, pp. 198–200.

15 'Disbandment', *Connacht Tribune*, 16 April 1966.

16 Claffey, *Glimpses of Tuam since the Famine*, pp. 198–200.

17 Frank Hynes, BMH WS 446, pp. 4–5.

18 Thomas (Sweeney) Newell, BMH WS 572, p. 2.

19 Michael Newell, BMH WS 342, pp. 1–3.

7 Path to Rebellion

1   C. Desmond Greaves, *Liam Mellows and the Irish Revolution* (1971), pp. 30, 34–44, 48, 50–1, 67, 71.

2   Martin Newell, BMH WS 1562, p. 6.

3   Kenny, *Galway*, pp. 18–19.

4   Greaves, *Liam Mellows and the Irish Revolution*, pp. 74–5.

5   Interview: Kitty Lardner, 5 May 1999.

6   Patrick Callanan, BMH WS 347, pp. 4–5.

7   Gilbert Morrissey, BMH WS 874, pp. 1, 3.

8   'The Coming of Mellows', *Connacht Tribune*, 2 April 1966.

9   'Seán MacDiarmada', *Galway Independent*, 20 October 2010.

10 The organising committee attending that day included W. Langley, W.

Cannon and W. Stockwell; Claffey, *Glimpses of Tuam since the Famine*, p. 202.

11 Greaves, *Liam Mellows and the Irish Revolution*, pp. 76–7.

12 Geraldine Plunkett Dillon, *All in the Blood: A Memoir of the Plunkett family, the 1916 Rising and the War of Independence*, edited by Honor Ó Brolchain (2006), pp. 278–9.

13 Greaves, *Liam Mellows and the Irish Revolution*, p. 77.

14 Ailbhe Ó Monachain, BMH WS 298, pp. 1, 4–5.

15 Martin Newell, BMH WS 1562, pp. 5–6.

16 Michael Kelly, BMH WS 1564, pp. 2–3.

17 Thomas (Sweeney) Newell, BMH WS 572, p. 2.

18 'Éamonn Corbett and 1916', *Galway Advertiser*, 24 April 2014.

8 A Rebel Call

1 Henry, *Supreme Sacrifice,* pp. 40–1.

2 'Patrick Henry Pearse', *Galway Independent*, 3 November 2010.

3 'The Peaceful Cottage of Revolt in Rosmuc', *Galway Advertiser*, 8 April 2004.

4 Daniel Kearns, BMH WS 1124, p. 1.

5 Micheál Ó Droighneáin, BMH WS 374, p. 3.

6 Henry, *Supreme Sacrifice,* pp. 41–2.

7 William Henry, *Galway and the Great War* (2006), pp. 39, 42, 44–8, 72–3.

8 Claffey, *Glimpses of Tuam since the Famine*, p. 186.

9 Greaves, *Liam Mellows and the Irish Revolution*, pp. 78–80.

10 Henry, *Supreme Sacrifice,* pp. 42–3.

11 Patrick Callanan, BMH WS 347, p. 6.

12 Michael Kelly, BMH WS 1564, p. 3.

13 'Journal of Brid, 25 May 1916', compiled by Galway Technical Institute (1979), p. 12.

14 Martin Newell, BMH WS 1562, p. 6.

15 Michael Newell, BMH WS 342, p. 2.

16 Thomas Courtney, BMH WS 447, pp. 2–3.

17 Greaves, *Liam Mellows and the Irish Revolution*, p. 81.

18 Thomas Sweeney Newell, BMH WS 572, p. 3.

19 Kenny, *Galway*, p. 20.

9 Orders and Countermanding Orders

1   Greaves, *Liam Mellows and the Irish Revolution*, p. 81.

2   Henry, *Supreme Sacrifice*, p. 44.

3   Greaves, *Liam Mellows and the Irish Revolution*, pp. 81–3.

4   Henry, *Supreme Sacrifice*, pp. 46–7, 90.

5   Martin Newell, BMH WS 1562, p. 7.

6   Greaves, *Liam Mellows and the Irish Revolution*, p. 85.

7   Mrs Seán McEntee (Margaret Browne), BMH WS 322, pp. 2–3.

8   Henry, *Supreme Sacrifice*, pp. 90–1.

9   Michael Newell, BMH WS 342, pp. 2–3.

10 *Ibid.*

11 Henry, *Supreme Sacrifice*, pp. 48–9.

12 Martin Newell, BMH WS 1562, p. 7.

13 Greaves, *Liam Mellows and The Irish Revolution*, pp. 83–5.

14 Martin Newell, BMH WS 1562, p. 7.

15 Micheál Ó Droighneáin, BMH WS 374, p. 4.

16 Mrs Martin Conlon, BMH WS 419, pp. 4–5.

17 Micheál Ó Droighneáin, BMH WS 374, pp. 3–5.

18 Michael Newell, BMH WS 342, p. 4.

19 Henry, *Supreme Sacrifice*, pp. 48–51.

20 Micheál Ó Droighneáin, BMH WS 374, pp. 4–5.

21 Greaves, *Liam Mellows and the Irish Revolution*, p. 86.

22 John Hosty, BMH WS 373, pp. 11–12.

23 Henry, *Supreme Sacrifice*, pp. 48–51.

10 Easter Monday 1916

1   Greaves, *Liam Mellows and the Irish Revolution*, p. 87.

2   Micheál Ó Droighneáin, BMH WS 374, p. 5.

3   Martin Newell, BMH WS 1562, pp. 7–8.

4   *Ibid.*, p. 8.

5   Greaves, *Liam Mellows and the Irish Revolution*, p. 87.

6   Brian Molloy, BMH WS 345, pp. 7–8.

7   Henry, *Supreme Sacrifice*, p. 59.

8   Interview: Nancy McDonagh, 3 June 1998.

9   William Henry, *Galway Through Time & Tide*, Vol. IV (2014), pp. 40–1, 54–7, 61–8.

10   Greaves, *Liam Mellows and The Irish Revolution*, p. 87.

11   Stephen Jordan, BMH WS 346, p. 4.

12   James Barrett, BMH WS 343, p. 2.

13   Greaves, *Liam Mellows and the Irish Revolution*, pp. 87–8.

14   Patrick Callanan, BMH WS 347, pp. 7–8.

15   Martin Newell, BMH WS 1562, p. 8.

16   Michael Kelly, BMH WS 1564, p. 5.

11 Mobilisation in County Galway

1   Martin Newell, BMH WS 1562, p. 9.

2   *Ibid.*, pp. 9–10.

3   Greaves, *Liam Mellows and the Irish Revolution*, p. 89.

4   Michael Kelly, BMH WS 1564, p. 5.

5   Martin Newell, BMH WS 1562, p. 10.

6   'Éamonn Corbett and 1916', *Galway Advertiser*, 24 April 2014.

7   Greaves, *Liam Mellows and the Irish Revolution*, p. 89.

8   Martin Newell, BMH WS 1562, pp. 10–11.

9   'The Police Account', *The Tuam Herald*, 3 June 1916.

10   'Germany's Insurrection', *The Galway Observer*, 29 April 1916.

11   Michael Kelly, BMH WS 1564, p. 6.

12   Martin Newell, BMH WS 1562, p. 11.

13   *Ibid.*

14   Greaves, *Liam Mellows and the Irish Revolution*, p. 89.

15   'Ireland Ablaze', *The Galway Express*, 29 April 1916.

16   Henry, *Supreme Sacrifice*, p. 91.

17   Micheál Ó Droighneáin, BMH WS 374, p. 8.

18   Greaves, *Liam Mellows and the Irish Revolution*, pp. 89–90.

19   Brian Molloy, BMH WS 345, pp. 8–10.

20   *Claregalway Parish History: 750 Years* (2002), pp. 33, 38.

21   Padraic Ó Laoi, *History of Castlegar Parish* (1998), p. 138.

22   Brian Molloy, BMH WS 345, p. 10.

12 Galway City – Swift Action

1 Margaret Peg Broderick-Nicholson, BMH WS 1682, p. 1.
2 'Sir Roger Casement Captured', *The Galway Express*, 29 April 1916.
3 Micheál Ó Droighneáin, BMH WS 374, pp. 5–7.
4 Martin Conneely, BMH WS 1611, p. 3.
5 Frank Hardiman, BMH WS 406, pp. 2–3.
6 Micheál Ó Droighneáin, BMH WS 374, p. 7.
7 *Ibid.*
8 Kenny, *Galway*, p. 23.
9 'Alleged General "Rising" in Ireland', *Connacht Tribune*, 25 April 1916.
10 Joseph J. Togher, BMH WS 1729, p. 1.
11 Thomas Hynes, BMH WS 714, p. 4.
12 Interview: Dr Mark McCarty, 3 March 2015.
13 'In and Around Galway', *The Tuam Herald*, 29 April 1916.
14 'Germany's Insurrection', *The Galway Observer*, 29 April 1916.
15 Forde, 'The Irish Party and Sinn Féin in Loughrea', p. 607.
16 'The Rising in County Galway 1916', *Connacht Tribune*, 9 April 1966.
17 'Alleged General "Rising" in Ireland', *Connacht Tribune*, 25 April 1916.
18 Minute Book: Irish National Volunteers, Galway: 1914–1916.
19 'The Rising in County Galway 1916', *Connacht Tribune*, 9 April 1966.
20 'Galway Round Up', *The Tuam Herald*, 6 May 1916.
21 'The Galway Rising', *The Tuam Herald*, 29 April 1916.
22 Thomas Courtney, BMH WS 447, pp. 4–8.

13 Wednesday's Actions

1 Brian Molloy, BMH WS 345, pp. 10–11.
2 Michael Newell, BMH WS 342, p. 6.
3 *An Chead Chath 1924 –1974: 50th Anniversary* (1974), p. 193.
4 Michael Newell, BMH WS 342, p. 6.
5 'Scenes in Galway', *The Freeman's Journal*, 6 May 1916.
6 'The Battle at Dawn', *Connacht Tribune*, 24 June 1916.
7 'Bloody Work', *Connacht Tribune*, 29 April 1916.
8 Michael Newell, BMH WS 342, pp. 6–7.
9 'The Attack at Carnmore', *Connacht Tribune*, 9 April 1966.

10 L. Blackmore and J. Cronin, *In Their Own Words: The Parish of Lackagh–Turloughmore and its People* (2001), pp. 202–4.

11 'The Real Leaders', *The Galway Observer*, 6 May 1916.

12 Brian Molloy, BMH WS 345, p. 11.

13 Martin Newell, BMH WS 1562, p. 11.

14 Michael Newell, BMH WS 342, p. 7.

15 Thomas Reidy, BMH WS 1555, pp. 2–4.

16 Michael Hynes, BMH WS 1173, pp. 2–4.

17 Thomas McInerney, BMH WS 1150, p. 4.

18 Claffey, *Glimpses of Tuam since the Famine*, pp. 187–90.

19 Patrick Dunlevy, BMH WS 1489, pp. 2–3.

20 Claffey, *Glimpses of Tuam since the Famine*, pp. 187–90.

21 'The Rising in North Galway', *Connacht Tribune*, 29 April 1916.

22 Kenny, *Galway*, p. 21.

14 Galway City – Shelling and Arrests

1 Thomas Courtney, BMH WS 447, pp. 9–13.

2 Micheál Ó Droighneáin, BMH WS 374, p. 8.

3 Donall Ó Luanaigh, 'A UCG Professor and the Easter Rising, 1916', *Galway Roots: Journal of the Galway Family History Society*, Vol. III, 1995, pp. 61–2.

4 Frank Hardiman, BMH WS 406, pp. 3–4.

5 Micheál Ó Droighneáin, BMH WS 374, p. 8.

6 Dillon, *All in The Blood,* pp. 278–9.

7 Thomas Courtney, BMH WS 447, pp. 11–13, 18.

8 Frank Hardiman, BMH 406, pp. 4–5.

9 *An Chead Chath 1924–1974*, p. 193.

10 Kenny, *Galway*, p. 22.

11 Thomas Courtney, BMH WS 447, pp. 12–13.

12 'Germany's Insurrection', *The Galway Observer*, 29 April 1916.

13 Thomas Courtney, BMH WS 447, p. 22.

15 Moyode

1 Martin Newell, BMH WS 1562, pp. 11–12.

2   Finbarr O'Regan, 'The 1916 Easter Rising in Athenry and County Galway', http://homepage.eircom.net/~oreganathenry/oreganathenry/localhistory/1916athenryandcountygalway.html.

3   Patrick Callanan, BMH WS 347, p. 9.

4   Ailbhe Ó Monachain, BMH WS 298, p. 13.

5   Martin Newell, BMH WS 1562, p. 12.

6   Greaves, *Liam Mellows and the Irish Revolution*, pp. 90–1.

7   Patrick Callanan, BMH WS 347, p. 9.

8   Greaves, *Liam Mellows and the Irish Revolution*, p. 92.

9   James Barrett, BMH WS 343, pp. 3–4.

10   'On to Moyode, Limepark and the End', *Connacht Tribune*, 16 April 1966.

11   Stephen Jordan, BMH WS 346, pp. 5–6.

12   Greaves, *Liam Mellows and the Irish Revolution*, p. 92.

13   O'Regan, 'The 1916 Easter Rising in Athenry and County Galway'.

14   Martin Newell, BMH WS 1562, p. 13.

15   Michael Kelly, BMH WS 1564, p. 8.

16   Thomas Courtney, BMH WS 447, pp. 14–17.

17   Greaves, *Liam Mellows and the Irish Revolution*, pp. 92–3.

18   Patrick Coy, BMH WS 1203, p. 1.

19   Stephen Jordan, BMH WS 346, p. 6.

20   Frank Hynes, BMH WS 446, p. 14.

16 The Rebels Disband

1   Michael Kelly, BMH WS 1564, p. 9.

2   Greaves, *Liam Mellows and the Irish Revolution*, pp. 93–4.

3   *Ibid.*

4   Martin Newell, BMH WS 1562, p. 14.

5   Michael Kelly, BMH WS 1564, p. 9.

6   Very Rev. Dr Thomas Fahy BMH WS 383, p. 2.

7   Martin Newell, BMH WS 1562, p. 14.

8   Greaves, *Liam Mellows and the Irish Revolution*, pp. 93–4.

9   Frank Hynes, BMH WS 446, p. 15.

10   'Break-Up of a Rebel Army', *Connacht Tribune*, 16 April 1966.

11   Brian Molloy, BMH WS 345, p. 12.

12   Greaves, *Liam Mellows and the Irish Revolution*, pp. 93–4.

13   Martin Newell, BMH WS 1562, p. 14.

14   Michael Kelly, BMH WS 1564, p. 10.

15   'Break-Up of a Rebel Army', *Connacht Tribune*, 16 April 1966.

16   Frank Hynes, BMH WS 446, p. 16.

17   Patrick Callanan, BMH WS 347, p. 10.

18   'Hunting and Jailing of the Rebels', *Connacht Tribune*, 23 April 1966.

19   Brian Molloy, BMH WS 345, p. 13.

20   Kenny, *Galway*, p. 22.

21   Very Rev. Dr Thomas Fahy, BMH WS 383, p. 3.

22   'In County Galway', *Connacht Tribune*, 6 May 1916.

23   Mrs Martin Conlon, BMH WS 419, p. 8.

24   Henry, *Supreme Sacrifice,* pp. 95, 98.

17 Rebels on the Run

1   Greaves, *Liam Mellows and the Irish Revolution*, p. 94.

2   Peter Howley, BMH WS 1379, pp. 12–13.

3   'In County Galway', *Connacht Tribune*, 6 May 1916.

4   Peter Howley, BMH WS 1379, p. 13.

5   Frank Hynes, BMH WS 446, pp. 17–29.

6   Greaves, *Liam Mellows and the Irish Revolution*, pp. 98–9.

7   Henry, *Supreme Sacrifice*, p. 93.

8   Frank Hynes, BMH WS 446, pp. 29–35.

9   'Éamonn Corbett and 1916', *Galway Advertiser*, 24 April 2014.

10   Patrick Callanan, BMH WS 347, p. 10.

11   Greaves, *Liam Mellows and the Irish Revolution*, p. 101.

12   'Tom Kenny of Craughwell', *The Tuam Herald*, 12 August 1916.

13   Greaves, *Liam Mellows and the Irish Revolution*, pp. 118–21, 154, 165.

14   'Éamonn Corbett and 1916', *Galway Advertiser*, 24 April 2014.

18 Rebel Round-Up

1   'Hunting and Jailing of the Rebels', *Connacht Tribune*, 23 April 1966.

2   'Germany's Rebellion', *The Galway Observer*, 13 May 1916.

3   *An Chead Chath 1924–1974, 50th Anniversary,* p. 193.

4   'Germany's Rebellion', *The Galway Observer*, 13 May 1916.

5   Sean O'Mahony, *Frongoch: University of Revolution* (1987), pp. 20–1.

6   Frank Hardiman, BMH WS 406, pp. 5–8.

7   Micheál Ó Droighneáin, BMH WS 374, pp. 8–9.

8   Frank Hardiman, BMH WS 406, pp. 8–9.

9   Micheál Ó Droighneáin, BMH WS 374, p. 9.

10   Interview: Luke Silke, 28 March 2015.

11   Frank Hardiman, BMH WS 406, p. 10.

12   Micheál Ó Droighneáin, BMH WS 374, pp. 9–10.

13   Villiers-Tuthill, *Beyond The Twelve Bens*, pp. 192, 194.

14   Brian Molloy, BMH WS 345, pp. 13–14.

15   Michael Newell, BMH WS 342, p. 8.

16   *Ibid.*, pp. 8–9.

17   Thomas (Sweeney) Newell, BMH WS 572, pp. 6–8.

18   Brian Molloy, BMH WS 345, pp. 14–16.

19   *Claregalway Parish History: 750 Years*, pp. 34–5, 39.

20   O'Regan, 'The 1916 Easter Rising in Athenry and County Galway'.

21   Stephen Jordan, BMH WS 346, p. 7.

22   Martin Newell, BMH WS 1562, pp. 14–15.

23   Ó Luanaigh, 'A UCG Professor and the Easter Rising, 1916', pp. 61–2.

19 Frongoch

1   'Hunting and Jailing of the Rebels', *Connacht Tribune*, 23 April 1966.

2   Frank Hardiman, BMH WS 406, pp. 15, 19.

3   O'Mahony, *Frongoch*, pp. 16, 24, 74, 76, 85, 99, 101–2, 217.

4   Frank Hardiman, BMH WS 406, pp. 20–3.

5   O'Mahony, *Frongoch*, p. 164.

6   Frank Hardiman, BMH WS 406, pp. 25–6.

7   O'Mahony, *Frongoch*, p. 164.

8   Martin Newell, BMH WS 1562, p. 16.

9   O'Mahony, *Frongoch*, p. 168.

10   'Frongoch: Thoughts of an Irish Man', *Frongoch*, 2005, pp. 13, 20, 23.

11   Brenda Furey, *The History of Oranmore Maree: A History of a Cultural and Social Heritage* (1991), p. 60; *Claregalway Parish History: 750 Years*,

p. 33; 'Deportation and Releases – More Arrests in Athenry', *Connacht Tribune*, 3 June 1916; 'Deporting Rebels', *Connacht Tribune*, 20 May 1916; Frank Hardiman, BMH WS 406, pp. 19, 21, 28; Gilbert Morrissey, BMH WS 874, p. 6; Patrick Coy, BMH WS 1203, p. 2; 'Penal Servitude – Clarenbridge Prisoners Sentenced', *Connacht Tribune, 27* May 1916; O'Mahony, *Frongoch*, pp. 165, 196–204.

20 Loyal to the Crown?

1   'The Riot in Dublin', *Connacht Tribune*, 6 May 1916.

2   Dillon, *All in the Blood,* pp. 278–9.

3   Forde, 'The Irish Party and Sinn Féin in Loughrea', p. 607.

4   'Journal of Brid, 25 May 1916', pp. 12–13.

5   'Galway Police', *Connacht Tribune*, 6 May 1916.

6   Thomas Courtney, BMH WS 447, p. 1.

7   Margaret Peg Broderick-Nicholson, BMH WS 1682, p. 1.

8   Forde, 'The Irish Party and Sinn Féin in Loughrea', pp. 605–8, 610.

9   Henry, *Galway and the Great War*, pp. 47–9.

10   'Craughwell Men's Loyalty to Ireland', *The Tuam Herald*, 20 May 1916.

11   *Ibid.*

12   Interview: Tom Joe Furey, 5 May 2004.

13   Claffey, *Glimpses of Tuam since the Famine,* p. 190.

14   'Sinn Féin Prisoners', *The Tuam Herald*, 10 June 1916.

15   'The Insurrection', *Connacht Tribune*, 20 May 1916.

16   Forde, 'The Irish Party and Sinn Féin in Loughrea', pp. 606–7.

17   'Mr Duffy, M.P., on the Rising', *Connacht Tribune*, 20 May 1916.

18   Forde, 'The Irish Party and Sinn Féin in Loughrea', p. 613.

19   Patrick Coy, BMH WS 1203, p. 2.

20   Forde, 'The Irish Party and Sinn Féin in Loughrea', pp. 610, 625.

21 Condemnation of the Rebels

1   'Great Public Meeting', *The Galway Observer*, 29 April 1916.

2   'City Branch U. I. League', *The Galway Observer*, 20 May 1916.

3   Forde, 'The Irish Party and Sinn Féin in Loughrea', p. 619.

4   'Galway Woman's Experience', *The Galway Observer*, 13 May 1916.

5   Seán O'Neill, BMH WS 1219, p. 40.

6   'The Aftermath of the Sinn Féin Rebellion', *The Tuam Herald*, 6 May 1916.

7   Forde, 'The Irish Party and Sinn Féin in Loughrea', pp. 610–11.

8   'Observer News', *The Galway Observer*, 6 May 1916.

9   *Ibid*.

10   'Mr. Redmond's Views', *The Tuam Herald*, 6 May 1916.

11   'Sir John Maxwell's Position', *The Irish Times*, 10 May 1916.

12   Interview: Tom Joe Furey, 5 May 2004.

13   Seán O'Neill, BMH WS 1219, p. 41.

22 The Aftermath of the Rebellion

1   'Galway Round Up', *The Tuam Herald*, 6 May 1916.

2   'Germany's Rebellion', *The Galway Observer*, 13 May 1916.

3   *An Chead Chath 1924–1974, 50th Anniversary*, p. 194.

4   Greaves, *Liam Mellows and the Irish Revolution*, p. 91.

5   Kenny, *Galway*, p. 23.

6   Thomas Courtney, BMH WS 447, pp. 18–22.

7   'American Opinion on the Dublin Rising', *The Tuam Herald*, 20 May 1916.

8   Henry, *Supreme Sacrifice,* pp. 28–9.

9   William Henry, *Blood for Blood: The Black and Tan War in Galway* (2012), pp. 27–9.

10   'Outcome', *Frongoch*, 2005, p. 23.

11   Kenny, *Galway*, p. 23.

12   'The Rising of 1916', Fr Levington: Furey Family Records.

13   'On the Irishmen Executed in Dublin', *The Tuam Herald*, 12 August 1916.

14   'The Year of the Rebellion', *Connacht Tribune*, 6 January 1917.

15   O'Mahony, *Frongoch*, p. 169.

16   'Who Fears to Speak of Easter Week?', *The East Galway Democrat*, 19 May 1917.

17   Greaves, *Liam Mellows and the Irish Revolution*, pp. 118–121, 154, 165, 221, 223, 218.

18   Eoin Neeson, *The Civil War 1922–23* (1995), pp. 118, 152.

19   Henry, *Supreme Sacrifice*, p. 131.

20   'Liam Mellows', *The Mantle*, Vol. 1–5, Spring–Autumn 1961, p. 18.

21   Lecture: 'History of Renmore Barracks' by Brian Smith, 20 November 2011.

22   'Bishop Unveils Mellows Memorial', *Connacht Tribune*, 24 August 1957.

23   'Their Deaths Rise Far Above the Clamour – Their Voices Insistent Still', *The Irish Times*, 28 January 2006.

Epilogue

1   P. F. MacLochlainn, *Last Words: Letters and Statements of the Leaders Executed after the Rising at Easter 1916* (1990), pp. 18–19, 45, 60–1, 95, 140–1, 170–1, 191, 193.

2   'They Gave All in Silence, Seeking No Reward, and Getting None', *Galway Advertiser*, 5 April 2012.

Appendix

1   'Galway Honours the Heroes of 1916', *Connacht Tribune*, 16 April 1966.

2   Interview: Maura Flaherty, 5 May 2005.

3   '1916 Commemoration Ceremonies', *Connacht Tribune*, 16 April 1966.

4   'The Boys of Castlegar', *Connacht Tribune*, 16 April 1966.

5   '1916 Commemoration Ceremonies', *Connacht Tribune*, 16 April 1966.

6   Martin Newell, BMH WS 1562, p. 5.

7   Ballymoe Commemoration 1966: Gallagher Family Records.

8   '1916 Commemoration Ceremonies', *Connacht Tribune*, 16 April 1966.

9   'Ballinasloe Sinn Féin Member's Wish for 1966', *Connacht Tribune*, 29 April 1966.

10   '1916 Commemoration Ceremonies', *Connacht Tribune*, 16 April 1966.

11   'When Donovan's Kid was Born', *Connacht Tribune*, 23 April 1966.

Bibliography

Bureau of Military History Witness Statements

298: Ailbhe Ó Monachain
  (Alf Monahan)
322: Mrs Seán McEntee
  (Margaret Browne)
342: Michael Newell
343: James Barrett
345: Brian Molloy
346: Stephen Jordan
347: Patrick Callanan
373: John Hosty
374: Micheál Ó Droighneáin
383: Very Rev. Dr Thomas Fahy
406: Frank Hardiman
419: Mrs Martin Conlon
446: Frank Hynes
447: Thomas Courtney
572: Thomas (Sweeney) Newell
714: Thomas Hynes
874: Gilbert Morrissey
1124: Daniel Kearns
1150: Thomas McInerney
1173: Michael Hynes
1203: Patrick Coy
1219: Seán O'Neill
1379: Peter Howley
1489: Patrick Dunlevy
1555: Thomas Reidy
1562: Martin Newell
1564: Michael Kelly
1611: Martin Conneely
1612: Peter McDonnell
1682: Margaret Peg Broderick-
  Nicholson
1729: Joseph J. Togher

Documents and Records

Ballymoe Commemoration 1966: Gallagher Family Records
Minute Book: Irish National Volunteers, Galway: 1914–1916
'The Rising of 1916', Fr Levington: Furey Family Records

Interviews

Christy Burke, 2 December 1998
Maura Flaherty, 5 May 2005
Tom Joe Furey, 5 May 2004
Kitty Lardner, 5 May 1999
Dr Mark McCarty, 3 March 2015
Luke Silke, 28 March 2015

Lecture

'History of Renmore Barracks' by Brian Smith, 20 November 2011

Newspaper Articles

'1916 Commemoration Ceremonies', *Connacht Tribune*, 16 April 1966

'A Memory of Ardrahan 50 Years Ago', *Connacht Tribune*, 2 April 1966

'Alleged General "Rising" in Ireland', *Connacht Tribune*, 25 April 1916

'American Opinion on the Dublin Rising', *The Tuam Herald*, 20 May 1916

'Ballinasloe Sinn Féin Member's Wish for 1966', *Connacht Tribune*, 29 April 1966

'Bishop Unveils Mellows Memorial', *Connacht Tribune*, 24 August 1957

'Bloody Work', *Connacht Tribune*, 29 April 1916

'Break-Up of a Rebel Army', *Connacht Tribune*, 16 April 1966

'Brutal Outrage', *The Galway Express*, 2 April 1887

'City Branch U. I. League', *The Galway Observer*, 20 May 1916

'Craughwell Men's Loyalty to Ireland', *The Tuam Herald*, 20 May 1916

'Deportation and Releases – More Arrests in Athenry', *Connacht Tribune*, 3 June 1916

'Deporting Rebels', *Connacht Tribune*, 20 May 1916

'Disbandment', *Connacht Tribune*, 16 April 1966

'Disorderly Conduct by Soldiers', *The Galway Express*, 2 June 1888

'Éamonn Corbett and 1916', *Galway Advertiser*, 24 April 2014

'Galway Honours the Heroes of 1916', *Connacht Tribune*, 16 April 1966

'Galway Police', *Connacht Tribune*, 6 May 1916

'Galway Round Up', *The Tuam Herald*, 6 May 1916

'Galway Woman's Experience', *The Galway Observer*, 13 May 1916

'Germany's Insurrection', *The Galway Observer*, 29 April 1916

'Germany's Rebellion', *The Galway Observer*, 13 May 1916

'Great Public Meeting', *The Galway Observer*, 29 April 1916

'Hunting and Jailing of the Rebels', *Connacht Tribune*, 23 April 1966

'In and Around Galway', *The Tuam Herald*, 29 April 1916

'In County Galway', *Connacht Tribune*, 6 May 1916

'I.R.B. Centre', *Connacht Tribune*, 16 April 1966

'Ireland Ablaze', *The Galway Express*, 29 April 1916

'Mr. Duffy, M.P., on the Rising', *Connacht Tribune*, 20 May 1916

'Mr. Redmond's Views', *The Tuam Herald*, 6 May 1916

'Observer News', *The Galway Observer*, 6 May 1916

'On the Irishmen Executed in Dublin', *The Tuam Herald*, 12 August 1916

'On to Moyode, Limepark and the End', *Connacht Tribune*, 16 April 1966

'Patrick Henry Pearse', *Galway Independent*, 3 November 2010

'Penal Servitude – Clarenbridge Prisoners Sentenced', *Connacht Tribune*, 27 May 1916

'Renmore Barracks – Foundation', *Galway Independent*, 16 April 2014

'Riot in William Street', *The Galway Express*, 31 December 1881

'Riotous Proceedings in Galway', *The Galway Express*, 18 September 1886

'Scenes in Galway', *The Freeman's Journal*, 6 May 1916

'Seán MacDiarmada', *Galway Independent*, 20 October 2010

'Siege of Loughrea', *Galway Independent*, 26 September 2012

'Sinn Féin Prisoners', *The Tuam Herald*, 10 June 1916

'Sir John Maxwell's Position', *The Irish Times*, 10 May 1916

'Sir Roger Casement Captured', *The Galway Express*, 29 April 1916

'St David's Day', *The Galway Express*, 1 March 1890

'The Aftermath of the Sinn Féin Rebellion', *The Tuam Herald*, 6 May 1916

'The Attack at Carnmore', *Connacht Tribune*, 9 April 1966

'The Battle at Dawn', *Connacht Tribune*, 24 June 1916

'The Boys of Castlegar', *Connacht Tribune*, 16 April 1966

'The Coming of Mellows', *Connacht Tribune*, 2 April 1966

'The Disgraceful Riots in Galway', *The Galway Express*, 2 April 1887

'The Fatal Riot Between Soldiers and Civilians', *The Galway Express*, 28 September 1889

'The Galway Rising', *The Tuam Herald*, 3 June 1916

'The Insurrection', *Connacht Tribune*, 20 May 1916

'The Loughrea Siege Ends', *Galway Independent*, 3 October 2012

'The Peaceful Cottage of Revolt in Rosmuc', *Galway Advertiser*, 8 April 2004

'The Police Account', *The Tuam Herald*, 3 June 1916

'The Police Attacked by the Military', *The Galway Express*, 15 November 1890

'The Position of the National Volunteers', *The Galway Express*, 13 March 1915

'The Queen's Birthday', *The Galway Express*, 5 June 1888

'The Real Leaders', *The Galway Observer*, 6 May 1916

'The Riot in Dublin', *Connacht Tribune*, 6 May 1916

'The Rising in County Galway 1916', *Connacht Tribune*, 9 April 1966

'The Rising in North Galway', *Connacht Tribune*, 29 April 1916

'The Significance of the Galway Revolt', *Connacht Tribune*, 2 April 1966

'The Year of the Rebellion', *Connacht Tribune*, 6 January 1917

'Their Deaths Rise Far Above the Clamour – Their Voices Insistent Still', *The Irish Times*, 28 January 2006

'They Gave All in Silence, Seeking No Reward, and Getting None', *Galway Advertiser*, 5 April 2012

'Tom Kenny of Craughwell', *The Tuam Herald*, 12 August 1916

'Trouble & Strife', *Galway Independent*, 30 April 2014

'When Donovan's Kid was Born', *Connacht Tribune*, 23 April 1966

'Who Fears to Speak of Easter Week?', *The East Galway Democrat*, 19 May 1917

Secondary Sources

Books

Blackmore, L. and Cronin, J., *In Their Own Words: The Parish of Lackagh–Turloughmore and its People* (Galway: Lackagh Museum Committee, 2001)

Claffey, J. A., *Glimpses of Tuam since the Famine* (Tuam: Old Tuam Society, 1997)

Dillon, G. P., *All in The Blood: A Memoir of the Plunkett family, the 1916 Rising and the War of Independence*, edited by Honor Ó Brolchain (Dublin: A & A Farmar Limited, 2006)

Duggan, E., *The Ploughman on the Pound Note: Farmer Politics in County Galway during the Twentieth Century* (Galway: self-published, 2004)

Finnegan, P., *Loughrea 'That Den of Infamy': The Land War in Co. Galway, 1879–82* (Dublin: Four Courts Press, 2014)

Forde, J., 'The Irish Party and Sinn Féin in Loughrea. Part I: 1914', in Joseph Forde, Christina Cassidy, Paul Manzor and David Ryan (eds), *The District of Loughrea*, Vol. I, 1791–1918 (Galway: Loughrea History Project, 2003)

Furey, B., *The History of Oranmore Maree: A History of a Cultural and Social Heritage* (Galway: self-published 1991)

Frazier, A., *George Moore, 1852–1933* (London: Yale University Press, 2000)

Gorman, T., Stanley, C., Lyons-Hynes, M., Roache, D. and McEneany S., *Clanricarde Country and the Land Campaign* (Galway: Woodford Heritage Group, 1987)

Greaves, C. D., *Liam Mellows and the Irish Revolution* (London: Lawrence & Wishart, 1971)

Henry, W., *Supreme Sacrifice: the Story of Éamonn Ceannt 1881–1916* (Cork: Mercier Press, 2005 (republished as *Éamonn Ceannt: Supreme Sacrifice*, Cork: Mercier Press, 2012))

Henry, W., *Galway and the Great War* (Cork: Mercier Press, 2006)

Henry, W., *Blood for Blood: The Black and Tan War in Galway* (Galway: Mercier Press, Cork, 2012)

Henry, W., *Hidden Galway: Gallows, Garrisons and Guttersnipes* (Cork: Mercier Press, 2011)

Henry, W., *Galway Through Time & Tide,* Vol. IV (Galway: Galway Independent, 2014)

Kenny, T., *Galway: Politics and Society, 1910–23* (Dublin: Four Courts Press, 2011)

MacLochlainn, P. F., *Last Words: Letters and Statements of the Leaders Executed after the Rising at Easter 1916* (Dublin: Government Publications, 1990)

McDonnell, N., 'The Ward Eviction 1906', in Joseph Forde, Christina Cassidy, Paul Manzor and David Ryan (eds), *The District of Loughrea*, Vol. I, 1791–1918 (Galway: Loughrea History Project, 2003)

Neeson, E., *The Civil War 1922–23* (Dublin: Poolbeg Press Limited, 1995)

Ó Comhraí, C., *Revolution in Connacht: A Photographic History 1913–23* (Cork: Mercier Press, 2013)

Ó Comhraí, C. and O'Malley, C. (eds), *The Men Will Talk To Me: Galway Interviews by Ernie O'Malley* (Cork: Mercier Press, 2013)

O'Mahony, S., *Frongoch: University of Revolution* (Dublin: FDR Teoranta, 1987)

Ó Laoi, P., *History of Castlegar Parish* (Galway: self-published, 1998)

O'Regan, C. and Lacy, A., *Abbeyknockmoy: A Time to Remember* (Galway: Abbeyknockmoy Community Council, n.d.)

Ryan, D., 'The Trial and Execution of Anthony Daly', in Joseph Forde, Christina Cassidy, Paul Manzor and David Ryan (eds), *The District of Loughrea*, Vol. I, 1791–1918 (Galway: Loughrea History Project, 2003)

Shiel, M. J. and Roche, D. (eds), *A Forgotten Campaign and Aspects of the Heritage of South-East Galway* (Galway: Woodford Heritage Group, 1986)

Villiers-Tuthill, K., *Beyond The Twelve Bens: A History of Clifden and District 1860–1923* (Dublin: self-published, 1990)

Booklets

An Chead Chath 1924–1974: 50th Anniversary (Galway: An Chead Chath, 1974)

Claregalway Parish History: 750 Years (Galway: Claregalway Historical and Cultural Society, 2002)

Internet Articles

O'Regan, F., 'The 1916 Easter Rising in Athenry and County Galway', http://homepage.eircom.net/~oreganathenry/oreganathenry/localhistory/1916athenryandcountygalway.html (accessed 2 February 2014)

Journal Articles

'Journal of Brid, 25 May 1916', Galway Technical Institute (Galway 1979)

Ó Luanaigh, D., 'A UCG Professor and the Easter Rising, 1916', *Galway Roots: Journal of the Galway Family History Society*, Vol. III, 1995

O'Sullivan, S., 'Popular Perceptions of the Royal Irish Constabulary during the Land War in Galway', *Journal of the Galway Family History Society*, Vol. V, 1998

'Reign of Terror at Craughwell: Tom Kenny and the McGoldrick Murder of 1909', *18th–19th-Century Social Perspectives*, Issue 1, Vol. 18, January/February 2010

Magazine Articles

'Frongoch: Thoughts of an Irish Man', *Frongoch*, 2005, Galway

'Liam Mellows', *The Mantle,* Vol. 1–5, No. 1, Spring–Autumn 1961, Galway

'Outcome', *Frongoch*, 2005, Galway

'Pearse As I Remember Him', *The Mantle*, Vol. 9–10, No. 33, Spring 1966–1969, Galway

INDEX

283